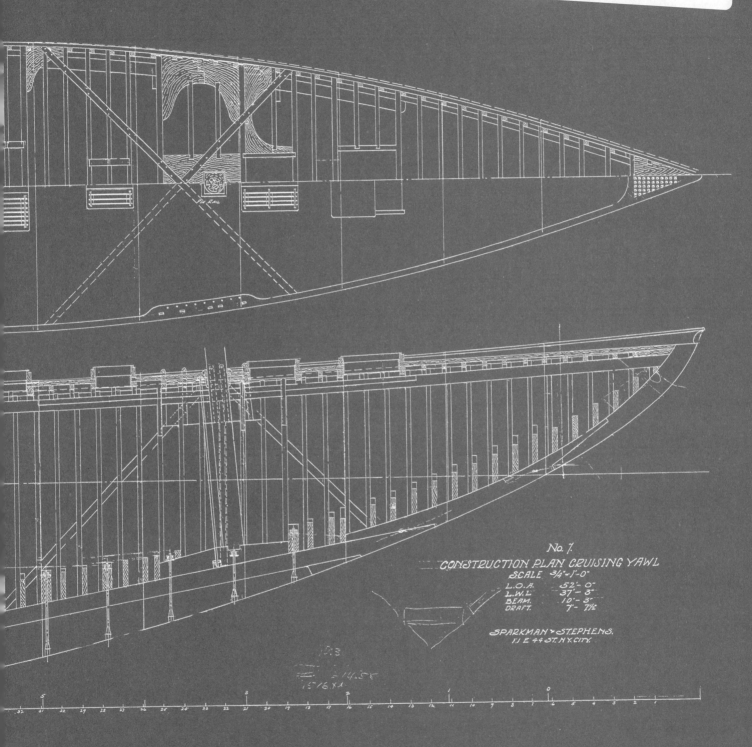

PIN RAIL

No. 7.

CONSTRUCTION PLAN CRUISING YAWL
SCALE ¾"-1'-0"

L.O.A.	52'- 0"
L.W.L.	37'- 3"
BEAM.	10'- 3"
DRAFT.	7'- 7½"

SPARKMAN & STEPHENS.
11 E 44 ST. N.Y. CITY.

Dorade

The History of an Ocean Racing Yacht

Dorade

The History of an Ocean Racing Yacht

DOUGLAS D. ADKINS

DAVID R. GODINE

Publisher · Boston

Cover photo: *Dorade*
Photo by Ken Ollar, © Guy Hoppen

First published in 2012 by David R. Godine, Publisher
Post Office Box 450
Jaffrey, New Hampshire 03452
www.godine.com

Adkins, Douglas D.
Dorade : the history of an ocean racing yacht / by Douglas D. Adkins.
    p. cm.
Includes bibliographical references and index.
ISBN 978-1-56792-447-3 (alk. paper)
1. Dorade (Yacht) 2. Yacht racing—United States. 3. Yacht building—
United States. 4. Yachts—Design and construction. I. Title.
GV822.D67A35 2012
797.1'40973—dc23

2011027376

Trade Edition ISBN: 978-1-56792-447-3
Deluxe Edition ISBN: 978-1-56792-449-7

First Edition
Printed in China

Foreword

BY LLEWELLYN HOWLAND III

The story is as old as that of the great artificer Daedalus and his impetuous and headstrong son, Icarus. To refresh your memory: Daedalus and Icarus find themselves consigned by King Minos to the Labyrinth, a fantastic maze of a prison from which there is no possible exit by land or sea. Undaunted, Daedalus fashions from feathers and wax a dandy pair of artificial wings for himself, another fine pair for his son. The wings not only fit well and look well, they work well, and Daedalus and Icarus take off from the Labyrinth, becoming the first mortals ever to fly through the air.

But there is one problem. Disregarding his father's firmly stated and very practical instructions, Icarus, having followed his father into the air and away from the Labyrinth, decides to take a quick joy ride up to the sun. All too soon, the wax begins to melt and the wing feathers to flutter away. Icarus stalls. Loses altitude. Crashes and burns.

Generations of schoolchildren have learned the moral of this tale: Father knows best; stay away from the sun; and, if you must fly at all, be sure to wear your seat belt. Translated into terms even sailors can understand, the story of Icarus teaches us that the prudent way is the best way. The maritime lesson to take away from the fall of Icarus is that the more orthodox in form an ocean racing yacht may be, the more conservative in design and rig, the better the likelihood that it will safely lead the fleet home.

Douglas Adkins' superb biography of the ocean racing yawl *Dorade* reads like a modern-day retelling of the Icarus legend. But it is a retelling with dramatic differences. For one thing, Adkins' account is as factual and as truthful as careful and extensive research can make it. For a second, it is not about an impetuous kid flying too close to the sun. Rather, it begins with two wonderfully able and self-assured young brothers—Olin and Rod Stephens Jr.—who not only fly, in a yachting context, as close to the sun as man has ever flown, but circle it repeatedly, successfully, and in seeming defiance of the laws of gravity.

It is a story in which the father, Roderick Stephens Sr., an early-retired New York coal merchant with limited sailing skill and experience—has a deep and abiding faith in his sons' talent and character and good sense and lets them take wing. Believing in the boys, the elder Stephens risks reputation, treasure and even physical well-being to support the construction of a boat to a largely unproven design by son Olin, scarcely out of his teens, for international competition against some of the finest offshore racing yachts of the day.

Most important of all, it is the story of a narrow, 52-foot yawl launched in May 1930, at the start of the Great Depression. Named after the blunt-nosed warm-water dolphinfish, *Dorade* has many characteristics of an International Rule metre boat. Her accommodations are Spartan. She is quite lightly and quickly built on a tight budget. She has no engine. She sails on her ear. She is a great roller in a seaway. Her berths are likened to coffins. Who in their right minds would want to own or go racing offshore in such a boat as this?

Dorade performed well in her shakedown summer, taking second in Class B and the All Amateur Prize in the 1930 Bermuda Race and silver in various club races. In this respect, she was a success from the very first. But it was her extraordinary victory under the command of Olin Stephens in the 1931 Transatlantic Race from Newport, Rhode Island, to Plymouth, England, that put her on the path to yachting immortality. Competing against the best that rival designers had to offer, she made the North Atlantic passage in 16 days and 55 minutes. The next boat to finish—a much larger boat at that—crossed the line two days later. When the final results were tallied, *Dorade* was the winner by over four days on corrected time. Winning, she brought about a revolution in the design of ocean-racing yachts.

Olin Stephens, a truly modest man with nothing to be modest about, always ascribed *Dorade's* victory in the 1931 Transatlantic Race to luck. No question *Dorade* was a lucky ship in that race, as she has proved to be in countless subsequent races and adventures over a career that now spans 80 years. However, as each new ocean racer, International Rule sloop, cruising class auxiliary, one-design daysailer, motor sailer, and America's Cup defender issued forth from the Sparkman & Stephens drafting room over the next many decades, wise sailors quickly learned to discount the fabled Stephens luck. Boats designed by Olin Stephens and tuned by his brother Rod earned their victories on merit, not chance. The characteristics that made *Dorade* a great and revolutionary boat in 1930-'31 have made her great and revolutionary ever since.

Douglas Adkins has written a long-awaited history of *Dorade*. But she herself is just one player in his narrative, and the Stephens brothers and their father were only the first of a long and colorful line who have owned, helped build or restore, cut sails for, sanded the bottom of, raced on or against, sailed or cruised on or in company with, and, in at least one instance, died for her.

As this book makes clear, the relationship between yachts and those who design, build, own, and sail them is dynamic and complex. Not every serious sailor, not even young sportsmen as wealthy and well-connected as *Dorade's* early West Coast owners, would welcome the celebrity—sometimes even notoriety—that *Dorade* has tended to confer those who have owned her. Conversely, not every owner of *Dorade* has won the silver he dreamed of or the recognition and acceptance he sought as the owner of such a fast and famous boat. To hold the tiller of *Dorade* as she takes the cannon at the finish line may be the fulfillment of a lifelong dream. To be involved in a spectacular collision and sinking on the race course, or even to suffer a succession of minor, but highly visible, lapses of seamanship or good judgment, can rapidly turn the joys of possession into psychic burdens too great to bear.

Variously owned on Long Island Sound, in San Francisco and Seattle, on Orcas Island, in the Mediterranean at Argentario in Italy and Antibes on the Cote d'Azure, and latterly in Newport, Rhode Island, *Dorade* has outlived her famously long-lived designer and many of her former owners. She has crossed the Atlantic often and visited Hawaii at least twice. She has endured countless repairs and undergone restorations both minor and massive. Love affairs have begun and marriages have ended aboard her. She has been a dry ship (under the Stephens ownership) and, at times, a very wet one. Races she has won (and lost) are now almost past counting.

What a life she has led! And with what grace and dignity and firmness of purpose she has sought to do the will of her many masters! This is not to say that *Dorade* is unique in these respects. Other sailing yachts, and not just those designed by Sparkman & Stephens, have lived as long or longer and have given as much pleasure (some even with a lot less rolling in a seaway and with berths far more comfortable than coffins). Their owners have been no less varied in temperament, background, and ambition, no less obsessed by the sea in all its moods and ways.

But these other yachts were not in signaling distance of the English lighthouse known as The Lizard at 5:45 on the morning of Tuesday, 21 July, 1931, when a narrow yawl named *Dorade* ghosted by on her way to Plymouth. In response to *Dorade's* request for her place in the order of finish in the Transatlantic Race, the station keeper hoisted the flags N A X: "You are first." As Doug Adkins demonstrates so convincingly, so entertainingly, and so eloquently, *Dorade* has been first ever since.

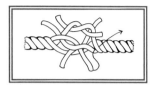

Acknowledgments

In many ways, the research involved in writing this history of *Dorade* has been its own reward. Throughout the process, I have been helped, directed and encouraged by literally everyone whom I have sought out concerning the project. Some of that support has come from friendship, some from a sense of graciousness and generosity and some from an unending love of the boat. The work in assembling these pages has involved interviews, photographic research and acquisition, fact checking, many original sources and the preparation of new photography. It has afforded me the chance to learn about the editing, assembly and publishing of a book, that being a new experience for me. All of it has been most satisfying.

There are many people to thank, and foremost in his contribution was Olin J. Stephens II. Olin shared generously of his time, knowledge and company in putting specifics to this story. With his grace, intellect and commitment to doing things the right way, he provided details, color and texture while lending his wonderful personality to the boat's image. He loved *Dorade* and he shared interviews and artifacts that make this history richer. My time with him was precious, and I only regret that he did not live to see the book in its hard covers.

I am also indebted to Sparkman & Stephens, Incorporated for their remarkable help. Mitch Gibbons-Neff gave early guidance and encouragement before his untimely death. Bruce Johnson offered support, made available the priceless plans that are included and helped whenever I asked. But most especially, Harry Morgan tracked down the answers to my questions, provided crucial introductions, lent enthusiasm and allowed me the use of the wonderful journals prepared by his stepfather, Albert Pratt, which document *Dorade's* return from Europe in the summer of 1933. Harry also helped in so many ways with access to the New York Yacht Club and its archives. I am lucky to have his friendship.

Dorade's very name gave me an opportunity to interview many of those whose lives had been impacted by her. My Orcas Island friend and neighbor Miles McCoy and his wife, Louellen, shared stories and photos. Mike Douglas related his years of ownership and *Dorade's* adventures at Camp Four Winds-Westward Ho. Elizabeth Dresser Flood and her son James C. Flood, through the kind introduction of my sailing and golfing friend Richard Taylor, filled in the story of the boat's years in San Francisco prior to the War. R. C. Keefe was invaluable in his detailed historical perspective on all of *Dorade's* West Coast experience and her connections with the St. Francis Yacht Club. Myron Doxon and Ray Rairdon shared their insights and background of the Franklin Eddy years. Edgar Cato held forth in *Dorade's* saloon, sharing his own fascinating background and his history as the boat's latest owner. Paul Buttrose could not have helped more with proofing facts and giving support and unflagging encouragement. Peter Cassidy was always on hand to answer my questions and give progress reports on *Dorade* in Newport. Giles McLaughlin filled in the blanks of the Italian years, and the irrepressible Federico Nardi added wonderfully to the story of the boat's European rebuild. Louise Daley generously shared photographs and stories of her mother's time on the boat. Barbara Parlapiano helped to provide background on her father, Ralph James, and his delivery of the boat to Seattle in 1943. Bill Button shared his experiences and stories to add to the tale of the 1979 Swiftsure Race. Jeroen Frech added photos and memories of *Dorade's* years under his father's ownership. It is hard to convey the fun I had during these interviews.

A large and invaluable influence on this work has been Llewellyn Howland III. Louie's writing skill and generous guidance have been critical, and I am very grateful to him for sharing them with me and for providing the foreword for this book. Malcolm Harris has guided me to the book's realization in an expert way, always mindful of my objectives. Maynard Bray has provided expert technical editing. David Godine, enthusiastic and accomplished publisher, has shown the temerity and grace to take on another yachting title and I thank him for taking mine. Darcy Magratten has given her wonderful eye and capable experience to the book as its designer, and I think she has come to love *Dorade*.

I am indebted to Mystic Seaport Museum and particularly to Louisa Watrous for wonderful help in locating and reproducing images from their collections and to the Museum of History and Industry in Seattle for opening their photographic archives to me. Other notable images include those in Guy Hoppen's collection of the beautiful Northwest yachting photography of Kenneth Ollar, which add so much to these pages. The world should see more of Ollar's work. Mark Welther of the Spaulding Wooden Boat Center in Sausalito, California, unearthed some gems, including Myron Spaulding's chart of *Dorade's* wartime voyage up the West Coast. The assistance of Jay Picotte of the Museum of Yachting added greatly. I am particularly grateful to Scott Rohrer for his scholarship, direction and friendship. He is a great repository of West Coast yachting history and colorful stories. Tony Dixon graciously allowed the use of drawings and graphs by his uncle, Uffa Fox. Finally, Tom Nye of City Island, New York, is a remarkable yachting historian as well as a sailmaker, and he could not have been more helpful and kind in providing background on Minneford's and the other great builders at City Island during the 1930s.

Personal encouragement in this project has been generous and welcome and has come from many kind friends. Christina Godshalk, an accomplished writer, added her perspective and push. Ernest L. Godshalk read and corrected an early draft and always urged me on. Robert Alasdair "Brodie" MacGregor, my friend of three decades at the Concordia Company, did everything I asked of him to provide introductions and unearth sources. George Moffett, the longtime captain of *Brilliant* and later *Belle Aventure*, brought his friendship and enormous yachting and design knowledge to bear on the book. Douglas Cole, a Northwest yachtsman, historian and writer, found references and sources and was always ready to assist. Knight Coolidge was critical in helping me in coordinating and working with Olin and in finding snippets to add to the story. My sailing friends Mike and Lee Brown have always put wind in my sails. James Robart and Mari Jalbing added good humor and sailing gusto. John B. Baker kept me engaged and on the water. David Skinner provided his friendship and media expertise. David Bicks provided friendship, access, enthusiasm and photographs. Matt Cockburn was always on the lookout for data and helped me with software. Stewart and Denny McDougall added important images from the 1970s as did Diane Beeston, Bill Button, Brad Read, Crayton Walters, Jim Allsopp and Green Brett. Mark Swope provided wonderful images taken by his father, John Swope, during the 1930s. Patrick Haskett contributed his delightful painting of *Dorade* on West Sound. Christopher White of *Yachting* gave much needed access to their archives. My lifelong pal Peter Phillips, whose father raced on *Dorade* during the 1950s, shared movies and photos and provided background which was personal and very important. He also served graciously as an editor for this book. Like the good coach he is, Capt. Pete always drove me forward with kind guidance and criticism.

But my most important thanks are to the three beautiful women who sail with me. Susan has smiled and suffered through over four decades on the water in our adventures together. She has sailed on both coasts in boats large and small, has even endured *Dorade*, and has been a tower of tolerance and assistance, even when she thought that the end was near. Caitlin has cheerfully and ably sailed all of her life, starting in a canvas hamper on our Concordia yawl *Coriolis* at the age of six months and not-quite-enough pounds. Her elegance never interferes with her clear thinking and competence on the water. Blakeley is waterborne at heart, drives a sailboat downhill with a touch unlike anyone I have ever known, gently shares her love of sailing with others, is hearty, cheerful, brave and adventurous, a great crew in any endeavor. These three ladies have been my constant support, lending their love to me and to this work. Without them, there would be nothing.

Clifford W. Ashley and
The Ashley Book of Knots

Illustrations from *The Ashley Book of Knots* are used to denote section and chapter headings throughout the text of *Dorade: The History of an Ocean Racing Yacht*. Published in 1944, Ashley's definitive collection of drawings and descriptions has served as a delightful and important history of the development, use and lore of knots and fancy ropework for generations of readers of maritime matters. Born in 1881 in New Bedford, Massachusetts, and surrounded by reminders of the whaling era so fundamental to the town's prominence, he soon set himself to a career in art and literature. Following his graduation from New Bedford High School, Clifford Ashley studied art at the Eric Pape School in Boston along with other students and friends N.C. Wyeth, Sidney Chase and Henry Peck. Further studies with the renowned teacher Howard Pyle in Wilmington, Delaware, followed, and Ashley's illustrations and paintings soon appeared in important magazines of the day including *Collier's, Success, Delineator, Scribner's* and *Sportsman Magazine*. His beautifully illustrated *Whaleships of New Bedford* was published in 1929 and included an introduction by Franklin Delano Roosevelt. Ashley spent 11 years identifying, describing and illustrating the nearly 4000 knots included in *The Ashley Book of Knots*, most with multiple illustrations of their tying along with charming descriptions of their lineage and purpose. Tiny notations such as ⚓, ☠ and ⊘ signify knots that are, respectively, reliable, dangerous, or difficult to untie. The symbol 🐎 signifies a knot that is "probably original" and ★ identifies a knot that is "best for the purpose."

I am deeply indebted to Clifford Ashley's daughters Phoebe Chardon, Jane Ashley and Polly Reid for allowing permission to include these illustrations in the book.

Dorade became the most famous ocean racing yacht in the world. As the first major blue water design to be built to the drawings of her 21-year-old designer, *Dorade*'s keel was laid just weeks after the Stock Market Crash of 1929, and her launching in the spring of 1930 coincided with the slide of the nation into the Great Depression. Despite such inauspicious timing, this yacht, her young designer and youthful, attractive crew became a sensation on both sides of the Atlantic and on both coasts of America. *Dorade* introduced and validated the early yacht design concepts of Olin Stephens and influenced, in one way or another, nearly all developments in yacht design for the next three decades. Her rigging and deck fixtures, developed in large part by Olin's younger brother, Roderick Stephens Jr., still make the name *Dorade* commonplace today. Her combination of speed, sea-keeping ability, stunning beauty and small size, coupled with her startling racing success, kept the eye of the public on her and on those aboard her. It is difficult to find a serious book about yacht racing in the 20th century that does not refer to her and to her impact on the popularity of ocean racing and the development of yacht design. *Dorade* was and is a breakthrough yacht, a unique point in the continuum of yacht architecture that defines a change in thinking about how an ocean racing yacht should be shaped and rigged and a present-day reminder of that inflection point. This is her story, from her genesis to her enduring fame, from her influence on design development to her long racing success. Most importantly, it is a record of her owners, triumphs, travels, travails and resurrections, and it is a biography of a singular, defining American yacht, continuously adored and still racing.

Table of Contents

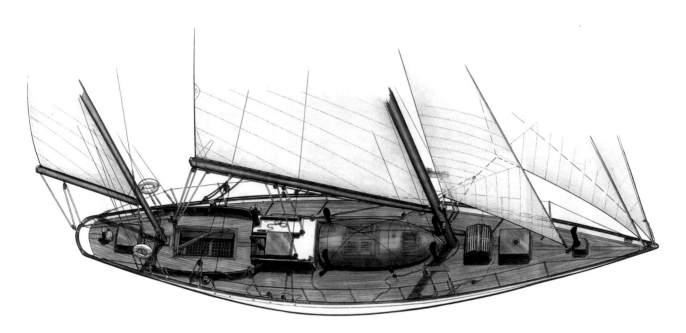

RENDERING BY ROBBERT DAS

Yachting

The Spirit of Ocean Racing

Painting by W. J. Burns

August, 1926

35 Cents a Copy

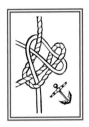

The Stage Is Set

Racing under sail began the first time two vessels propelled by scraps of cloth encountered one another on the water. There is no occasion since of two sailing vessels meeting and traveling in generally the same direction which has not been, at some level, a test of speed.

Boatbuilding in America began in 1613 in New Amsterdam with the launching of the coastal trader *Onrust*. While isolated examples of pleasure yachts emerged in the late 1700s and early 1800s, the purposeful building of American yachts for recreation and racing really took hold in the 1840s, grew until the hiatus imposed by the Civil War and then blossomed and flourished through economic cycles and design developments into the yachting of today. The New York Yacht Club's founding in 1844, with yacht racing as its important underpinning, marked a seminal moment in American yachting. That club's successful challenge of the British for the Hundred Guinea Cup by the schooner *America* in 1851 solidified the nation's standing in the sport and galvanized the attention of the American public in the often excessive displays of wealth at sea. Commencing with the first Transatlantic Race of 1866 and followed by other races to Europe and 10 America's Cup challenges and successful defenses, the 19th century ended with yachting and yacht racing firmly established in the United States. America continued to lead the world in ocean racing in the new century, with a 330-mile race from Brooklyn, New York, to Marblehead, Massachusetts, for small boats in 1904, a second Transatlantic contest in 1905 and inaugural races from the American coasts to Bermuda and Honolulu in 1906. Design developments and the broadening popularity of recreational boating, from canoes to very large yachts, increased the public's involvement in and appetite for yacht racing. Spurred on by the rivalry with British designers and yachtsmen and led by the exciting exploits of racers in a wide variety of vessels, the early decades of the Twentieth Century saw racing yacht design characterized by both a rich tradition of innovation and a settled, deliberate pace of change. Great designers such as Edward Burgess and Nathanael Herreshoff had proven that America could lead in yacht design. Great fortunes such as those of the Morgans and Vanderbilts had supported development and competition. Yacht racing was perceived as a well-developed, closely-followed and fundamental activity within American society,

—opposite—

This exciting and rugged image entitled, "The Spirit of Ocean Racing," by W.J. Burns, graced the cover of *Yachting*'s August 1926 issue.

COURTESY *YACHTING*

The Doubled Sheet Bend is primarily decorative for curtains and girdles but is reliable and secure. Ashley's anchor symbolizes "Reliable."

ASHLEY KNOT 1424

1

despite its generally upper class trappings. Through the years of World War I and into the 1920s, the sport expanded and grew measurably more populist. Ocean cruising and racing, largely with the leadership of the Cruising Club of America, became a small but growing adjunct to near-shore racing. As the 1920s ended, four massive J-Boat America's Cup defenders were being designed and built for the up-coming 1930 contest. But storm clouds gathered.

Current observers view 1929 as a year of change and crisis. The year began with the vestigial exuberance of the Roaring Twenties and finished with the Great Stock Market Crash that ushered in the Great Depression. Seen from today's perspective, the incorporation of a yacht brokerage and design firm and the laying of the keel of its first significant design in November 1929 following the tumultuous declines of the stock markets in October, appear improbable and ill-timed. However, a closer look reveals something about the state of the markets, the economy, the yachting world and the designing of that yacht.

The risks of stock speculation had been heralded broadly in late 1928 and throughout 1929. A significant decline in stock prices had already been experienced in many prominent companies' shares during the 12 months leading up to Black Thursday, October 19, 1929. While the Dow Jones and *New York Times* indexes were registering record highs, other prominent companies' shares were materially lower in September of 1929 than they had been in 1928. Pepsi Cola was down 47 percent from its high of the previous year. Similarly, shares in large companies of the era such as Cluett, Peabody, Consolidated Freeport Sulphur, Celanese, New York Shipbuilding, Phillip Morris and Consolidated Cigar were at levels 40 to 70 percent lower than those seen during 1928. Despite the tales of unbridled buy-ing with borrowed capital and the consequences that accrued from such leverage to those involved, many investors had already left the stock market, eliminating their exposure by selling rather than buying. Further, the markets, although made sensational in the popular press because of the exploits of Jessie Livermore and others, were, in reality, populated by relatively few investors—only one percent of Americans owned shares of any kind. But the banking system owned securities, had borrowed them, lent against them and operated on the thinnest of capital bases. When their securities positions and depositor confidence evaporated simultaneously, there was neither the liquidity nor the safety net to save many of them and their depositors.

Roderick Stephens Sr. navigated these financial reefs successfully. In 1929, whol-ly aside from market uncertainties, generational considerations or the competitive landscape of the fuels business, he received an attractive offer to sell the Stephens Coal Supply Company. Stephens was prominent and important in the New York coal business, but he accepted the offer nonetheless. The timing was prescient and propi-tious. Founded by his grandfather and passed to him by his father, the family's suc-

The Stephens brothers' early penchant for the water and for overloading is seen here; the two teenagers (Olin forward and Rod at the engine) and friends Buck and Bob Moore Sr., greet the camera, circa 1924.

© MYSTIC SEAPORT

cessful anthracite coal distribution business in the Morris Heights section of the Bronx was sold to new owners, and the Stephens family's finances became comfortably liquid. His eldest son, Olin J. Stephens II, would describe his family as "upper middle class" and their carriage and appearance would make obvious the modesty of that description.

The Stephens family's two sons, Olin James II and Roderick Jr., a year and a half apart in age, and their younger sister, Marite, born in 1913, grew up in Scarsdale, not far from the Long Island shore. Olin graduated from Scarsdale High School in 1926. That fall, he entered the Massachusetts Institute of Technology to study naval architecture, only to leave within six months to recuperate from bouts with academic disenchantment and jaundice. He returned home in the spring of 1927 to begin drafting boats. His younger brother, Rod, was playing high-school football as captain that year with the vigor and physicality that would mark his entire life, and the family was being catapulted by these two energetic sons into the world of yachting.

Starting with a small powerboat on Lake George when the boys were very young and coming to water sports naturally through the active participation of their grandfather, Olin Stephens Sr., in rowing, the family graduated successively through a series of small sailboats. They expanded their horizons from fresh to salt water with a summer house at Barnstable on Cape Cod after Roderick Sr. returned in 1919 from Army tank corps service in Europe. On the Cape, young Olin and Rod learned to drive and sail small watercraft, devoured yachting magazines, dreamt of new designs and equipment and involved themselves with everything about boats. In a pattern that would be fundamental to their emerging success, their father supported them and underwrote their sailing passion in a remarkable way. It is difficult to tell whether or not Roderick Stephens Sr. deeply loved sailing, but he clearly loved his boys. From both the Cape and a yachting base closer to home at Larchmont, they sailed, raced, hitched rides as crew with the active sailors of the area and employed their enthusiasm, commitment and grace to find friends and supporters in the sailing fraternity of Long Island Sound. In this way, they laid the groundwork for *Dorade.*

The winner of the 1928 Bermuda Race *Rugosa II*, a New York Forty designed by Nathanael Herreshoff. Her tall rig, mizzen and relatively light construction influenced Olin Stephens' thinking about offshore design.

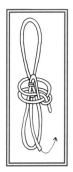

Foundations of Design

In order to evaluate the genesis of *Dorade*'s design and her unique contribution to the development of ocean racing yachts, it is helpful to evaluate the state of the art and science of yacht architecture in the mid-1920s. The principal testing grounds for offshore sailing were two ocean races on either side of the Atlantic. On the American east coast the Bermuda Race, from Gravesend Bay, New York, to St. David's Light, Bermuda, had been started in 1906 and, after a 14-year hiatus, was re-inaugurated with the support, if not the formal sponsorship, of the newly-formed Cruising Club of America in 1923. In Britain, the Fastnet Race, from the Isle of Wight to the Fastnet Rock in the Irish Sea and back, had begun under the sponsorship of the Ocean Racing Club in 1925. These races of 660 and 608 miles, respectively, were participated in by those vessels deemed appropriate to the tests of the open ocean and vigorous sailing.

The entrants in ocean contests derived their designs primarily from the working schooners of the day. Typically, they were relatively small but heavily-built vessels with gaff rigs, sailed in part by professional crews along with their amateur owners. The designs of John Alden dominated the Bermuda Races of the late 1920s. His modified fisherman schooner hull forms were successful and refined developments of the type of yachts sailed in the prior century and at the new century's turn. Those yachts followed *Atlantic*, the great 185-foot, three-masted schooner which set the Transatlantic record of 12 days, four hours in 1905.

The new designs of the 1920s were small in comparison to their turn-of-the-century ocean-racing forebears. Alden's long succession of 50- to 60-foot Malabar schooners were designed by him, built for his account, and typically raced for a year or so. They were then sold to make way for his next iteration. They were well sailed and very successful. Yachts for coastal racing of finer proportions and more daring sail plans were actively developed under or influenced by the forms of the Universal and International Rules, but the relatively fragile and lightweight concepts of those designs were not considered to be suitable for ocean racing. Vessels such as William Fife III's 1926 *Hallowe'en*, an elegant and drawn-out sloop of 80 feet with a Bermuda rig, might serve as one example. She successfully won the Fastnet Race in her first season only to later bow under pressure to reduce her sail plan to a gaff in concern for safety.

Although Americans tended toward sturdy, husky designs with greater beam than those popular in Europe, the deeper and narrower design ideas of Dr. Claud Worth and George L. Watson found some adherents in North America. Indeed,

The Holdback with Turk's Head is a multi-loop knot used when fancy knotwork is favored.

Ashley Knot 1112

Watson's design of *Dora* of 1891 would be strikingly similar to the boat that emerged as *Dorade*. Examples of narrow design in larger boats, such as the 94-foot-overall, Fife ketch *Eileen* (the first of that name, later named *Belle Aventure*), were being introduced in Europe by the late 1920s. Some American designers were also drawing more slippery and lightly-built boats by the later part of the decade, an example being the New York 40 *Rugosa II* by Nathanael G. Herreshoff, which was yawl rigged to be taken offshore. Despite her inshore racing design, she influenced Olin's views as she sailed past him to win the 1928 Bermuda Race while he crewed on the heavier, fisherman-style schooner *Malabar IX*. Starling Burgess advanced the notion of a staysail schooner with the revolutionary rig and narrower lines of *Niña* in 1928. She was taken to sea successfully, winning the Queen of Spain's Cup for yachts of waterline length less than 55 feet, sailed from New York to Spain, the so-called Santander Race. She combined a fisherman style with lighter construction and a more radical schooner rig, and pointed the way to a different combination of elements. The late 1920s were, in some ways, a collision of old and new ideas. Although traditional hull forms still predominated, narrower boats were beginning to make their presence felt. Building methods were being examined for weight saving. New sail plans were being introduced and others refined. Many forces were in flux, and the environment was ripe for a new direction.

Ocean yacht design in the 1920s had become a matter of art coupled with a kind of developmental science that was dictated by trial and error. Small-scale improvements and relatively little deviation from the norm characterized most new work. Breakthroughs in yacht architecture which found their way into practice on smaller vessels were not readily adopted by ocean racers, who relied on far less radical but proven approaches. Safety at sea was paramount. Mathematics was an adjunct to reliable and fundamental concepts of shape, but ratios did not lead design. Tank testing and computational comparative analysis would begin to appear in the next decade but were not yet a part of the process. Designers found it more fruitful to design for ocean racing with sheer speed relative to waterline length in mind rather than designing to loopholes of a specific handicapping rule. There was much reliance on the "eye" of the designer, a concept as long-standing as the work of Donald McKay on clipper ships.

The experiments and innovations commonly adapted to ocean racing yachts in later decades from all corners of naval architecture, from dinghies to submarine hydrodynamics, did not make their way easily into ocean racers in the 1920s. *Dorade* permanently changed the way that smaller vessel design was perceived in relation to ocean yachting development. It took until 1934 for a Bermuda Race to be won overall by a yacht influenced by *Dorade*'s trailblazing design, *Edlu*, but the transformation to a narrower, smaller and more aggressively-rigged boat with lighter building specifications and more effective hull form had been set in motion by *Dorade* with the success of her first season of 1930. Because of her there was no turning back.

The stalwart channel cutter *Jolie Brise*, hero of the 1932 Bermuda Race, exemplified the designs favored for ocean racing in the 1920s. Derived from working schooners and cutters, ocean racing sailors took to sea with heavy, proven hull forms and rigs.

Dorade is remarkable when set within the context of Olin Stephens' design experience. His exposure to yacht forms as a little boy began with powerboats on Lake George but was importantly nurtured and soon converted to an interest in sailing by experiences on a series of relatively common sailboats during his teenage years. Those included a small, centerboard, gaff-rigged cutter called *Corker*, a 30-foot Great South Bay centerboarder named *Token*, a 24-foot auxiliary cruising yawl called *Tradscantia*, a 40-foot William Atkin auxiliary ketch called *Sou'wester* and a Nova Scotia One Design of 30 feet called *Scrapper*. The pace of Roderick Sr.'s boat acquisitions and sales was quite remarkable and afforded his sons experience with various sizes, hull forms and rigs. It continued with the purchase in 1926 of *Alicia*, an older 41-foot Sound Schooner Class racer designed by B. B. Crowninshield, to be followed by *Alicia's* sale in order to purchase an older Six Metre, *Natka*, a boat that would importantly influence Olin's early design work. Olin and Rod often sailed without their family, just teenage boys ranging the coast from Long Island Sound to Maine, but in the summer of 1927 they raced *Natka* with their father. Over the period between 1920 and 1927, the family generally bought and sold at least one boat every year and sometimes several, although one boat, *Scrapper*, perished in a fire. This velocity of change in boating platforms created variety and wide opportunity for Olin and Rod.

Olin's return from MIT in 1927 allowed him to do what he wanted most: to design boats and to be near his high-school sweetheart, Florence "Susie" Reynolds, whom he would later marry. Olin had found his way to the Six Metre Class prior to college. Six Metres, designed to the International Rule, are a development class racer of approximately 36 feet in overall length and 23 feet on the water. Each is unique. They played a significant role in Olin's early design career and in the development of *Dorade*. Sailed on both sides of the Atlantic and competed in by many of the most prominent yachtsmen in America, Britain and Bermuda, Six Metres were the almost perfect early platform for Olin's racing experience and design development. He recalls in his autobiography being asked, along with Rod, to crew on a pair of Sixes sailed by Clinton Crane and Sherman Hoyt, two of the most important yachtsmen of the day. Despite having just completed a wet and miserable passage across Long Island Sound on *Scrapper*, they leapt from their hot yacht club showers at the chance to race in the most sought-after class of the day. It was only natural for Olin to begin his design efforts by drawing a Six Metre that spring of 1927. He drew it on a drafting table at his family home in Scarsdale and the effort produced a roll of drawings which the 19-year-old took to the leading lights of yachting that summer in hopes of attracting attention for his design and a client to build it.

One of the notable aspects of Olin Stephens at this early age was the number of important contacts he had made within yachting and design circles by the time he was 19. He was serious about boats, enthusiastic about racing, studious about design and infectious in his desire to learn more. As teenagers, he and Rod had crawled through the yacht yards of City Island in the Bronx, the building site of many of

Foundations of Design

A Six-Metre Boat Design with Interesting Features

AT the conclusion of the recent international six-metre races off Oyster Bay, most of the critics agreed on at least two things, i.e.: American designers had been left far in the rear by their foreign contemporaries, and "something should be done about it."

Just what should be done about it is a question. But at least, the ideas of young designers should see the light of day, in the hopes that they might succeed where more experienced naval architects have progressed but little in the past year or so. It is with this idea in view that we publish the accompanying plans from the board of Olin J. Stephens, II, of New York, which show a six-metre boat with possibilities.

The dimensions of this craft are as follows: l.o.a. 34′; l.w.l. 22′ 10″; beam, 6′ 4½″; draft, 5′; sail area (measured), 525 sq. ft.; sail area, actual, 589 sq. ft.; displacement, 8620 lbs. In explanation of the design, Mr. Stephens has the following to say:

"The design is intended primarily for light weather. In any design the most important factors of speed seem to be long sailing lines and large sail area, with moderate displacement and small wetted surface. Then comes beauty, by which is meant clean, fair, pleasing lines. Though *per se* beauty is not a factor of speed, the easiest boats to look at seem the easiest to drive.

"To produce long sailing lines there are two methods available. First, by using a long water line coupled with fine ends; second, a shorter water line and full ends. The former method has been used in this design. The water line is about the longest of any existing American 'Six.' Though this long water line would ordinarily result in small sail area, this has been avoided by reducing the girth and girth difference measurements to the very minimum, which also lessens the wetted surface. The measured sail area is good, while with overlapping jibs of various sizes it may be said to be ample for the lightest of weather."

To predict what a boat will or will not do, from a study of her design, is a dangerous undertaking, as experienced designers and critics well know. Nevertheless, this design shows a great deal of promise, and it would be decidedly interesting to see her built and tried out.

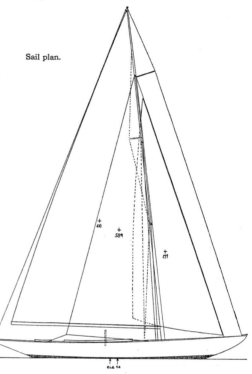

Sail plan.

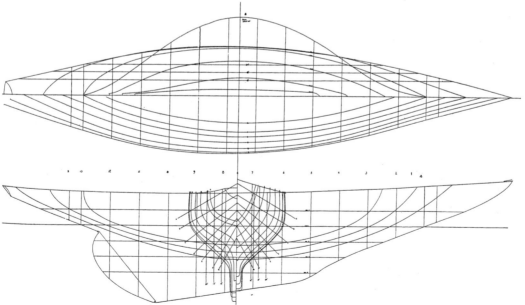

Lines and sections of the six-metre boat designed by Olin J. Stephens, II.

the most important American yachts. Rod would ride his bicycle from Scarsdale and later work at Henry Nevins' yard. The Stephens brothers' experiences in racing and sailing brought them into contact with many of the well-known sailors of the era. Their father encouraged and supported their interest and, as polite and courteous young men, Olin and Rod were welcomed by many who were in a position to advance their careers.

During that summer of 1927, Olin took his Six Metre design to Herbert Stone, editor of *Yachting* magazine and to others whom he hoped would show an interest in building it. He found his way to a meeting with Starling Burgess, ultimately the designer of three America's Cup defenders, to ask for his reactions. As that summer ended, through effort and introductions, Olin joined the yacht design office of Henry J. Gielow on City Island. Gielow was known more for designs of powerboats than sailing yachts. Olin had nevertheless found for himself an association with a recognized firm as a draftsman. Within a few short months he left Gielow to join Philip Rhodes, who became one of the most famous yacht designers of the century and whose boats were more in line with Olin's interest in sailing designs.

From his work base on City Island, he came to know the great yacht builders, such as Nevins, Minneford and Jacob, and to find his way again into the offices of *Yachting*. In January 1928, his design for the Six Metre was published in the new design section under the caption "A Six Metre Boat Design with Interesting Features". He would claim later that his design was published because he haunted the hallways of *Yachting* magazine and that Herbert Stone, its publisher, and his assistant Sam Wetherill thought the work of such a young designer might appeal to *Yachting*'s readers.

It is important to note that five of Olin Stephens' first 10 designs were Six Metres and another of this first group was an Eight Metre, *Conewago* (Design No. 9). His Six Metre in *Yachting* was never built and his first constructed Six Metre, *Thalia* (Design No. 5) was, by his own admission, less than a breakthrough. However, he was directed new work by such luminaries as Clinton Crane, who sent clients his way. He attracted other design commissions by virtue of his early participation and success in the class. Six Metres, designed to the International Measurement Rule are beautiful, deep racers with slack bilges and full hull forms. Even into the 21st century, Six Metres are still designed, built, restored, and raced. Mitch Gibbons-Neff, then the president of Sparkman & Stephens, commented around 2004, "Six Metres are like long-legged blonds, and if you like long-legged blonds, you've got to have one." Their concept of modest beam enhanced their windward performance, and they went downwind with progressively larger and more radical spinnakers.

The measurement of righting moment (the amount of torque, measured in foot pounds, required to incline the hull to a specific angle from an upright position) is determined by ballast, the depth of that ballast and the shape and total displacement of the hull. This measurement is a proxy for the force of the breeze on the sails. By virtue of the penalties inflicted by the constraints of the Six Metre design formula,

A gaggle of Six Metres wait for a rising tide after having their bottoms scrubbed, circa 1929.

Sixes have generally similar shapes that are deep and narrow. That metre hull form is the basis of *Dorade*. By early 1928, forces were in motion that would bring her into being. She is the natural outgrowth of the International Rule designed into an ocean racer. She is deep and very narrow for her length, with 10 feet, 3 inches of beam to carry her 37 feet, 3 inches of designed waterline length. Her ends are relatively drawn-out for an ocean racer of her day, and her Marconi or Bermuda yawl rig is very large in relationship to her hull form. She caused consternation in the yachting world by virtue of her light construction and ample sail plan, and questions were raised about her suitability for ocean contests. Her combinations of diverse design elements made her a revolutionary concept.

Drake Sparkman's yacht brokerage office at 205 City Island Avenue on City Island, New York, in 1928.

COURTESY TOM NYE AND CITY ISLAND NAUTICAL MUSEUM

Sparkman & Stephens

Drake Sparkman was a 29-year-old yacht broker with offices in New York City and City Island when he entered the Stephens family's life in 1927. He found a buyer for their 41-foot racing schooner *Alicia*, and the senior Stephens purchased through him the Six Metre *Natka*. Sparkman raced in the Victory class and successfully sold boats with his knowledge and enthusiasm for yachting. His affability and his associations with members of the New York and Larchmont Yacht Clubs helped as well. In addition to brokerage, Sparkman also guided his clients in the design and building of new boats. In early 1928, he encouraged Olin Stephens to leave Philip Rhodes' design office and join him in what was informally known as Sparkman & Stephens, a firm that was not legally incorporated until November 11, 1929. It certainly must have helped Sparkman to make his offer with Olin's Six Metre design appearing in *Yachting* in January. Such advertising could not hurt. One thing was leading to another.

In the early months of 1928, Sparkman relied on Olin, drawing from home, to handle the design work for sailboats while Sparkman's then retiring associate, Roger Haddock, managed the drawing of powerboats. Olin's designs found clients beginning with a 21-foot one-design called the Sound Junior Class (S&S Design No. 1, later known as the Manhasset Bay One Design) of which 20 were built. The yachting fraternity was collegial and friendly, and that summer Sam Wetherill of *Yachting* again helped Olin by arranging an invitation for him to crew with John Alden on his *Malabar IX* in the Bermuda Race amongst a fleet well-populated with Alden-designed schooners. The boat finished adequately, and Olin sailed back to Marblehead after the race to compete with Alden on his Universal Rule Q-Boat *Hope*. Afterward, Alden asked Olin to join his design office, but Olin felt that he had set a course on his own with Sparkman, his third association in eighteen months. Although flattered to be asked, he declined. It would prove to be a momentous decision.

That fall, Sparkman inveigled Henry Nevins to make a drafting table available to Olin, allowing him to supplement his own design work with work for Nevins

The Double Sheet Bend, shown with lashing, connects two lines and is designated as "strong" by Ashley, although not as secure as the Double Bend.

ASHLEY KNOT 1434

The crew of *Kalmia,*
Olin's second design, in 1929
with Olin at the tiller and
the two Rods forward.

© MYSTIC SEAPORT

———opposite———

Kalmia under sail.
Her club jib heralds her cruising
intentions, but she proved able
on a race course.

© MYSTIC SEAPORT

and no longer to work primarily from home. Henry B. Nevins was a full service design and build operation, famous for building to both their own designs and to the designs of others. Henry Nevins himself owned the yard and was known for his commitment to perfection and strength in the building of yachts. "The Nevins Way" was synonymous with seaworthiness, the best materials and fine craftsmanship. The yard manager was Rufus Murray, who had come from the Herreshoff Manufacturing Company in Bristol, Rhode Island, a yard notable for great advances in yacht building, designs and efficient construction systems. Nevins fittings and mechanical devices, some developed from the hardware of Merriman Brothers, were legendary, particularly machined equipment such as winches and windlasses. Working in the Nevins yard gave Olin firsthand experience in building methods and organization. The relationship of the Stephens family with Henry Nevins was to grow deeper as the years progressed. A sort of semi-independent incubation occurred where Olin was associated with Sparkman, was provided space and some work by Nevins and yet was able to operate on his own. It must have been his devotion to yacht design, coupled with youth, hard work, talent and personality, that made possible such a system of support. There he was, launched as a yacht designer at the age of 20.

The Six Metre *Cherokee* was designed in 1929 at the same time that the lines for *Dorade* were drawn. Both boats were launched in the spring of 1930.

© MYSTIC SEAPORT

In the fall of 1928, Drake was approached for the design of a 30-foot yacht with small accommodations below, to be used for "afternoon sailing" and just maybe a bit of racing. Olin was asked to turn to the task for the owner, Arthur Hatch. *Kalmia* (S&S Design No. 2) was launched in the spring of 1929, having been built by the Minneford Yard at City Island over the winter. She was drawn with ability to windward in mind but was in no way radical, just an able and attractive cruiser/racer. Olin and his family were invited by Hatch to take *Kalmia* on the Gibson Island Race that next summer, a race from New London, Conn., to the Chesapeake Bay, and she won class honors in the smallest class. As Olin stated, "*Kalmia*'s performance seemed to give confidence to both prospective clients and my associates, offsetting likely doubts due to my youth and limited background."

Next came a commission for a slightly larger version of *Kalmia*, the sloop *Cynara* (Design No. 4), for Robert Moore of Huntington, New York, built again at Minneford's. Finally came Olin's first constructed Six Metre, a design drawn for Louis G. Young, who raced in the Six Metre class and had some ideas for a new boat to replace one he owned designed by Johan Anker. *Thalia*, (Design No. 5), as this first Six Metre was named, was not the design that Olin had carried around in his roll of plans in 1927 but was a new effort with Long Island Sound's light summer racing winds in mind. She was built by Nevins and was ready for trial in the fall. She had full midship sections and, although she fared acceptably in early match racing, Olin counted her as a design misjudgment and felt lucky, yet again, that her competitors in the closely-watched speed trials at her early testing were Sixes with fouled bottoms which seemed slower in the eyes of prospective clients looking at the early efforts of an untried designer. This experience made a great impression on the young yacht architect, and he immediately incorporated refinements into a subsequent series of Sixes, an Eight Metre (*Conewago*) and several cruising design commissions, which flowed into S&S. As Olin would write, "In early 1929, people were taking chances."

By 1929, boats to Olin Stephens' designs were being built at Nevins, Minneford's and the Robert Jacob yards, side by side in City Island. The scope of business and the need for a separate space prompted the opening of a Sparkman & Stephens office in a storefront there. Olin was immersed in the designs for the Sixes *Mist* (Design No. 6), *Comet* and *Meteor* (Nos. 8 and 8.1) and *Cherokee* (No. 10). Yet the volume of work during 1929 did not keep Olin from his and his family's fervent objective—the design and building of a real ocean racer. The sale of the coal company made it possible to contemplate such a yacht. Design No. 7, sandwiched between the paying commissions for the flock of International Rule Metre boats, was to become *Dorade*.

Olin's stiletto-thin *Comet* of 1929.

© MYSTIC SEAPORT

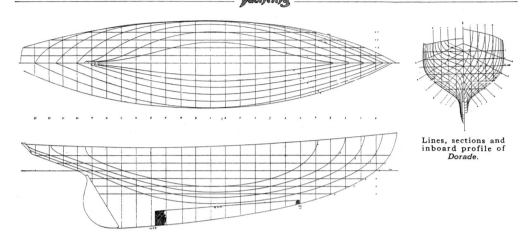

Lines, sections and
inboard profile of
Dorade.

Dorade—a Fast Cruising Cutter Designed by Sparkman & Stephens

THE objective towards which the designers, Spark-man & Stephens, aimed in working out the accompanying design of *Dorade* was the production of a fast cruising boat for use without an engine in both coastwise and deep water cruising and racing. Though realizing that windward work comprises but a small part of most cruising, they believe that a smart boat to windward is always a source of great satisfaction, and further, that without an engine, good light weather performance is decidedly desirable. Therefore they have endeavored to incorporate in the design weatherly qualities for any kind of going.

Dorade is 50′ 5″ o.a., 40′ l.w.l., 11′ beam, and 7′ 6″ draft, with sail area of 1565 sq. ft. and displacement of 46,400 lbs. She is somewhat long and narrow, with deep sections and generous displacement. Bow and stern sections are sharp, and the overhangs are moderate. All ballast is outside. Plenty of forefoot and a raking keel should promote good steering, and the design throughout shows good proportion and balance.

A jib-headed mainsail was adopted for speed and ease of

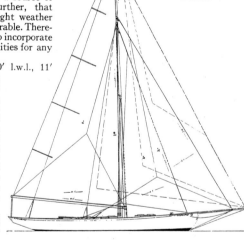

Sail plan of
Dorade.

handling, and because there is no gaff to slat and bang around in a calm. The bowsprit is carried out beyond the tack of the working jib so that a large ballooner or reacher may be set easily.

The interior accommodations are laid out for four people aft and two forward. A navigator's chart table is shown, and generous locker space is provided. All berths are built in. There is a toilet room amidships, on the port side, large galley forward, with berth and crew's toilet in the forecastle.

The short bow and deep hull are decided advantages when measurement rules are taken into consideration, *Dorade* rating but 41.8 under the Bermuda Race Rule. The rig might easily be reduced for ocean cruising, while a roller reefing gear would facilitate reefing the mainsail, making sail shortening easy.

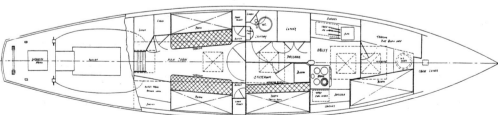

Accommodation plan of *Dorade*, a fast cruising cutter designed by Sparkman & Stephens.

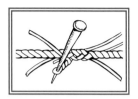

Birth of an Offshore Racer

The idea for an ocean racer had germinated over a long period of time in Olin's thinking, and the July 1928 issue of *Yachting* contained the drawings and description of a 50-foot cutter credited to the Sparkman & Stephens firm with the name *Dorade*. It was the second design by Olin to be published in the magazine in six months. The layout and rig looked much less modern and radical than the yacht that was actually to become the famous yawl and emerge two years later. It is interesting that this trial balloon was released in the yachting press, later altered substantially and still retained the same name. The plans show an almost typical yacht of the period and, although this initial design was never built, it is unlikely that she would have achieved anything like the success of the ultimate *Dorade*. Her waterline length and subsequent rating would have made her less competitive under the CCA Rule. She is laid out with a paid hand forward near the galley at the mainmast. She is beamier and probably much less handy with her foreshortened bow and long bowsprit. Major changes evolved over the next year as Olin refined his design thinking. The published plans leave a wonderful record of that evolution.

In mid-1929, Olin began the redrawing of a revised offshore racing yacht, sometimes more modestly called a fast cruiser by S&S, to be commissioned by Roderick Stephens Sr. to his son's design. Unlike his published design of 1928, this time she would be a yawl. Olin's autobiography describes the underpinnings of his ideas for this boat and stresses several fundamental notions. The reduction of weight, smooth and drawn-out lines, a high ballast-to-displacement ratio, all ballasting carried externally rather than higher inside in the bilge and minimal wetted surface are his stated approach. The most defining feature was a relationship of beam to waterline length similar to his Six Metres. Stephens also alludes to beauty and voiced an early devotion to art as a fundamental and even essential component of successful yacht design. Beauty was a defining aspect of his designs throughout his career, for they are, to whatever purpose, consistently striking and beautiful boats. Weight saving was accomplished in a wide variety of ways. Steam-bent frames were specified to replace the more closely spaced, heavier, sometimes doubled, sawn frames used in the fisherman types. Deck beams, where practical, were to be made of spruce rather than the heavier and more commonly used oak. A flush deck combined with full breadth deck beams, even under skylights, gave the structure strength despite the overall lighter building approach.

The Marlinspike on Hoisted Hitch shows a three-strand splicing of two ropes together used by a sailmaker for a boltrope or a rigger for standing rigging.

ASHLEY KNOT 2625

———opposite———

Olin's first *Dorade*, published but never built.
COURTESY *YACHTING*

Full width spruce deck beams, even beneath the main skylight, added to the boat's structural strength. This contemporary photograph shows the notches in the beams made to accomodate standing rods for the non-original saloon table, later removed.

PHOTOGRAPH BY GREEN BRETT

The yacht was given deck planking of white pine rather than the teak more typically used. Pine was softer and less durable but still afforded a good footing for the crew. When asked how much weight was saved by not using teak, Olin replied that they never calculated the weight savings. They just knew that pine was lighter and that was all that mattered. The racer's interior floorboards were made of a solid cork material, again lighter than a teak and holly sole and still providing a good grip in a pitching seaway. The use of pine and cork are telling. They are not particularly durable materials, but they are light. She was designed to race, and Olin knew that less weight meant greater speed. Her lines were easy in the sense of a smooth continuum and a drawn-out waterline that ended naturally without significant or radical curvature. Her keel was long—over 21 feet—in relationship to her designed waterline of 37 feet, 3 inches. Further, her overhangs were not as drawn-out as was typical of International Rule boats, and this saved weight and diminished hobby-horsing in a seaway. All of these features gave her a confident motion at sea, and there is no doubt that she was and is a famously competent, lightly steered, well balanced vessel when sailed to weather.

The matter of the positioning of ballast was still somewhat of a question in 1929. External ballast concentrated the center of gravity and positioned it lower and more centrally fore and aft than internal ballast spread through the bilges. External ballast was thought to be deleterious to an easy motion at sea, causing the vessel to roll and pitch too quickly. Internal ballast distributed the weight more evenly along the waterline, albeit at some sacrifice to stiffness because it was placed higher. Stephens believed that weight (i.e. the verticle center of gravity) should be as low as possible, and so *Dorade*'s relatively deep keel was fitted with 16,600 pounds of external lead ballast.

It was not uncommon for new designs to fail to float on their designed waterlines, given the complexity of weight calculations. Oftentimes, small amounts of internal ballast in the form of lead "pigs" were added to the bilge for obtaining correct fore and aft trim. *Dorade* was heavier than expected, and her waterline had been painted too low before her launching. It was simply repainted higher. Of course, such a change lengthened her waterline and gave the hull greater theoretical speed, which resulted in some penalty in rating. A scrap of calculations and notes from the S&S technical file show Rod's recording of weights for the boat. He had deduced her ballast weight by calculating actual floating displacement and deducting the weight of everything other than the lead ballast keel. He noted that lead pigs totaling 238 pounds was added internally and placed 11 feet, 1 ½ inches ahead of the calculated balance point, which is itself 10 feet, 10 inches ahead of the stern tip of the lead keel. The pigs were used to trim her bow down slightly and probably extended her waterline even further.

All of the deliberate and detailed attention to weight saving, its distribution, the boat's ballasting and the selection of materials combined to produce an oceangoing vessel that was significantly lighter than her principal competitors. Olin was devoted to lowering weight as a way to improve speed, and the combined effect of his efforts with *Dorade* made her at least one-fifth lighter than would have been the case for a similarly proportioned boat built with sawn frames on closer centers using thicker and heavier materials overall. This was a notable but less obvious element of her revolutionary design, but it contributed as much as nearly anything else to her racing success.

Dorade's hull shape itself also advanced two other conceptual elements. First, her bilges were slack, meaning that her hull was full as the bilge turned into the keel and did not make a sharp turn downward. Secondly, the lateral plane or side surface of her keel was smaller in area than a fisherman-style underbody. This was combined with a continuous leading edge to the stem and keel, not extended or cut away at any point. The total plane was more representative of onshore racers than of oceangoing competitors. The rudder was relatively small to minimize resistance. These elements were criticized for ocean work, with the view that *Dorade*'s hull form was less stable than was desirable, but Stephens saw these elements as efficiencies that added speed and could successfully be incorporated into an ocean racer.

Significantly, the boat's most radical and notable element was found in Olin's approach to beam. *Dorade* is very narrow, and it is interesting to compare her lines to other boats in order to evaluate just how narrow she really is. One benchmark is the ratio of waterline length to maximum beam. An International Rule boat of the era, such as a Six Metre, has a ratio of waterline to beam of 3.7 to 3.9. *Conewago*, Olin's first Eight Metre, is at the high end of that range. An Alden schooner such as *Malabar X* carried a ratio of 2.9, clearly by this basic measurement a beamier boat. Fife's *Hallowe'en* of 1926 was drawn to a ratio of 3.23 and *Eileen* of 1929 had a ratio of 3.75. Charles Nicholson at the turn of the century had drawn *Flame*, a 63-foot cutter, later a yawl, with a 48-foot waterline and a beam of 12 feet, producing a ratio of 4.0. The notion of a narrow boat was not new, particularly in Britain. Extreme English racing cutters of the 1880s, such as William Fife Jr.'s *Clara*, had an astonishing ratio of 5.86.

Dorade was drawn to be 52 feet on deck in length with a beam of 10 feet, 3 inches and a datum or load waterline of 37 feet, 3 inches. However, despite the saving of weight at every turn, she still floated lower than her designed waterline at nearly 39 feet. At this figure, she carried a waterline to beam ratio of 3.8, a big, muscular Six Metre or, more appropriately, a Ten Metre.

The matter of beam relative to waterline was explored later in the 1930s, as new designs and descendants of *Dorade* were launched. The graph above appears in Uffa Fox's book of 1934, *Sailing, Seamanship and Yacht Construction*, and describes this

IDEAL PROPORTIONS OF CRUISING YACHTS

BEAM

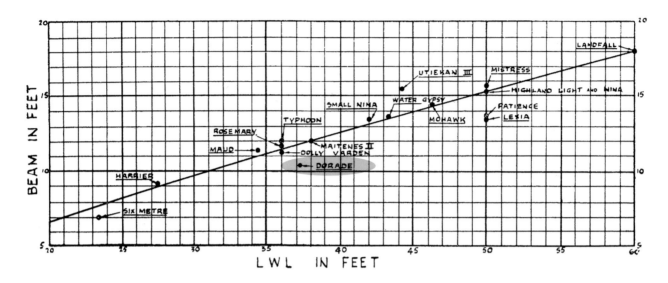

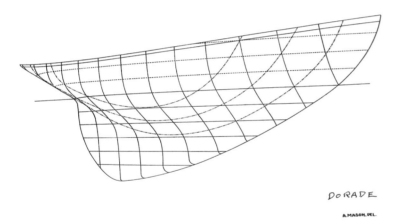

DORADE

A. MASON. DEL.

Top—Dorade is narrow, as shown in this comparison of beam to load water line by Uffa Fox for Sailing, Seamanship and Yacht Construction, *1934.*

Below—Dorade, in perspective, rendered by Al Mason of S&S.

COURTESY
SPARKMAN & STEPHENS

relationship. It is clear that *Dorade* lies at the far edge of narrowness and would be seen as even more radical on this graph if her real waterline were to be used in the calculations. Fox reported in his *Racing, Cruising and Design* of 1937 that *Dorade* actually measured 41 feet on the water and drew 8 feet, 3 inches when she was measured fully loaded for the 1936 Honolulu Race.

The combination of a narrow hull form and a generous sail plan produced a boat that was tender, possibly too tender given that rigging changes were made after her first season to reduce her sail area. However, there is no doubt that Olin Stephens sought to achieve a design that would heel easily to extend its waterline length and thus increase its theoretical hull speed. *Dorade*'s drawn-out lines added to the combination and produced a singularly fast yacht for her size. Olin had mixed the elements of weight and shape to create a breakthrough.

Her rig was Marconi and not gaff, a contemporary choice which was becoming common, and she was given ample sail area totaling 1,192 square feet. Her yawl configuration would allow for more manageable handling under a wide variety of wind conditions and maneuverability in close quarters using her mizzen. The rating rules of the day did not count the sail area of the mizzen or its staysail in any

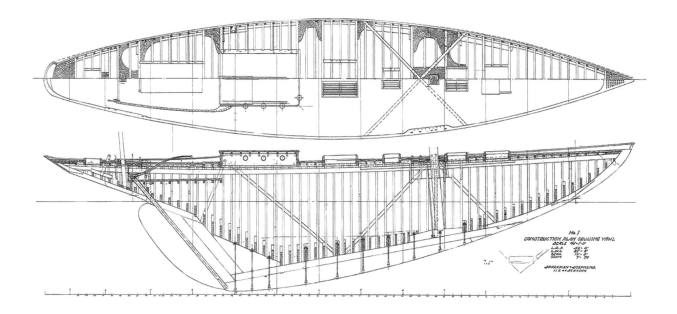

Dorade's construction plan clearly shows her bronze strapping, continuous forefoot profile and abundant use of lodging knees for strength in her deck.

COURTESY
SPARKMAN & STEPHENS

way, and thus these additions were free. It was a rating convention that persisted through the next 30 years. Her masts were raked aft, for balance and a more aerodynamic attack to weather. It is a feature that makes her distinctive and very easily identified from a distance and it was a device used on yachts of the prior century but was not employed as aggressively by Stephens ever again. She was drawn to carry three headsails, thereby offering many combinations of easily handled jibs to balance the boat in a variety of wind and sea conditions. She was also masthead rigged and could carry a large single Genoa jib in light air. She had two sets of running backstays with her rig, one set for the main and one set for the mizzen. *Dorade* was equipped with 12 winches for running rigging, a remarkable abundance of machinery that raised eyebrows in a sailing world still employing some block and tackle. Olin wanted power to handle the large sailplan. She was originally fitted with a two-spreader heavy-section, hollow and round mainmast and a short bowsprit. While tangs were employed for part of her rigging to attach shrouds to the spars, she also used strops with wooden keepers, an old-fashioned approach using less metal and punching fewer fasteners into the spars. Modern sailors may consider asymmetrical spinnakers a new innovation, but *Dorade*'s early spinnakers were fashioned with an unequal leech and luff. Her first small chute was 41 feet, 7 inches on one side and 43 feet, 9 inches on the other.

The development of Marconi or Bermudian rigs had created some anomalies in the 1920s, particularly in Britain as they replaced the gaff rig. The tendency of some designers to position the Bermudian mast too far forward created overly large mainsails and unbalanced boats that were difficult to reef. *Dorade*'s proportions were very nearly right the first time out, with a foretriangle fitted to accommodate multiple headsail combinations balanced by her mizzen. Refinements conducted in the winter of 1930-'31 included cutting down the main mast and removing the bow-

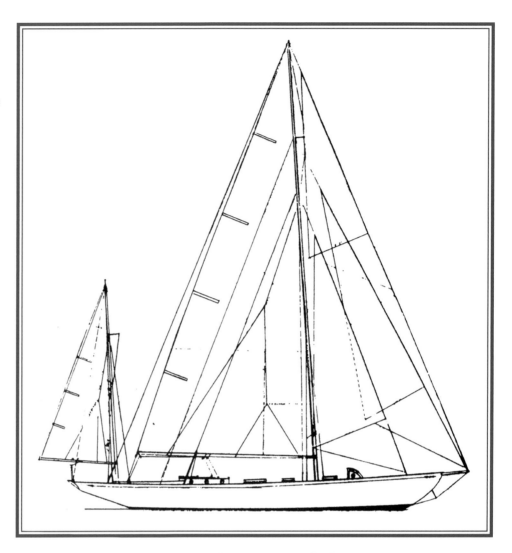

Dorade's original rig incorporated the salvaged and cut down mast of the six-metre *Natka* as a mizzen. Both masts had solid upper sections.

Dorade with her original rig in 1930. Her deep varnished bulwarks and bowsprit hide the beauty of her sheer, making her look somewhat inelegant and old fashioned. This same image and an advertisement appeared in *The Rudder* following the Bermuda Race.

© MYSTIC SEAPORT

sprit, which gave *Dorade* her legendary balance and a helm that was light. *Dorade* needed that sailing balance. She had no engine and would sail without one for the next decade. A real sailboat.

It is worth noting that, while Olin drew the lines for *Dorade*, the construction and accommodation drawings were developed by an "elderly marine draftsman, a Mr. Clark" and by Jim Merrill within the Sparkman & Stephens office. It was to be an often repeated pattern, for Olin was an absolute master at setting down lines beautifully and quickly, but he did not excel at drafting and utilized those more able to prepare detailed construction drawings for the yard to use in building the boat. It was a good division of talents. Olin's extraordinary eye clearly led the basic design, but the draftsmen's work was also essential in producing the finished product to the correct specifications. Down below, *Dorade* was designed as a racing yacht for an all-amateur crew of up to eight. The forepeak held a pipe berth but was not designed for a paid hand, as was so common during the day. The peak was used instead for sail stowage, and with her rig there were lots of sails. Next aft from the forepeak

Counterclockwise, from top— 1. The saloon, looking forward.
2. The fold-down, "Pullman" sink in the head. 3. The strops for the
lower shrouds on the mizzen employed an older style, rather than using
tangs. These are retained today. 4. *Dorade*'s galley, rebuilt to original
specifications, not including the salt water sink.

GREEN BRETT / AUTHOR

Birth of an Offshore Racer

Elements of the cabinetry were copied from familiar furniture and drawers in the Stephens' home in Scarsdale.

GREEN BRETT / AUTHOR

were berths to port and starboard, and further aft to port a small head with an elegant fold-down "Pullman" porcelain sink. Across the passageway to starboard were cupboards. This passageway was tight, only 2 feet, 8 inches across. The main saloon was fitted with an L-shaped bench to port, a very narrow bench to starboard and bunks outboard on both sides.

There were various configurations for a table in the early years, some mounted to the floor, some gimbaled and some hung from the deck beams. There wasn't a great deal of room for any of these designs given her beam, but the earliest gimbaled version received good reviews from those who sailed offshore in the yacht. There is a lovely cabinet for bottles forward of the settee to port, but in her early days she was generally a dry ship, particularly to the Stephens brothers.

The galley was aft to port, making it accessible to the cockpit. It held two sinks, one in the initial plans for fresh water and another, added later, for pumping salt water to wash dishes. It was also fitted with a coal stove and a coal scuttle, located under the bridge deck and cockpit, which served as storage for this fuel. A kerosene two-burner stove was added later. Across the galley to starboard was a six-foot-long navigation table which, in reality, served as a small bunk for the navigator, allowing easy access to the cockpit. Outboard to starboard over this bunk was the flag locker, an absolutely necessary fitment for racing.

It is interesting to notice the placement of the companionway 13 inches to starboard with its port edge on the centerline. The placement makes the galley to port more spacious. Olin was not concerned about this lack of symmetry, and his later design for *Stormy Weather*'s cockpit companionway placed it just off center. John Alden had also used such an off-center approach. Olin as a young designer embraced the practical advantages of proportioning spaces in a variety of ways, and they worked very well. *Dorade*'s configuration with a galley aft and no accommodation for a paid hand confirms her design as one for amateur racing and family cruising. By comparison, Olin's designs for similar boats, such as *Edlu*, *Stormy Weather*, *Sonny*, and the New York 32s, all laid out a galley near the mainmast and provided for a hand close by in the forepeak. *Dorade* singularly approached her layout with the Stephens men in mind. And with the women in mind, the seams on the cockpit seats were payed in white rather than black compound, so as not to smudge their white yachting skirts.

Finally, *Dorade*'s cockpit was carefully designed for ocean work. The shallow footwell avoids the accumulation of large amounts of water in heavy going, while her coamings are low for easy access to deck. This made for a wet ride but was a sensible design for working at sea. She was fitted with a tiller, not a wheel, and the tiller was tucked under the cockpit deck slightly. Its movement was moderately constrained by the sides of the footwell. The tiller itself was originally built in a very sturdy, faceted solid section and looked a bit beefy for the fine lines of the boat. It was not going to break.

City Island yacht yards with Consolidated, Minneford and Nevins.

Minneford's

City Island and its major yacht yards played an important role in the story of the Stephens brothers and *Dorade*. The relationship of the Stephens family with Henry Nevins was a close one and developed in small steps, over a short period of time. As teenagers, Rod and Olin were fascinated by the work of the yard, visiting on Sundays to see boats under construction. Olin had taken on drafting work for Nevins when he returned from MIT. It would have seemed likely that the family would go to Nevins for the building of their new yawl, but in the summer of 1929 Nevins was full of work and could not take on the project until the following year. The shared objective was to have a boat finished in time to participate in the Bermuda Race the following summer. If they missed that window, they would have to wait until the next race two years later. Given the velocity of learning and progress, such a wait seemed impossible to the young Stephens brothers, and so Roderick Sr. took the project to build the 52-foot ocean racer to H.S. Sayers at the Minneford Yacht Yard.

Founded in 1926 by H. Schiefflin Sayers and sandwiched between the well-established Henry B. Nevins and Robert Jacob yards on what had been known as Sugar Loaf Beach on City Island, the Minneford Yacht Yard was the upstart. Named in the language of the Minnifer Indians, the yard was to outlast both of its better-known neighbors. H.S. Sayers was a yachtsman and lawyer with active membership in the City Island Yacht Club and a law office in Manhattan. He and his brother held property investments, including ownership of the Bronx Swimming Pool. The Sayers family lived on Eastchester Bay on City Island and sailed a 1920 Robert Jacob-built yawl named *Squall*. The yard he established built for him the 36-foot *Margenita* as one of its earliest projects. By 1930, the Minneford yard was building four sailing yachts to Olin Stephens' designs as well as the important keel/centerboard ketch *Tidal Wave* to the design of Philip Rhodes. If the Nevins yard was full, the Minneford Yard was at least very busy that year. The next years of a deepening Depression would take a toll and there would not be as much activ-

The Pocket Shaped Multi-Strand Stopper is elaborately made up from four strands and is sometimes fitted with a leather washer for strength and to lessen chafe.

Ashley Knot 772

Minneford Yacht Yard in the late
1920s. *Dorade* was built in the
brick building to the right.

COURTESY TOM NYE AND
CITY ISLAND NAUTICAL MUSEUM

ity at Minneford's during any future year until the war effort began in early 1942.

Dorade's construction began alongside *Tidal Wave* at the same time that Sparkman & Stephens added "Incorporated" to its name, in November 1929. The new firm had five shareholders: Drake Sparkman; his younger brother, James Sparkman; Roderick Stephens Sr.; Olin J. Stephens II; and James Murray, another salesman in the office.

Rod had started studies at Cornell University following his graduation from high school but had left college after one year with the same urgency to get at the yacht building business that had characterized Olin's departure from MIT. Henry Nevins had asked Roderick Sr. for permission to offer young Rod a job in the yard, stressing that he felt Rod would learn more in boatbuilding than in his studies at college. The senior Stephens agreed to try it for one year. Rod never returned to Cornell. Henry Nevins took every opportunity to support both Stephens brothers; some say the pair would have been his successors in the yard had they not found such enticing independent success at S&S. Nevins' relationship with Roderick Sr. was also a close and generous one, and when the yard sought capital for a new marine railway in the early 1930s, it was the senior Stephens who supplied it. Minneford's had the contract for building *Dorade*, and they also had Rod Jr., who would monitor progress daily and seek the counsel of Nevins and Rufus Murray to be certain a first-class product was being produced.

Dorade was built to scantlings applied under the Universal Rule with reference to Herreshoff's practices. Her planking was of 1¼-inch Honduras mahogany on steam-bent oak frames 2 inches by 2 inches arranged at intervals, or centers, of

Right—Minneford's showroom
in the late 1940s.

Below—City Island and
its bridge, looking up Long
Island Sound.

COURTESY TOM NYE AND
CITY ISLAND NAUTICAL MUSEUM

The launching of the Eight Metre *Conewago* in April 1930, just weeks before *Dorade*. Henry Nevins is second from right. Olin, without glasses in front of his masterpiece, appears almost out of place in his youthful countenance.

9 inches. Later designs would call for a more conventional framing interval of as much as 11 or 12 inches and planking became lighter, but *Dorade* was lightly built for her time. Her deck beams were 1 ¾ inches wide by 2 ¾ inches deep, beefy but still conservatively sized, given that they were of spruce. Lodging and hanging knees were of oak. Her 16,600 pounds of lead ballast was carried outside the hull, and she displaced a total of 37,720 lbs as drawn. She was fastened with 2 inch, No. 12 Everdur bronze screws through her single layer of planking, and ⅞-inch bronze keel bolts were fitted through her oak keel and deadwood. Her hull was bronze strapped diagonally with ³⁄₁₆- by 2 ½-inch material in way of the mainmast, and her deck was similarly strapped at the mainmast partners. The use of bronze fasteners and strapping was relatively new. Herreshoff, Nevins and others had led the way with these

materials in America, but it had not been as commonly adopted in Europe. Many attribute the European reluctance to use non-ferrous metals to the lower salinity in the Baltic waters resulting in less steel corrosion and to the fact that bronze was so much more expensive. However, there is no doubt that the use of silicon bronze added importantly to the long lives of yachts built in America during the 1930s and 1940s. Her deck furniture, skylights and a short, low house were all constructed of mahogany. The deckhouse was topped by tongue-and-groove fir covered in canvas. Her spars of Sitka spruce were partially hollow and glued with resorcinol, and her winches and windlass were bronze fitments to Nevins' designs. Olin would call this approach to building "The City Island Way."

She was a solidly built, straightforward ocean racer, balanced and purposeful. Uffa Fox, the great British sailor, racer, designer, author and sailing master to the Royal Family, would say of *Dorade* in *Sailing, Seamanship and Yacht Construction:*

"*Dorade* is easy throughout, her easy sections made for ease in draughting her lines, this in turn made for ease in building, the final result being an easy seaboat, one easily driven and easy on her gear." " Her narrow beam is balanced by her deep draught, her light displacement by a small sail area, and her narrow floor space forces her freeboard higher, for headroom." "*Dorade's* tiny tiller shows that she is easy on her helm, and proves her to be a well-balanced boat." "Her ability and success does not lie so much in any special point, but in the perfection of every detail."

Despite the accolades, the boat was not perfect. Her bunks outboard to port and starboard in the main saloon were unconventionally narrow, and this made rolling over in them very difficult. They were deep and secure at sea but felt to some like coffins. Olin stated that they were only "tolerable" when in port, particularly when it was warm. In many ways, they seemed to have been designed for Olin, Rod and Roderick Sr., who were all "convenient" in size. Her extreme narrowness made her a famous rolling platform at sea when she was sailed downwind. Her crews uniformly describe the dipping of the main boom followed by the dipping of the spinnaker pole as she rolled from side to side downwind with a sea running. They certainly got used to it, as her motion was active, although not violent, on a run. Adjustments made to allow for greater ease at sea included a special reefing clew set three feet up the leech on the mainsail to keep the boom out of the water when running.

And run she did with her light displacement. Many of her great victories were to come as a result of her remarkable speed off the wind. She was aggressively rigged with her original bowsprit and a mainsail that was 680 square feet on a hoist of 55 feet, 1 inch. But by the following season her bowsprit was gone, a change that brought her entire rig inboard and interestingly made her look more modern. The elimination of a bowsprit was soon adopted avidly by Olin and many others in later designs. At the same time, *Dorade's* mainmast was reduced to 52 feet, 6 inches on the hoist, and her boom was cut down by nearly 10 inches, thus reducing her

Dorade rolling wildly and dipping her boom despite the lifting reef. This painting by R.F. Paterson was captioned, "July 15, 1931: Day's Run 205 Miles" and appeared in Uffa Fox's *Sailing, Seamanship and Yacht Construction* of 1934.

© MYSTIC SEAPORT

mainsail area to 617 square feet, a reduction of nearly 10 percent. The combination worked, and she became easier to handle, better balanced and faster after these seemingly small rig changes were made by her second racing year of 1931. Importantly, her sailplan could be matched well to her inherent lines to allow her to be sailed easily and quickly in heavy weather with a very moderate amount of canvas. Her rig had struck the right balance.

Dorade was launched in May 1930. Her name was taken from the dorado or dolphinfish (coryphaena hippurus), an exotic, colorful, bluff-headed, offshore, warm water trophy fish. Presaging the triumphs of the boat, the fish is found in both the Atlantic and Pacific oceans. *Dorade* had taken only seven months to build, a testament to Minneford's efficiency and to the amount of available labor applied to the project but also to the ease of her lines and relative lightness of her construction. The Bermuda Race was approaching, and she needed to be ready. Her waterline was repainted to suit her floating level, and sails (built by Fuller on City Island) and other equipment were purchased. The cockpit compass in a binnacle was supplemented with a "sighting compass" mounted on the far afterdeck below the mizzen boom. This large pyramid of gear, often seen with a canvas cover in her early pictures, was designed to sit as far away as possible from any metal that might impact its accu-

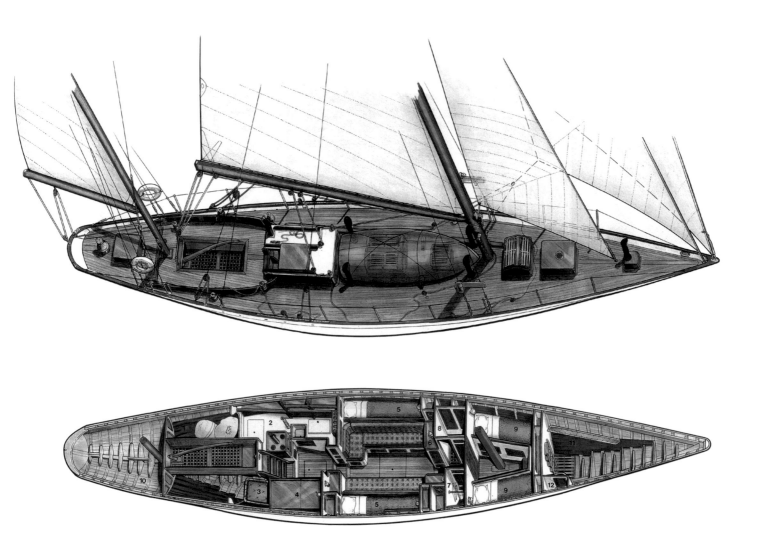

Renderings of *Dorade*'s 1931 deck and accommodation plan.

ROBBERT DAS

racy. In later years, this instrument was moved to the house top. Despite the fact that *Dorade* carried no engine to give magnetic interference, this aft perch seemed at first to be the best place for a clear directional reading, but the housetop later proved to be easier and more secure at sea. Like other yachts of the day, *Dorade* carried a taffrail log, an instrument that towed a wire line with a small spinner astern and recorded its rotations and in this way calibrated the distance traveled. She was later to receive a Kenyon Knotmeter, an early model given by the maker.

Dorade's building cost was an agreed-to $20,000, and her sails and other equipment added another $8,000 to the total figure.

Dorade being provisioned at the Nevins Dock on City Island circa 1934.

© MYSTIC SEAPORT

Minneford's

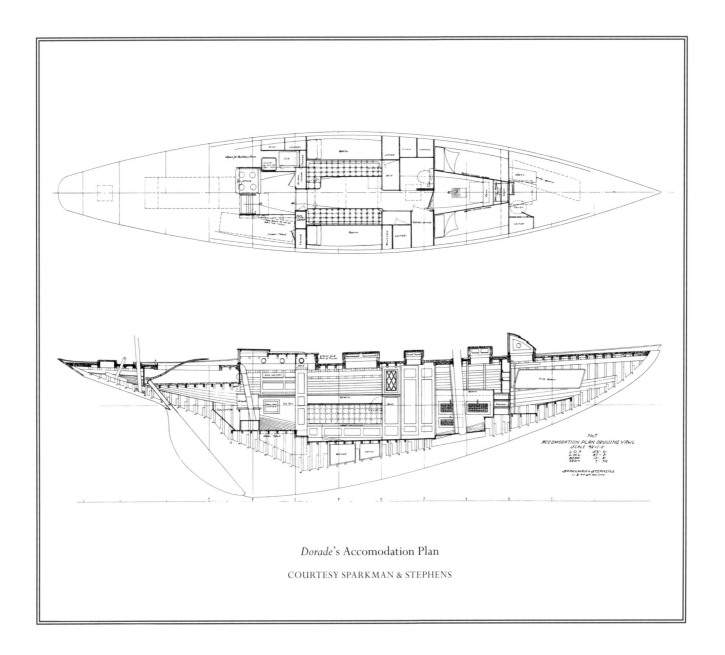

Dorade's Accomodation Plan

COURTESY SPARKMAN & STEPHENS

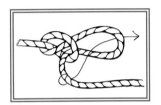

First Lessons from the Onion Patch

The first major test for the new yawl was to be the Bermuda Race in the summer of 1930, the Atlantic Ocean contest to "The Onion Patch." Five new boats had been designed to race under the measurement rule of the Cruising Club of America, which had been recently revised as an adaptation of the Britain's Ocean Racing Club. *Yachting* fanned interest in the race with an article in April 1930, entitled "Three New Yachts for the Bermuda Race." At the article's publication, *Dorade* was not yet in the water. Other designs included a 61-foot schooner to be named *Mistress*, drawn by Sherman Hoyt for George Roosevelt, and the cutter *Viking*, by F. Jay Wells for himself. John Alden brought his newest *Malabar X*, a schooner of 58 feet, 3 inches.

Forty-two boats assembled off New London, Connecticut, at 0800 on June 22 for the start. The finish lay 660 miles to the south, southeast off St. David's Light. The fleet was composed of 30 schooners, five yawls, four ketches, two cutters and a sloop. Aboard *Dorade* were Roderick Sr., Olin, Rod Jr. and three young men who would figure prominently in her future—Buck Moore, Johnny Fox and Jim Merrill. Also adding importantly to the crew were the experienced Arthur Knapp and Marshall Rawle. The start headed out toward Montauk Point on Long Island and then southeast into the Atlantic. It was to be a race of moderate breezes, never over about 18 knots.

As the fleet approached Bermuda after four days at sea, a cloudy sky made navigation difficult. *Dorade*'s crew realized that they had sailed low of the finish line and hardened up. First to finish, with an average speed of 6.7 knots, was *Yankee Girl II*, a 66-foot schooner designed by William Hand and owned by G. W. Warren. *Malabar X* and her experienced skipper, John Alden, also finished ahead of *Dorade* to win

The Monkey Chain shortens a line for easy handling and storage. It is not a knot but is, in fact, nothing more than a crochet chain stitch.

ASHLEY KNOT 1144

———opposite———

Dorade in 1930, driving to weather with all sails flying from her original rig. With her original tall mainmast and stubby bowsprit, *Dorade* looks a little tender.

© MYSTIC SEAPORT

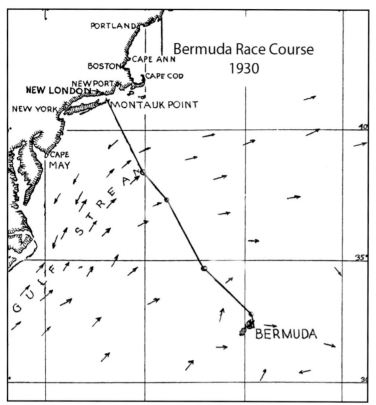

Bermuda Race Course
1930

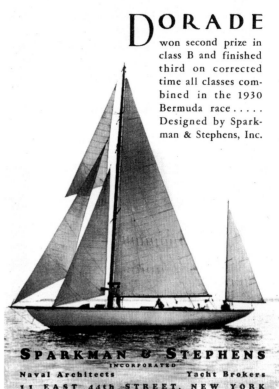

DORADE won second prize in class B and finished third on corrected time all classes combined in the 1930 Bermuda race..... Designed by Sparkman & Stephens, Inc.

SPARKMAN **&** **S**TEPHENS
INCORPORATED
Naval Architects   Yacht Brokers
11 EAST 44th STREET, NEW YORK

Above—The 1930 course from new London to Bermuda.

Right—Sparkman & Stephens boasts in this advertisement from *The Rudder.*

in Class A. *Malay*, a smaller boat in Class B, finished behind *Dorade* but saved her time to win first on corrected time, take first in class and carry home the Bermuda Trophy.

In his autobiography, Olin described the scene as *Dorade* hardened to the wind and headed for the finish:

"There was some compensation in the fact that we saw twelve larger boats ahead of us toward the finish and on the way passed them all, crossing the finish line ten seconds ahead of the leader.... Looking back, that beat, as we ticked off one boat after another, is still a high point in my sailing experience because it confirmed all I had hoped for in Dorade—*a real sea boat that could go to windward with the out-and-out racers."*

She had finished fourth to the line, beating a group of larger boats by seconds after 660 miles of racing and captured second in Class B. She had not won the Bermuda Trophy, but she had proven herself fast and able beyond any doubt. She had been well sailed and would be even better sailed as her crew grew in knowledge and confidence. She had won a wonderful trophy, treasured by Olin all his life, presented by Paul Hammond to the first finisher with an all-amateur crew.

On corrected time, the top three boats' times were *Malay* at 84 hr 20 min, *Malabar X* at 85 hr 5 min and *Dorade* at 85 hr 50 min. It was a great beginning race for *Dorade* and a great triumph for the CCA. Alfred F. Loomis, in his book of 1936 *Ocean Racing: The Great Blue-Water Yacht Races 1866-1935*, wrote of the 1930 race

First Lessons from the Onion Patch

Above — Overloaded again, the festivities at the 1930 CCA Lloyd's Harbor Rendevous may not have been as "dry" as normal.

© MYSTIC SEAPORT

Right —The All Amateur Crew trophy won by *Dorade* in the 1930 Bermuda Race and presented by Paul Hammond.

AUTHOR'S COLLECTION

"Unquestionably the twelfth running of the Bermuda race was the most successful ever. So enthusiastic was everybody that it needed something drastic like a world-wide depression to keep the next fleet from pushing all the water in Hamilton Harbor up into the hospitable city. But the depression came."

The remainder of that season of 1930 saw the boat returned to New York with a successful entry in the CCA Rendezvous at Lloyd's Harbor over the Columbus Day holiday. *Yachting* reported her winning "by a big margin" for boats over 40 feet.

Olin had just begun to receive the public attention that would continue throughout his life. He was, at some level, already famous, and so was *Dorade*, having finished her maiden season as a success. But her biggest year, 1931, was about to launch her into unprecedented fame.

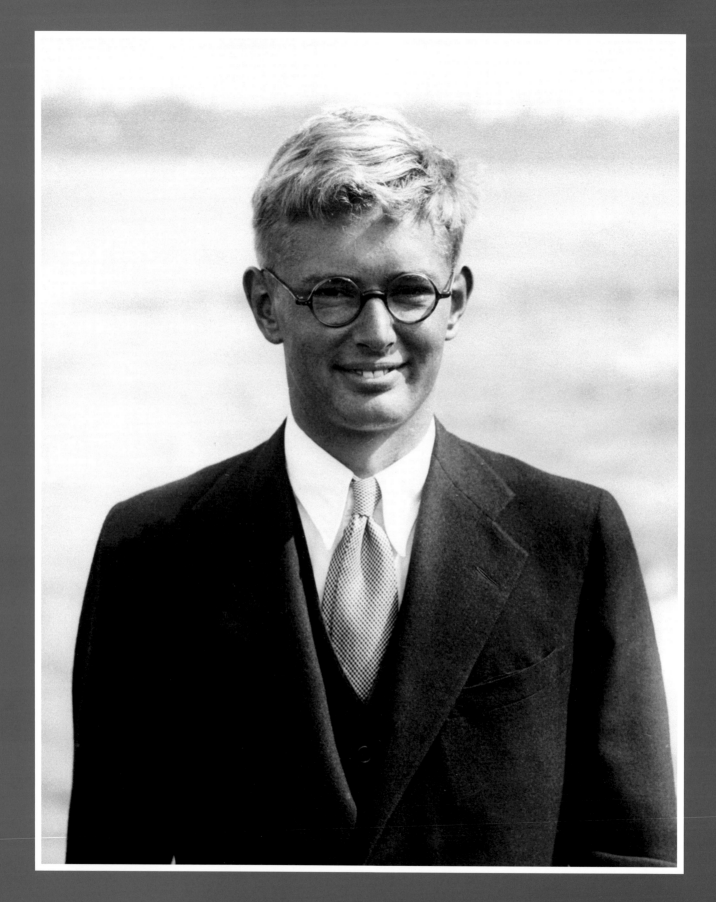

IN THE WORLD OF YACHTING

OLIN J. STEPHENS, 2nd

TO HAVE *achieved a reputation as a clever helmsman and successful racing skipper, and at the same time to have earned a name as a naval architect with many fast yachts to one's credit, is something that does not often fall to the lot of anyone at the age of twenty-two. Hence it is with satisfaction that we present this month the portrait of Olin J. Stephens, 2nd, of whom all the above can be said.*

It was, of course, his early training in yachts and his love of the sport that decided the young man in taking up yacht designing as a career. Like most of our best sailormen, Stephens started sailing at an early age in a small boat, when as a youngster he explored thoroughly the waters of Barnstable Bay aboard an ancient but honorable 14-foot Crosby-built knockabout. That was no longer ago than 1922. Since then there followed, successively, a 28-foot cruising yawl, a 40-foot ketch, a Sound schooner which he raced with success during 1926 and 1927, and then a number of six-metre yachts, all of which added to his experience in handling boats of different types. During the early part of the season just closed he sailed the six-metre "Comet," of his own design.

Not content with racing on sheltered waters only, young Stephens designed the 30-foot sloop "Kalmia" and sailed her to victory in her class in the ocean race of 1929 to Gibson Island, and in this year's Bermuda Race he was skipper and navigator of the 52-foot yawl "Dorade," which he also designed, making an excellent showing. "Dorade" took second prize in Class B, won the All-Amateur prize, and finished third on corrected time out of a fleet of 42 boats.

In the past year Stephens designed several six-metre class sloops, including the "Cherokee," Long Island Sound champion of her class and a member of the American team which defeated the British team so decisively, "Meteor," and "Comet." He also designed the Canada's Cup candidate "Conewago." All of which would indicate that Olin had quite a busy season.

Mr. Stephens is a member of the Cruising Club of America, the New York Yacht Club, and a junior member of the Larchmont Yacht Club.

A famous image of *Dorade* in 1931 with Olin at the helm and Rod splayed over the cockpit coaming looking forward. Partially hidden to Olin's right is probably Florence "Susie" Reynolds. Forward of Rod are Margaret Morton, her sister, Eleanor Smith, and Allen Smith. The ladies are keeping weight to windward and not taking advantage of the drier cockpit and the white seam compound designed to protect their clothing from smudges.

The Multi-strand Stopper or Lanyard
Knot secures the end of a line.
Variants are Buttons and
Turk's Heads.

ASHLEY KNOT 125

The Greatest Year

By the spring of 1931, *Dorade*'s bowsprit had disappeared, and
her mainmast had been shortened by 3 feet, 6 inches. The high
scuttle on her forward companionway had been replaced by a
flat hatch cover, allowing for sails to be taken more easily to and
from the forepeak. A heavy bulwark and rail fixture at the bow over the bowsprit
had been removed, saving weight, and her bulwarks had been painted white, inside and out, lightening her looks. She had found her wonderful balance.

The Stephens family, or at least two of them, longed for the challenge of an
even greater contest than the race to Bermuda. The 1928 Race to Spain had
whetted many appetites for another Atlantic competition, and so the Cruising
Club of America and the Ocean Racing Club (later that year to be graced with
the Royal Warrant and renamed the Royal Ocean Racing Club) jointly organized
a race from Newport to Plymouth, England. Rod and Olin could imagine nothing
better than a transatlantic test for their yawl. Others in the Stephens family were
not so sure. Certainly, their mother, Marguerite, was apprehensive about sending her three men 2,950 miles to Plymouth. Olin and Rod's grandparents were
also opposed to the trip, but, as momentum built and it became apparent that the
trip was on, they relented and even went so far as to present a new, hand-stitched
mainsail, built by Ratsey Sailmakers to fit *Dorade*'s newly shortened rig.

The yachting press swung into action. Articles in *The Rudder* and *Yachting*
heralded the upcoming event with discussions of alternative course strategies,
comparing the southerly route and its potential kick from the Gulf Stream with
the more northerly route of fewer miles and the greater hazard from icebergs.
The publications seemed to favor the southerly course.

Designs for newly-built competitors were published, including *Highland Light*,
an elegant, 62-foot cutter designed by Frank Paine for himself and D. F. Wolfe,
as well as *Landfall*, a 71-foot Herreshoff ketch built for Paul Hammond to replace
his offshore racer, *Niña*. The fleet included 10 boats, two of which came from
England for the race, as well as *Skål*, the 48-foot Philip Rhodes cutter that had

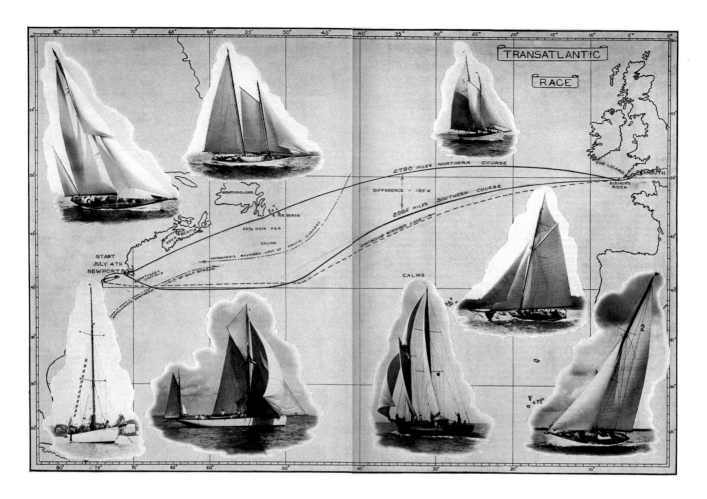

A two-page spread in *Yachting* featured the competitors in the 1931 TransAtlantic race and showed *Dorade* (upper left) with her rig before being modified.

competed in the Bermuda Race of the prior summer. Rigs other than schooner were beginning to be seen. Four cutters, two ketches and *Dorade* as the only yawl joined three schooners to make up the fleet. Olin and Rod made preparations. Food was organized and labeled. The crew of the two brothers and their father was filled out with Jim Merrill, Johnny Fox (the "Lone Wolf"), Hartwell "Buck" Moore and Ed Koster, all Scarsdale and yacht-racing friends and, true to form, all amateurs. Jim Merrill was truly a natural addition, as he had helped to draft the drawings for the boat. Roderick Stephens Sr. was 46, but the average age of the rest of the crew was less than 22 years. It is no wonder that they referred to the senior Stephens as "The Commodore" in deference to his superannuation. The race was to begin off Brenton's Reef Lightship on the 4th of July. *Dorade* was delivered to Newport, Rhode Island, but only after a stop on Block Island to take on water. Asked why, Olin explained that they didn't trust the city water of Newport and wanted to take aboard a fresher, sweeter supply from the island. Her tanks held 150 gallons. (Crewman John Fox in an unpublished manuscript described water holding capacity of 240 gallons and reported that they completed the Atlantic passage with 75 gallons left and continued to drink "American" water while at Cowes awaiting the Fastnet Race.)

An old sign for the Ratsey Sail Loft on City Island, now affixed to a nautical antique emporium.

This compass was used on *Dorade* in the Transatlantic Race of 1931 and in subsequent *Dorade* cruises. The courses in the yacht's log were given in 32 points and not in degrees.

The CCA held a grand dinner two nights before the start, and George Roosevelt, then Commodore of the CCA and owner of the big black schooner *Mistress*, was reported to have expressed the view that it was wrong of the CCA and ORC to allow such fragile boats as *Dorade* to compete in a sail across the Atlantic. It is notable that amongst the crews of the 10 competitors were to be found 89 men, one woman and some of the best known names in yachting. They included an abundance of offshore sailors, including such participants as Sherman Hoyt, Uffa Fox, Sam Wetherill, John Quincy Adams and Waldo Howland, of later Concordia fame.

The press was transfixed by the notion of a group of small boats braving the North Atlantic. The *New York Times* on June 28 called out the dangers with the headline, "Ten Tiny Craft Set For Ocean Crossing. First Time for Yachts of their Size to Race Across the North Atlantic. Must Brave Dreaded Fog."

The Fourth of July arrived with light breezes from the southeast. *Dorade* was towed to the line by the tug *Cynara* and was cast off at noon. The fleet, anxious for a good start, relatively tightly bunched, headed east toward Nantucket Shoals and the open Atlantic. Their order at the start was *Mistress*, *Highland Light*, *Landfall*, *Ilex* (Brit.), *Maitenes II* (Brit.), *Dorade*, *Lismore*, *Water Gypsy*, *Lismore*, *Skål*, and *Amberjack II*. Bolstered by extensive weather studies and consultation, Olin had evaluated the northerly great circle route which promised to save as much as 200 miles from the southerly track through the Gulf Stream. He had spoken with Casey Baldwin, a friend in Baddeck, Nova Scotia, about the wind conditions and the ice. As the fleet headed east that first afternoon on a starboard tack, *Dorade* eased to a slightly more northerly path. While they had not made up their mind at the start, as night fell they continued to go north. They were to be alone in that choice. *Dorade* disappeared into the first night as she passed the southern shore of Martha's Vineyard and Nantucket, and it would be 18 days before anyone in the fleet would see her again. Within several days the wind would back, allowing *Dorade* to first reach and eventually run, carrying a spinnaker. As the warm waters of the Gulf Stream collided with the colder seas from the Arctic in the North Atlantic, the resulting fog plagued the crew in the early days of the race, creating difficulties with celestial navigation. Yet she was moving well and her speed was building, at times approaching 11 knots. She was to average 7.83 knots "as the crow flies" over the nearly 3,000 miles. As those on the southerly track sailed a longer course in less wind and less fog, *Dorade* sped toward Plymouth. Only *Skål* went north, but only after keeping with the rest of the fleet for 13 days and finally choosing a route even further north than *Dorade*'s.

The ship's log faithfully recorded the passage with notes punctuated with the delight of her crew at their adventure. The passing of dolphins at night leaving phosphorescent trails in the water, the wet and enveloping fog, the sighting of mys-

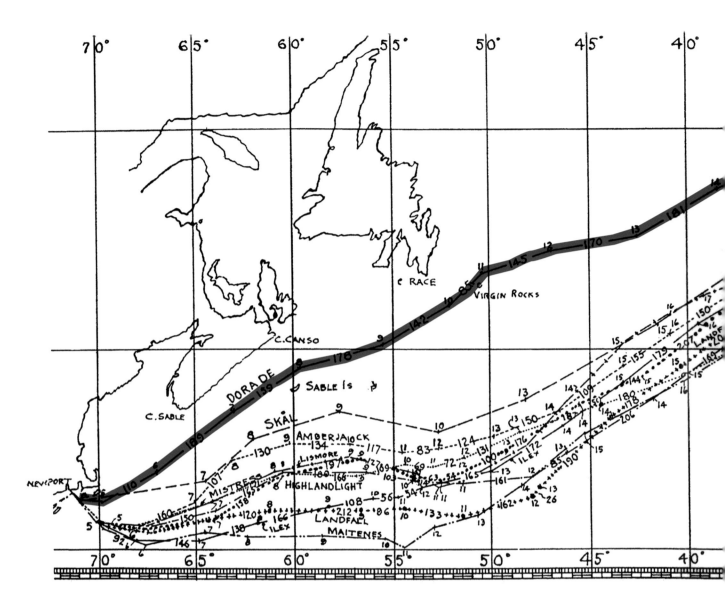

Dorade's northerly track across the Atlantic in 1931. During the race, no yacht other than *Skål* ever crossed north of her.

FROM FRANCIS KINNEY, *"YOU ARE FIRST"*

terious, green-watered shallows in the North Atlantic, the consistent recording of astonishing speeds between 9 and 11 knots—all of this found its way into a stenographer's notebook purchased from Shapiro's Stationers in the Bronx. As they neared their first landfall, a fishing boat approached over a flat sea to give them two gifts. The first was a batch of fresh-caught crabs, and the second was the opinion that *Dorade* stood first in the fleet.

Francis Kinney in his delightful book *"You Are First"* chronicles the yawl contacting their first landfall 25 minutes later:

The Scilly Islands are the first land a vessel approaching England from the Atlantic can pick up. They are off Land's End, the rocky southwestern tip of Cornwall. Entering the English Channel, a vessel on a course bound for Plymouth must round Lizard Point, about 55 nautical miles after passing the Scillies. There on a high green headland stands

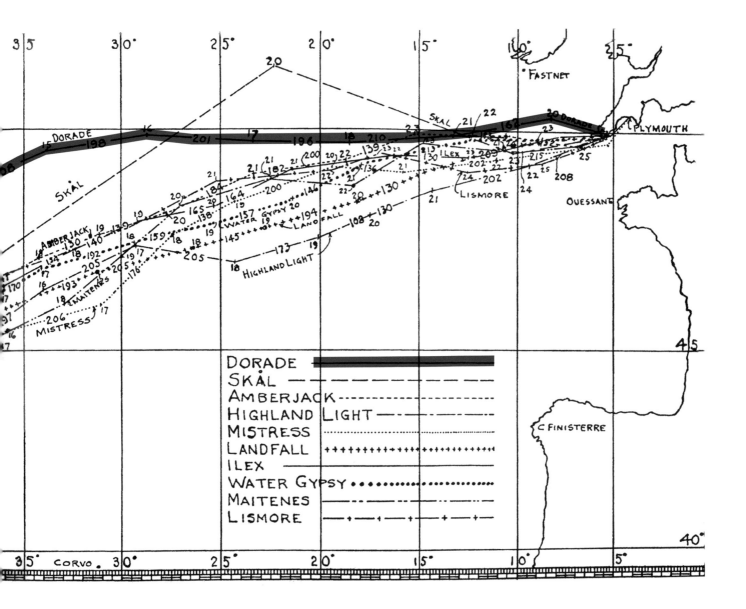

a lighthouse tower with a signal station next to it, affectionately called by seamen "The Lizard." At 5:45 a.m. on Tuesday, July 21, 1931, the signalman on duty there sighted a small white yawl, close-in beneath his station and almost becalmed. At 11 p.m. the night before she had picked up the Lizard light and ghosted along in light air to come as close as possible to exchange signals clearly. The signalman took a look through his spyglass, then hoisted two international code flags. They were the letters "E" and "C", one above the other, barely fluttering in the light breeze from the north-northwest. Their meaning: "What ship is this?" Quickly on the little yawl went up the code flag "H." It's meaning? "Dorade." After a brief interval that flag was lowered and the station keeper watching the yawl saw the letters "CPV" hoisted. He checked his book of international code flags and saw the meaning: "Which am I?" Then, without the slightest hesitation he went to his flag locker and pulled out the flags "NAX" to hoist in answer. They meant "You are First."

Dorade sailed down the Channel to Plymouth to complete her trip across the Atlantic in 16 days, 55 minutes. Two days later, *Landfall* and *Highland Light* finished within 14 minutes of one another. To their horror, they were greeted by the little white yawl with the entire Stephens family, ladies and all on board, sailing on an afternoon out to meet them. Given her time allowance, *Dorade* had won by nearly four days. Second on corrected time was *Skål*, who had taken a meandering course, first south and then north, to find better winds. Olin would say that the winning of the 1931 Transatlantic Race was "luck"—the luck of simply picking the right course. But the margin was enormous, she had been extraordinarily well sailed and navigated and her name was permanently made in the annals of yachting.

The drama of the Transatlantic Race and *Dorade*'s triumph were big news on both sides of the Atlantic. Maybe the image of a small boat with a young designer beating the established names in yachting fueled the interest of the press. Maybe the margin of winning or the "risk" of the ice-strewn, northern route created the attention. Maybe her beauty drew the coverage. All of it added up to a sensation. The Stephenses were converged upon by the British yachting establishment at Cowes,

Above—The victorious *Dorade* on the afternoon of July 21, 1931, entering Plymouth harbor alongside a photographer's boat and her mizzen coming down as she enters Plymouth harbor.

CYRIL H. GILL

including the Royal Yacht Squadron. The crew was asked aboard the Royal Yacht *Britannia*, moored in Cowes Roads, and was introduced to King George V and feted at a Royal dinner. Olin, as navigator, was presented an elegant sextant by Paul Hammond, *Landfall*'s owner, who had also donated the All Amateur Cup from the prior year's Bermuda Race. *Dorade* participated in one Royal Yacht Squadron Race, garnered a trophy and then prepared for the second great test of that special summer, the Fastnet Race.

Crew of "Dorade."

A charming staged picture of the crew. From left: John B. "Jack" Fox, Rod Jr., Edwin Koster, Roderick Sr., Owen "Jim" Merrill, Olin, and Hartwell "Buck" Moore.

© MYSTIC SEAPORT

This postcard was sent by Roderick Sr. to his father, Olin Sr., on the eve of the Fastnet Race.

Back row, left to right: Ed Koster, Roderick Sr., Jack Fox, Jim Merrill.

Front row, left to right: Rod Jr., Olin, Buck Moore.

COURTESY SPARKMAN & STEPHENS

Highland Light

As the yachting press scoured the list of 10 entries for the 1931 Transatlantic Ocean Race tying to pick the winner, *Dorade* was not a favorite. The scratch boat was *Landfall*, a 71-foot schooner built for Paul Hammond to replace his *Niña*, winner of the Santander Race. If she could save her time on the fleet, she had a good chance. George Roosevelt's powerful schooner *Mistress* was tested and ready. Most interesting was the newly launched *Highland Light*, drawn by the famous Frank C. Paine, of Boston. At 61 feet, she carried an immense cutter rig with a prominent boomkin to support a backstay and allow her boom to be sheeted well outboard of her transom. This appendage attracted a number of anatomically explicit nicknames. Her owner was wealthy adventurer and sportsman Dudley Wolfe. As a student, Wolfe had abruptly left Phillips Andover Academy at the outbreak of World War I to join the ambulance corps and, subsequently, the French Foreign Legion. Following the armistice, he returned to Harvard College to play football. Wolfe sailed a series of yachts through the 1920s and had commissioned the schooner *Mohawk* to compete in the 1928 race to Spain. The boat's slowness to weather prompted Wolfe to seek a new ocean racer and, *Highland Light* raced with *Dorade* across the Atlantic, to the Fasnet Rock and to Bermuda dur-

ing the early 1930s. She famously became, in 1932, the first yacht to race to Bermuda in less than three days and was a fixture on the ocean circuit. Her designer, Paine, loved her and had chartered her for that record Bermuda run while Wolfe spent the summer pursuing his passion for skiing and mountain climbing in Europe. Sailing out of Marblehead, Wolfe cruised and raced through 1938, taking *Highland Light* to Bermuda again. In 1939, he joined a much-publicized German-American expedition attempting to scale K2. The world's second-tallest peak had never before been conquered, and Wolfe and two others reached a level 600 feet short of the summit. The story of the climb portrayed Wolfe as continuing on alone and never having been seen again. His remains were finally found in 2008, and a less heroic tale of altitude sickness and a lonely death emerged as his compatriots went for help and could not return. Wolfe's death made big news as had his recent divorce and, with some foreboding, he left a will donating *Highland Light* to the United States Naval Academy, along with an endowment for her care. She was sailed by midshipmen in every Bermuda Race until 1958 and generally placed very well in Class A.

Dorade's crew gather before the 1931 Fastnet Race. Joining the seven-person Transatlantic Race crew are Cmdr. F.W. Hawkridge (third from left) and Briggs Swift Cunningham (fourth from left).

From Fastnet Rock
to City Hall

With the establishment of the Cruising Club of America in 1922 and the re-inauguration of the Bermuda Race in 1923 under the CCA's organization (but not sponsorship), the gauntlet's sting had been felt as far afield as Cowes. The Americans were on the move. British yachtsmen including Weston Martyr, George Martin and Malden Heckstall-Smith had vowed to uphold Britain's seagoing reputation and had organized the first race to Fastnet Rock, in the Irish Sea, and back. Through discussions with yacht clubs and a notice in *The Morning Post* (London), the three advocates then announced an "Ocean Race" to be sailed under the flag of the Royal Western Yacht Club. The instructions described a course from Cowes, on the Isle of Wight, out around Fastnet Rock, off the Irish coast, and back to Plymouth, and called for both coastwise navigation, with its attendant tides and shipping traffic, and off-soundings sailing. The passage included 360 offshore miles and a total of 615 miles for the race. Seven boats started the first Fastnet in 1925 and, unlike their American counterparts, were not schooners but, instead, were all cutters and ketches. With the published invitation to race had come the common public outcry regarding the dangers of the deep. Dr. Claud Worth, whose designs would influence Olin Stephens, remarked in *The Field*, "I venture to express a doubt which arises in my mind—are our latitudes suitable for a public ocean race? If two owners, experienced in ocean cruising, arrange a match involving several hundred miles of deep water, they know exactly what they are doing. But a public race might very well include some owners whose keenness is greater than their experience."

Despite such concerns, the race was successful and spawned, after its first running, the Ocean Racing Club, which organized and sponsored the contest each summer until 1931. Beginning in 1926, the Fastnet Race became an international affair, with the American schooner *Primrose IV* sailing from Boston to join eight British yachts for the event. The fleet grew to 19 in 1927. Although only two of the entrants finished the extremely rough race that year, with attendant public criticism, the contest had become firmly established and brought more American entries in 1928.

The Fastnet course leads up the Solent and around the eastern end of the Isle of Wight, thence to the west-southwest, down the English Channel and the chalky southern cliffs of England to Cornwall and the Lizard. At Land's End, the fleet

The Jib Sheet Eye is designed to absorb a portion of the slatting impact of the sheet. It is tied with a stopper knot.

ASHLEY KNOT 2783

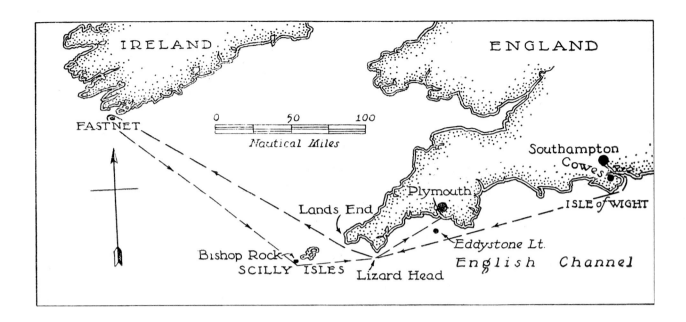

The Fastnet Race course sailed
by *Dorade* in 1931 and 1933, both
times scoring victories.

COURTESY *YACHTING*,
OCTOBER 1947, ALFRED LOOMIS

turns toward the northwest and Fastnet Rock, which lies three miles off the Irish coast at Cape Clear. Being in England and having triumphed in the Transatlantic Race, it seemed only right that Roderick Stephens Sr. and his two sons should challenge this ocean course as well.

On August 11, 1931, at 1100 hours, off Cowes, the starting cannon sent 17 ocean racers off into the Channel and the Irish Sea on what was to be the toughest Fastnet Race yet. Eight of the 10 boats in the fleet had competed in the Transatlantic Race just weeks before. *Dorade's* seasoned crew of seven was bolstered by two important additions. The first was Briggs Swift Cunningham, who joined for his first ocean race. Known to the Stephens' from his successful Six Metre sailing, Cunningham, was to become very famous in yachting and automobile racing circles throughout his long and exciting sporting life. Also aboard was Commander F.W. Hawkridge, of the British Naval Reserve, who brought to the team his experience with the local waters and their tricky currents. The race began normally enough, sailing to weather out the Channel in moderate breezes. By the third day, the fleet had passed the Lizard, beating into a building sea. *Dorade* stood third by a narrow margin to *Water Gypsy*, the 59-foot Alden schooner skippered by Olin's friend and supporter from *Yachting*, Sam Wetherill. At the turn of the Lizard began the broad reaching, downwind run in a freshening breeze, which carried away gear and prompted reefing and general shortening of sail—on all except *Dorade*. Olin attributed his Transatlantic win to luck, but he viewed the performance of *Dorade* and her crew in the 1931 Fastnet as skill. Under spinnaker, they drove into the night toward the rock and only shortened sail when Roderick Sr. roused Olin from his off-watch bunk and insisted that the chute come down. They rounded the Fastnet Rock still third to begin the close reach home at speed. Others in the fleet suffered. In the first loss

From Fastnet Rock to City Hall

Onlookers, including possibly Olin's wife, Susie, watch *Dorade* being offloaded in New York in 1931. Ever acrobatic, Rod observes from his perch on her foredeck.

of life in the modern ocean racing era, the English cutter *Maitenes II*, veteran of the Transatlantic Race, lost Col. C. H. Hudson overboard during the night after running under bare poles for 24 hours. He was highly respected and deeply mourned. Competitors reported winds as high as 50 knots, and seemingly all struggled, except for the little yawl that bounded home fourth and corrected out to win by nearly 19 hours. It seems that the only alarmed crewman aboard *Dorade* was Commander Hawkridge, who feared that the youthful crew would drive their racer at speed directly into the Irish Coast. *Dorade* had gained a marvelous and well-deserved victory, adding to her luster.

The British press was quick to seize upon the triumph, and her competitors began to see *Dorade* as unbeatable. Generally, when a boat becomes unbeatable, it is time to consider a change in the handicap rules. That was to come, but not right away. Weston Martyr, one of the founders of the Ocean Racing Club, wrote in *Yachting* with the title "A Hard Chance Around the Fastnet."

"The first six yachts to finish would appear to be in a class by themselves," Martyr wrote. "All these speeds are remarkable but *Dorade* is the miracle. She is a tiny thing compared with the yachts just mentioned, but she sailed nearly as fast as they did in their own weather, maintaining an average speed of 7.62 kn. She deserves the Cup, and there is no doubt about it—she is the heroine of the occasion."

The American press, for their part, began a field day of reporting, serving up to the public immediate news of the exploits of the young Americans and their "little yacht." In many ways, it was romantic stuff and a good human-interest story, but yachting was a more carefully watched sporting activity during the 1930's than it

was later in the century. The nation was distracted from its financial woes by stories of the glamour and optimism of wealthy and even not-so-wealthy yachtsmen and their vessels. It was society news on one the hand, sporting news on the other, wrapped around the appeal of the daring exploits of Americans doing battle with Europeans. In *Dorade*'s case, the story also exulted in youth.

The Stephens men, the remaining crew, Mrs. Roderick Stephens Sr., Olin's new bride, Susie, and the yawl were hurriedly bundled aboard the White Star liner *Homeric* within days of the Fastnet finish. Plenty of people were waiting for them to return to New York. The sailors and their boat had left Newport eastbound only seven weeks earlier, but in that time their names and that of *Dorade* had become famous. They would remain so for the rest of their lives, not entirely because of the two races but because of what those races had started. Olin Stephens II would ultimately be considered the greatest designer of racing yachts of the twentieth century. Rod would become legendary for racing, rigging, yacht construction and design.

From Fastnet Rock to City Hall

HOMERIC OFF THE ISLE OF WIGHT

White Star Lines advertising of 1930 described the *Homeric* as "the world's largest twin screw vessel." She provided an elegant platform for *Dorade*'s triumphant return to New York.

CHARLES DIXON

Roderick Stephens Sr. would be recognized as the support that launched his sons' remarkable careers. The *Homeric*'s deck cargo allowed the Stephenses to show fascinated fellow passengers the reason for their fame and pride as they returned across the Atlantic.

In New York Harbor preparations for their welcome had been put in place in early August, before the Fastnet was even run. The Transatlantic win was enough to celebrate, and the Fastnet would be icing on the cake. As the *Homeric* entered the harbor, the municipal tug *Macom* met them at quarantine with the Department of Sanitation Band "in new cream and gold uniforms," there to serenade the yacht's crew.

Olin and Rod's grandparents joined the proceedings, coming from Lake George. An automobile convoy waited at the Battery for the tug to make its way through the fleet of water-shooting fireboats and horn-blowing watercraft, collecting the Stephenses and proceeding to City Hall for a reception and photo session with the acting mayor, Joseph McKee. He might possibly have been Irish. He rose to the maritime occasion by noting that *Dorade* "'which would fit in this room with two feet to spare' was only half as large as Columbus's Santa Maria." The speeches were broadcast on Station WNYC. The City Hall reception was followed the next day by a luncheon in their honor given by the Bronx Board of Trade, the Bronx Real Estate Board and the Lions and Rotary Clubs. They were really home. The headline read, "Officials Welcome Youthful 'Vikings' Who Won Ocean Race In Little Yawl." The following week, Drake Sparkman and other members of the Larchmont Yacht Club held a grand dinner in their honor, recognition for the fame they had brought to the club and to the nation. Olin would write of all of this ceremony in his down-to-earth way. "It was an experience, fun," he wrote, "but the best was getting back to normal family life and work." Plenty of work awaited him, and Olin used the experience of that great summer to refine his design thinking. In an article for the September issue of *Yachting* entitled, "Along the Great Circle Track in *Dorade*," he wrote about the Transatlantic Race:

> If I had this race to sail over again, or almost any other ocean race. I should stick very close to Dorade *both as to hull and rig, but I should give her somewhat more initial stability and raise up both her booms. I do not think that speed and comfort in a boat are qualities which cannot be readily combined, and I think that these changes would make for improvement in both respects.*

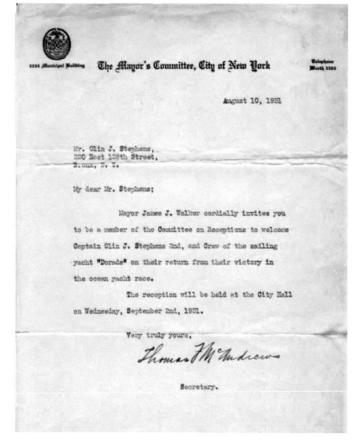

2224 *Municipal Building*   The Mayor's Committee, City of New York   Telephone Worth 5504

August 10, 1931

Mr. Olin J. Stephens,
220 East 138th Street,
Bronx, N. Y.

My dear Mr. Stephens:

Mayor James J. Walker cordially invites you to be a member of the Committee on Receptions to welcome Captain Olin J. Stephens 2nd, and Crew of the sailing yacht "Dorade" on their return from their victory in the ocean yacht race.

The reception will be held at the City Hall on Wednesday, September 2nd, 1931.

Very truly yours,

Thomas J. McAndrews

Secretary.

Top left and right—*Dorade*'s deep-sea victories— and the use of Everdur fastenings—gave Minneford's and Anaconda Copper & Brass a chance to crow, as in these 1931 advertisements from *Yachting* and *Rudder*.

Right—Larchmont Yacht Club celebrated its victorious members with a dinner in September at $5 a plate.

"Dorade"
WINNER
OF THE OCEAN RACE
FROM NEWPORT TO PLYMOUTH
AND THE
FASTNET RACE
1931

*Dinner
in honor of
Vice Commodore Roderick Stephens
and the
Crew of the "Dorade"
Given by
The Members of The Larchmont Yacht Club
September eleventh, Nineteen thirty-one
at the Club House*

THE SPARKMAN & STEPHENS DESIGNED, MINNEFORD BUILT - DORADE

ANTHRACITE CLUB OF NEW YORK CITY
DINNER HONORING

"ROD" STEPHENS

CAPT. OLIN J. STEPHENS II, "ROD" JR. AND
HIS VALIANT AMATEURS OF THE VICTORIOUS

DORADE

WEDNESDAY, SEPTEMBER 16th—7 P.M. - 1931

Hotel McAlpin. Broadway at 34th Street

TICKETS, $5.00

INFORMAL

Top—The scene at City Hall with the broadcast microphone front and center. Olin and Roderick Sr. take the first row, with Rod and the rest of the crew and family sprinkled in behind.

COURTESY SPARKMAN & STEVENS / ATTRIBUTED TO "CAMERAVIEW, N.Y."

Left—The coal distribution fraternity honors one of its own with a dinner at Broadway and 34th.

COURTESY SPARKMAN & STEPHENS

Working sails flying, *Dorade* tunes up for the 1932 Bermuda Race.

Off and Running

While *Dorade* slept away that winter of 1931-'32 in a shed at Min-neford's, it is possible that Olin Stephens slept very little. Despite the deepening Depression, he was able to attract design work with con-tinuing orders for Six Metres and the commission by Walter Barnum of a very different kind of boat for S&S, the 62-foot schooner *Brilliant*. Designed for extreme offshore conditions, *Brilliant* was launched by Nevins in 1932 and represented an unusual combination of heavy scantlings incorporated into a much more perfor-mance-oriented hull form than her specifications and appearance might at first have indicated. She reflected Olin's continued commitment to a high waterline length to beam ratio, and, despite the extraordinary heft of her building materials, she proved to be remarkably fast. She was built for a price tag of $100,000, of which $15,000 represented a design fee and $85,000 was spent on actual building, a very low fig-ure to Nevins, given the boat's complexity and size. Deep into the Depression, it is thought that she should have cost $160,000. Nevins needed the work. Though not designed for racing, in 1933, *Brilliant* set a Transatlantic record for a yacht with a waterline length under 50 feet—15d, 1h, 23m. The record was not surpassed for over four decades. She was Olin's largest commission to date. It was clear that, de-spite the enormous importance of *Dorade* to his career, Olin was off and running and sometimes in new and varied design directions. He returned to England that summer of 1932 to race Six Metres, feeling an obligation to support his own de-signs by racing for his customers. It was an obligation that he honored throughout his career. The Bermuda Race again loomed, and *Dorade* was an obvious partici-pant, but, in what was to become a more common pattern, Rod skippered her. Her designer was not aboard.

The 1932 Bermuda Race was sailed from Montauk Point, on Long Island, rather than New London, Connecticut. The race organizers felt that the stretch from the western shore of Long Island to the more abundant winds at Montauk made the

The challenge of tying a small and large line together is mastered by the Rolling Hitch or Magner's Hitch, one of the most frequently used knots on shipboard.

ASHLEY KNOT 1465

U.S. bidders for the Seawanhaka
Cup on the River Clyde, August
26, 1932, *(left to right):* Seward
Johnson, Hayward Dill, Olin
Stephens, Briggs Cunningham
and Phil LeBoutillier.

© BETTMAN ARCHIVE, CORBIS

race less dramatic and interesting, and so the course was shortened and the start
was held further to sea. It was the only year that the shorter course of 628 miles
was ever sailed. The new location made the logistics of supplying more complicated,
and the organizers returned to New London for the start in 1934. While economic
forces took their toll and would continue to do so, the 1932 fleet included 27 entries, down from 42 in the prior race of 1930. Nevertheless, seven new designs appeared for the contest. Seventeen of the racers, including Olin's new *Brilliant*, were
schooners. Six were yawls or ketches, and six were sloops or cutters. An additional
participant was the schooner *Adriana*, which sailed with the fleet but was too large
to be allowed to compete. Her presence proved to be very significant in the history
of ocean racing.

The 1932 Bermuda Race was memorable in a number of ways. The first was the
weather, which delivered a record-setting and, to some, startlingly fast passage to
"The Onion Patch." A steady southwest wind allowed for a close reach all the way to
St. David's Light, and the Class A boats bounded away right at the start. The end
result was a passage by *Highland Light* (under charter to her designer, Frank Paine,

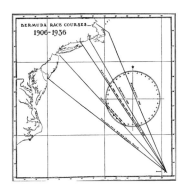

The Courses to Bermuda.
Ocean Racing 1866-1935 by
Alfred F. Loomis

from her owner, Dudley Wolfe) in a time of 25 minutes less than three full days, a result unthinkable to many. A single tack and a very fast passage, the finish was a sure relief for those crewmen who had tried to sleep hanging onto the high ledges of their starboard-side bunks all the way!

Also memorable were the events of the first night at sea. *Jolie Brise*, the famous Channel Cutter, had sailed in every Fastnet Race. Her new owner, Bobby Somerset, had Paul Hammond and Sherman Hoyt aboard, and this complement of three very experienced ocean sailors was to be brought to test. Hoyt saw flares, and Somerset, along with Hammond, knew that danger lay in the darkness astern. They turned back to help. Hoyt recalled the scene in his *Memoirs*:

As we neared her (Adriana), flames were shooting out of hatches and skylights. Some halyards, burned through, had let go, sails were in utter confusion, and her crew were in a naturally wild state of panic preparing to launch a boat, the spinnaker gear and other floatable deck gear. Passing close to her weather side we jibed across her stern intending to range close along her lee. It was blowing hard with a considerable sea running as we drew alongside. With our headsail becalmed, Jolie took a shear and in spite of efforts to keep clear ranged into her, beam and beam, with a horrible crash and fouling aloft. We were at once boarded by her complement, some wildly hysterical, including their cook, a Peruvian Indian, stark naked and brandishing a huge knife.

With tarred lanyards used in our old-fashioned rig to set up shrouds already on fire: with the confused mob on our deck crowded with both excited crews and, momentarily fearful of an explosion of what we erroneously assumed to be her gasoline fuel tank, we managed to get clear and pull away.

Just as we did so, to my horror, I saw a man, hitherto obscured by the half lowered mainsail and boom sagged on deck, appear around the mainmast and running to leeward, make a wild leap for us. This was Clarence Kozlay, who, bravely sticking by the helm trying to hold Adriana on course until the last moment, had not joined her wild boarding party in time to come on board of us while we were in contact. The poor fellow fell short, but I managed to heave him a line which he grabbed and I pulled him in until he was almost within reach when, either due to our accelerating speed or to becoming fouled in the mess of gear floating alongside, he let go. We at once heaved over our two life rings with flares attached, but by the time we could clear our decks sufficiently to handle our craft, put her about and return, there was no sign of him.

The schooner *Adriana* burned and sank into the Atlantic, and the Bermuda Race recorded its first fatality, joining the Fastnet in that unhappy distinction. *Jolie Brise* returned to Newport for repairs and to deliver the ten survivors, while the hulk of the schooner still burned and was encountered hours later by another competitor. Without *Jolie*'s crew and their great courage and seamanship, there would have been no survivors. Unknowingly, *Dorade* and most of the rest of the fleet continued on their single starboard tack to Bermuda.

An Improved "Dorade"—with Schooner Rig

MANY people have doubtless wondered what Olin Stephens, of Sparkman & Stephens, would do if called upon to turn out an improved *Dorade*. The answer is to be found in the accompanying plans, which show a craft quite similar in hull form to the famous ocean race winner, but with the more conventional and popular jib-headed schooner rig. The dimensions are: l.o.a. 54′6″; l.w.l. 40′; beam, 12′; draft, 8′2″; sail area, lowers, 1352 sq. ft.; displacement, 19 tons; lead keel, 18,000 lbs.

The object of the design was to produce a boat with the same characteristics which produce speed in *Dorade*, but with improved accommodations below and increased deck space, plus auxiliary power. The increased beam makes it possible to combine built-in berths and extension transoms in the main cabin, and still have good floor space. She will sleep four in the cabin, two in the stateroom, and two men forward.

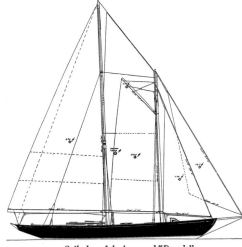

Sail plan of the improved "Dorade"

The galley, with motor installed under a dresser, concentrates the crew's work forward, and releases the after part of the boat for berths, lockers, bureaus, etc. The companionway is aft, with chart table to starboard and toilet room opposite. The large after double stateroom has a bureau and three hanging lockers. There is an oilskin locker near the companion steps. In the forward end of the main cabin, to starboard, is another large hanging locker, and writing desk opposite.

With flush deck forward of the mainmast and small trunk cabin aft, added room is gained below as well as on deck, where a dinghy may easily be lashed and still leave plenty of room for lounging or handling sails.

The motor is a Gray 4–44, with Morse silent chain reduction gear with ratio of 1.74 to 1, which should drive her 8 miles or better under power. Ample fuel and water tanks are located under the cabin floor.

The designers believe that she should be fast under sail, particularly to windward, and should combine to an unusual degree those qualities which make a comfortable cruising yacht with those desirable in ocean racing or club runs.

By placing the motor forward, the space aft usually set apart for a motor compartment is utilized to advantage in enlarging the after quarters and providing a better lazarette and other stowage space. Placing the water and fuel tanks under the cabin floor keeps this weight low, and results in added stability and more speed.

Inboard profile of the schooner developed from "Dorade" by Sparkman & Stephens

Olin gave his version of *Dorade* as a schooner in this design published in *Yachting* in February 1932. Her gaff foremast and marconi main harken to a re-rigged *Brilliant*.

COURTESY *YACHTING*

Rod's first major ocean race as skipper was a success, and he brought *Dorade* to the finish line in 88h, 33m, which corrected out to 72h, 11m. It was to be her best Bermuda finish ever and fastest time. She took first place in Class B and again won the All-Amateur Cup. She was setting a pace that was to align the rating forces against her, for her margin of victory was large enough to ensure that she would find tougher time allowances to overcome in the years ahead. Rod and his young crew sailed *Dorade* back to Larchmont, and she raced very successfully in the New York Yacht Club Cruise that July. During the course of that year, she had acquired new owners, as Roderick Sr. had made a gift of the yawl to his sons Olin and Rod Jr. They had certainly shown their ability to sail her and keep her, and now she was theirs. The economic slide had worsened, and even the Bermuda Race Committee

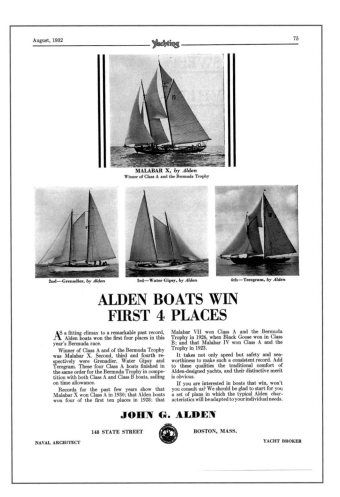

In 1932, S&S was challenging John Alden for supremacy in ocean racing design, but the Alden firm still had many victories to trumpet, including the Bermuda Trophy won by *Malabar X*. This advertisement in *Yachting* makes the point.

COURTESY *YACHTING*

had attempted to place restrictions on the number of new sails allowed for each competing boat in order to limit costs. The year 1933 would be an eventful one for *Dorade*, but she would spend many more days cruising than racing. Still, her exploits were worthy of the press, and their continued reporting and her fame continued to grow.

It is interesting to watch how competitors within the yacht-design fraternity began to react to Sparkman & Stephens' success. There was a natural, albeit friendly, competitiveness, but the battle was waged to some extent in the advertising pages of *Yachting* and *The Rudder*. John Alden had dominated ocean racing during the 1920s, and Olin Stephens was making inroads. *Dorade*, particularly, was fast and small, and with her rating was nipping at Alden's heels. In August, John G. Alden, Naval Architect and Yacht Broker, ran a full-page advertisement in *Yachting* showing pictures of *Malabar X*, *Grenadier*, *Water Gypsy* and *Teragram* with the banner "Alden Boats Win First 4 Places." It was true, and the big, heavy Class A boats had delighted in the breezy conditions. Still, *Dorade* had beaten the next Class B boat by eight hours.

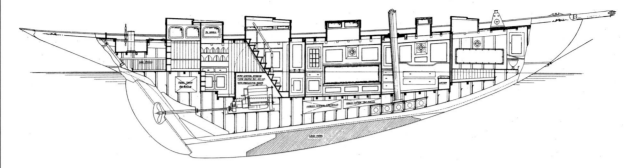

J. Read's Winning Design for a 55-Foot Rater

The British Battle Back

While the 1932 Bermuda Race tested the latest ideas of ocean racing yachts on the American side, the British were trying to regroup. The long-held British view—that ocean racers had to represent heavy, comfortable cruisers derived from working boat designs—had been chastened by *Dorade*. The Royal Ocean Racing Club altered its rating rule during the winter of 1931-'32 to encourage faster boats, and the Royal Corinthian Yacht Club formed a committee to announce a design competition to provoke new thinking for yachts to be raced at sea. Designs for 55- and 35-foot ratings under the RORC Rule were specified, and a special award was offered for designers under 30 years old. Plans were due in April, and many designers throughout Europe and a few North Americans participated. The contest was judged by Malden Heckstall-Smith and Charles E. Nicholson. Entrants to the under-30 category included Olin Stephens, K. Aage Nielsen, David Boyd and Charles A. Nicholson. Established designers such as Laurent Giles weighed in, and designers Jac. M. Iverson, of Sweden, and H.W. de Voogt, of Holland, also also submitted designs. A selection of the submissions was published by the RCYC in a wonderful book of lines entitled, *A Book of Designs of Deep Sea Racing Craft*, giving a representative sampling of the best work. It is notable that, in many cases, hull form was beginning to evolve to a type exemplified by *Dorade*, an inshore racer's form adapted to the open ocean. Lateral planes were being reduced. In some cases, the leading edge of the keel and stem were cut away to improve maneuverability. Overhangs were being drawn out. However, rigs were another matter. In most cases, the designs included bowsprits and boomkins and, in some cases, both. Mainmasts with large mainsails and small headsails were placed far forward in the boat. Gaff rigs were favored by some, and one entry showed both gaff and Bermudian rig alternatives of the same sail area. Only a few yawls were drawn.

Olin Stephens' entry was a 72-foot yawl with an all-inboard rig. Narrow, with a waterline to beam ratio of 3.6, she looked a lot like *Dorade* in hull form, with a continuous sweep to her keel but with more beam. The design moved closer to what would become *Stormy Weather*. Her rudder was small and she was drawn with an engine but given an offset prop to eliminate a propeller aperture. She did not win the young designer prize

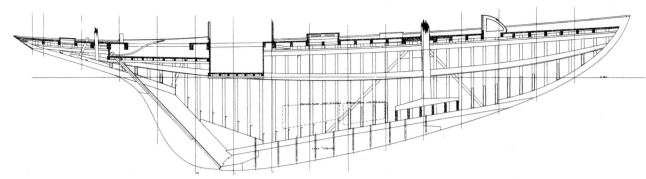

Olin's RCYC entry in the 55-Foot Rater Class

for Olin. It went instead to J. Read of England for his narrow cutter with bowsprit and a waterline to beam ratio of nearly 4.0. The winner in the 35-foot category was H.W. de Voogt, with a cutter named *Filibuster*, fitted with a bowsprit, a boomkin, a cutaway forefoot and a very large main. She looked like a real handful. All entries were drawn to Lloyd's scantlings but evoked workboat concepts. Many look very heavy. Comfort was not completely abandoned. One entry was fitted with a bathtub.

In the introduction of the RCYC design book, Heckstall-Smith goes to some lengths to make the case for "ocean cruisers" as an improved type:

A criticism which has been levied against deep sea racing yachts is that they are racers and not cruisers and that, while they may be very interesting craft in their own particular line, the lessons that they may teach are of no particular value to the purely cruising man. The obvious answer to this criticism is that the best deep sea racing craft which have yet been produced are far better cruisers than the majority of so-called cruising yachts. They are faster-by any reasonable standard: they are better sea boats: and they are far better and more substantially rigged and equipped. They are, in fact, deep sea <u>cruisers</u>, and not just "occasional" cruisers. The American ocean racing yachts, Mistress, Highland Light *and* Landfall *are all far better all-around cruisers than the average yacht which is designed as a cruiser."*

Heckstall-Smith egged the British on, implying that their thinking about ocean racers was antiquated and stodgy. He referred to the heavier, yet advanced American designs by John Alden, Frank Paine and Francis Herreshoff as being of a better "cruising" type, but he failed to mention *Dorade*. Maybe the little yawl was still seen as a radical outlier, successful but uncomfortable and even dangerous at sea, but things were moving in her direction. Despite the Royal Corinthian Yacht Club Designing Contest, no yachts were ever built to the submitted designs. The next year's Fastnet Race beckoned, and the British still tarried.

Rod, his mother, Marguerite Dulon Stephens (far right), and sister, Marite (second from left),
pose with Brita (at tiller), Porter Buck and Vally.

To Norway and Cowes

Ocean racers had really only one event to look forward to in the spring of 1933—the eighth Fastnet, now held in years alternating with the Bermuda Race. Olin and Rod sized up their schedules, and it was clear that Rod, still a bachelor and by now considered amongst the most prominent of the "young veterans" of ocean racing, would find the time to sail. Olin, with a burgeoning schedule of design work before him, would remain in New York. Rod made plans for crossing the Atlantic to cruise in the Baltic Sea, do some racing there, return to the Solent for the Fastnet Race and then sail back across—in all, a course of over 8,000 miles. He enlisted his longtime sailing friend and competitor Everand C. "Ducky" Endt, veteran of the 1928 Santander Race, two Bermuda Races and the 1931 Transatlantic. Porter Buck, who had been aboard for the successful Bermuda Race of the prior summer, added his experience. A young cook named David Leeson signed on, and Rod convinced the esteemed Sherman Hoyt, now in middle age, to join. A crew of five would be enough for a cruising voyage. The route crossed the North Atlantic, passing through Pentland Firth and past Scapa Flow in the north of Scotland, thence to Bergen, Norway. It was a cold passage, beginning so early in the spring, but the Fastnet had been moved up to July from August, and the crew wanted to enjoy some exploring in Scandinavia. The passage went easily, and Rod, always one to innovate, set a squaresail on a long yard at the mainmast. It was cumbersome and cranky, and the boat rolled horrifically. They struggled for hours to lower and stow it, never to be set again.

In his *Memoirs*, Sherman Hoyt describes in absolute certainty his sighting of a sea monster as they approached the Scottish shore. "Headed by something shaped like a horse's head (but not spouting smoke and flame, depicted in the old woodcuts) and followed by convolutions which I had earlier taken for porpoises, was an enormous something," he wrote. The "something" broke off the spinner from the taffrail log, and although the remaining crew found Hoyt's report of his visions improbable, days later the British papers validated his claims by reporting other sightings in the area. The mystery of the Loch Ness Monster was born.

This lovely trophy was inscribed with *Dorade*'s name and presented to Rod Stephens for winning the Oslo to Hanko Race in 1933.

© MYSTIC SEAPORT

Diamond Knot and Block Strap elegantly secures a block on running rigging.

ASHLEY KNOT 716

Ducky Endt, photographed in
the 1950s by Carleton Mitchell.

Dorade and her crew enjoyed the early summer in Norway and lingered through midsummer's night in the Baltic, cruising, racing successfully in Hanko and enjoying the hospitality and the beauty of the fjords. They visited with old friends from the Six Metre fraternity. Then it was back across a lumpy and unpleasant North Sea to join the fleet in Cowes. Unfortunately, it was not much of a fleet. Initially, only one British yacht had shown an intention to compete, that being *Ilex*, the veteran racer sailed by the Royal Engineers. Finally, somewhat shamed by the absence of British participants, the famous yacht designer and builder Charles Nicholson Sr. entered his 33-year-old, slender and fast cutter *Flame*, and Major T.P. Rose Richards weighed in with his cutter *Lexia*. *Dorade* was joined by two American schooners to round out the sparse fleet of six. *Brilliant*, fresh from her record-setting passage across the Atlantic, and *Grenadier*, sailed by a crew of very recent Harvard graduates and a sole professional, were both yachts eager for the test of their first Fastnet. So it was three British cutters, two American schooners and a famous and feared little yawl which came to a nearly windless starting line on July 22 at Cowes.

The Ocean Racing Club may have become Royal, but the lack of British participants drew great notice and, in some cases, criticism. Some foresaw the end of the Fastnet Race, and others lambasted their countrymen for their lack of competitive fervor. Some of the reticence to participate may have been *Dorade*'s doing, for she was clearly favored to win. Weston Martyr, no shrinking violet he and a veteran of two Bermuda Races when living in New York, weighed in sarcastically with the following from *Yachting*, slightly altered from a piece he wrote for the British magazine *Yachting World and Motor Boating Journal*:

I should like to tell you of those inspired words I uttered about our young yachtsmen who have the boats and the time, but not the stomach to sail around the Fastnet. But I won't. After all it is a family matter and Yachting *is a respectable magazine. So I will just hand on the rumor that the Royal Ocean Racing Club has decided to abandon the Fastnet Race and substitute a race for punts on the Upper Thames. Japanese paper lanterns of any color may be carried in lieu of navigation lights; and the punts must be equipped with at least one silk cushion for each member of the crew, together with a gramophone, an adequate supply of sucking bottles and a certified wet-nurse."*

Martyr went on, in the September issue of *Yachting*, to describe the British competitors' view of *Dorade* after he visited the boat before the start:

How do you expect us to defend our Fastnet Cup against Dorade *anyhow? It isn't fair to send her over. But when you go and put a crew in her such as she has this year, it isn't only*

Sherman Hoyt joined Rod for the trip to Norway in May of 1933 and then on that year's Fastnet Race. Hoyt had already sailed in two Bermuda Races, one Transatlantic, two Fastnets and had actively raced Six Metres in America, Britain and Scandinavia. He had served as a draftsman at Henry J. Gielow in 1927 and helped bring Olin into that firm. He had been helmsman aboard Bobby Somerset's *Jolie Brise* during the daring rescue of most of the crew of the burning schooner *Adriana* during the 1932 Bermuda Race, and his America's Cup experience was deep. He served as the American observer aboard Sir Thomas Lipton's *Shamrock IV* in 1920 and in the afterguard of *Enterprise* for the 1930 defense of the America's Cup. Hoyt had graduated from Brown University in 1901, studied naval architecture at Edinburgh University and served as a Lieutenant Commander during World War I. He designed the schooner *Mistress* for George Roosevelt and the Six Metre *Navajo* (US 40), which won the Silver Medal at the 1932 Olympics. Now in his mid fifties, Hoyt was Rod's oldest crew member as they set off across the Atlantic again. Rod Stephens lacked confidence in few things, but in those years, one was celestial navigation, in which Hoyt gave important instruction. The description of the trip across the Atlantic that follows is from his letter to Herbert Stone, editor of *Yachting*, written on June 12, 1933, "at sea, North Sea":

Dorade is really an extraordinary little ship and I can now understand better her excellent record. An extremely fine sea-boat, she is … able to keep going when others would heave to. When even the discretion of age such as I possess would deem such a course desirable, youngsters of the type Dorade *breeds continue to scud before it. Her rig is handiness personified. Only*

SHERMAN HOYT'S MEMOIRS

THE BEST KNOWN YACHTSMAN IN THE WORLD
TELLS THE INTERESTING STORY OF HIS UNIQUE EXPERIENCES AT HOME AND ABROAD

Dust cover of *Sherman Hoyt's Memoirs*, published by D. Van Nostrand Sporting Books in 1950.

once was the off watch called on deck as two were ample for ordinary handling, and major operations were generally left until the shifting of watches. We had some really hard weather, first a near gale some 100 miles south of Sable Island, in which we hove to for four or five hours under forestaysail and mizzen. Our next real blow came later after clearing the Banks. It was of real strong gale strength for some 36 hrs. and we took it on our port quarter, under mizzen and forestaysail alone most of the time. At that we logged between 8 and 9 and got our biggest day's run of 190. The sea was quite the heaviest I have yet met in any of my sea ventures in small boats, yet Dorade *took it without a whimper, and once convinced we were not going to be properly pooped, coasting down the big waves was exhilarating."*
"Have only one fault to find with Dorade. *Perhaps it is more an acquired vice than an intrinsic fault and whisper it softly among the ocean going crowd, but* Dorade *is a rollormaniac. At any time running free with or without provocation she is prone to indulge in orgies of rolling. Unreasonable, unrestrained, free wide and handsome she rolls with blissful abandon. Perhaps it is our deep loading, her narrow beam or the rather heavy mast, but my can she roll!*

Sherman Hoyt went on to defend a second America's Cup with Mike Vanderbilt in 1934 on *Rainbow* and was credited with important tactical decisions and helmsmanship, which kept the Cup in America in the face of a faster challenger, T.O.M. Sopwith's *Endeavour*. He raced Twelve Metres in the 1930s and returned to the Navy during World War II. Then in his early 60s, Hoyt applied his maritime talents to the design and construction of submarine chasers and PT Boats. Hoyt died in 1961 at the age of 83.

This vivid painting by Charles Dixon shows *Dorade* rounding Fastnet Rock. The boat behind likely represents—with artistic license—the competitor *Lexia*, which was not this close at the rounding.

© MYSTIC SEAPORT

unfair, it's an outrage! I'm all for fair sport myself, and I admit it. So when I left Dorade *I went ashore to see if I couldn't arrange with the Royal Yacht Squadron to shoot Sherman Hoyt with the starting gun."*

In the light winds, which some attributed to the earlier, July start, the tide nearly swept the fleet across the line early, with dim prospects for an easy return to restart. But all started fairly, with *Grenadier's* youthful crew taking the best position, followed by Rod and *Dorade*. Westward they went to face the significant currents of the English Channel. Boat speed and handicapping over the fixed mileage of the course conspired to leave *Dorade* at the wrong places at the turn of several tides. *Flame*, with greater boat speed, was able to arrive at the Lizard and the Nab in time to avoid foul current. The slower *Dorade* missed the turn of the tide and sat stalled for hours as *Flame* sailed away. Those competitors behind the yawl made up time, while the foul current eased as they arrived at the turn. It was just a matter of timing, wind speed and boat speed, but it did not help. Nevertheless, throughout the light airs of six days of racing, *Dorade* battled with the swifter *Flame*, *Brilliant* and

To Norway and Cowes

Grenadier. The fleet also battled with shipping traffic, and *Dorade* narrowly avoided a nighttime collision with a British liner on her way up the Channel, an encounter close enough to include angry and profane shouts from the bridge of the liner. The finish line loomed, but no one was there to take the finishers' times. They did so themselves. Nicholson and *Flame* crossed the line at 5:15 a.m. on the 28th; *Dorade* came in five hours later, finishing first overall on corrected time. She was followed within less than an hour by the two American schooners *Grenadier* and *Brilliant*, which finished two-minutes apart. It was great racing for these two at the finish, but they could not have found less advantageous winds for their heavy rigs. *Lexia* followed in close order, and the aging *Ilex* finished the next day. As predicted, *Dorade* had done it again, adding a second Fastnet Cup to her growing collection of silverware.

The start of the 1933 Fastnet Race was frustratingly calm, and the tide—seen on the buoy—swept the fleet through the starting area.

ALBERT PRATT'S 1933 JOURNALS

Rod and ladies four enjoy a swim and a lunch on deck in the Baltic.

British Yachting Press

The paucity of British competitors in the 1933 Fastnet Race was not forgiven by the sailing press, which also questioned the direction of ocean racing design. *Yachting World* presented what were considered fair interpretations of developments and, by the end of 1933, editorialized the common British viewpoint with the following, later quoted in *British Ocean Racing*:

(The Fastnet) was an experiment and, like all experiments, its success was a matter of conjecture. Now when the race has become an institution and nearly ten years have passed since its inauguration, it seems time to take stock whether the high hopes of its originators have been realized. Looking back on this year's contest, when only six competitors, three of which were American, took part, it seems hard to believe that it has not fallen far short of its original promise....

The modern ocean racing machine represented by such as Dorade, Niña, Highland Light *and* Landfall, *has not been produced simply by retaining and developing the virtues of the cruiser and blending thereto something of the speed of the racing yacht. The type has vices of its own. It requires a large and well-trained crew to sail these yachts, sacrificing as they do comfort and even safety for the sake of speed. Their deep outside keels give them weatherlyness and speed at the expense of seakindliness....*

To date this country has not produced a single ocean-racing yacht, surely adequate proof that the type makes no appeal whatever to the cruising yachtsman....

Let us face the fact that the great experiment has broken down...

Douglas Phillips-Birt wrote in *The History of Yachting*, "While Ocean Racing in Europe thus appeared to be a fire guttering soon after it had been lit, the Bermuda Races of 1932 and 1934 which bracketed the unfortunate Fastnet of 1933, presented a picture of virility which defied the prevailing Depression."

Acceptance of the strength and seakeeping ability of *Dorade* and her sisters in design would have to wait until the European sour grapes had dissolved.

Above and opposite right—*Dorade* drives into the Atlantic westerlies, heading home to Larchmont.

ALBERT PRATT'S 1933 JOURNALS

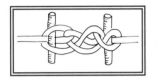 # Across the Pond Home

Rod Stephens prepared for the last leg of the trip, the return across the Atlantic. He knew that a return voyage across the northern route would mean sailing to windward for many days, but he did not dare to chance the southern route, through warmer waters and fairer winds. They stood on the cusp of the hurricane season, and *Dorade*, with no engine, could not chance being caught in a major storm unable to alter position to avoid it. His crew was game for the trip, but a number of events transpired to change his plans. Sherman Hoyt chose to stay in England, race Twelve Metres for a month or so and then return on *Brilliant* in the fall via Madeira and the warmer southern route. Ducky Endt, a Dutchman, encountered difficulties with his American visa and ended up staying behind as well. However, bad luck in Cowes Road spelled good fortune for *Dorade* in filling out her crew. As the fleet lay rafted awaiting a Royal London Yacht Club regatta delayed by high winds, the Southern Railway steamer *Whippingham* went adrift in the gale and was swept down on the yachts. *Grenadier* suffered damage to her bowsprit and rig. *Brilliant* was damaged at the stern. (She was so stoutly constructed that it was not until a major refit in 2007 that the full extent of the damage was unearthed.) *Dorade* slipped her mooring. The *Daily Telegraph* reported dramatically, "Only the prompt action of the *Dorade*'s amateur crew in cutting away their anchor ropes saved the yacht from serious injury." They also reported that the King's yacht *Britannia* had not been damaged and that the *Whippingham* had not suffered significantly, but took four passes at her pier before landing to unload passengers. The damaged American yachts would have to change their plans for the return to the United States and in doing so would serve up the crew that *Dorade* needed.

One of the remarkable features of ocean racing in the 1930s was the youth of the sailors and the latitude and support given them to go heading off across the Atlantic. Roderick Stephens Sr. had allowed his sons, at very early ages, to sail alone. *Grenadier*, a 59-foot Alden schooner from Marblehead owned by the Morss family, was sailed by their young men and had set off to England for the Fastnet with a group of seven amateurs in their 20s and a single paid hand. Among the youngest of the crew

A Monkey Chain Doubled Toggled converts the slipping Chain into a secure knot at last.

ASHLEY KNOT 1145

The Southern Railway steamer *Whippingham* altered the return of the American competitors from Cowes. Above, she is fully underway, her paddlewheel churning. Below, she is seen tangled with the competitors in Cowes Road.

© MYSTIC SEAPORT

were two recent Harvard College graduates who savored the excitement of the sea, the sailing and the society that they encountered in Britain. With the return trip on *Grenadier* abandoned because of the *Whippingham* accident damage and knowing that Rod Stephens was short by two, they pleaded with him to fill out his crew and each found a berth on *Dorade*. As was common in those days, these two young men memorialized their experiences in articles to the yachting press which were promptly published. Further, private journals and photographs have left a charming record of the trip. Albert Pratt, a 1933 graduate of Harvard, was the last member to find a berth. He wrote articles for *Yachting* and his private journals of that summer have survived. Samuel Morse Lane, whose serialized articles were published in *The Sportsman*, added his youthful perspective, and these two writers helped to give a picture of the voyage home that brought to life the image of *Dorade* at sea for readers in both Britain and America.

The voyage began with frustratingly calm winds, but the easy weather gave the crew a chance to organize the boat and learn their duties. Aboard, along with Stephens, Pratt and Lane, was Joe Appleton, an experienced sailor who had come over on *Brilliant*. Dave Leeson served famously as cook. Also along was Porter Buck, a *Dorade* crewman from both the Fastnet and the prior year's Bermuda Race. After a crowded send-off, which included Rod's mother and sister, they were aweigh just before noon on August 5. In bathing trunks and hot weather, the crew headed west for four days, and Pratt and Lane both reflected on how well the boat went in light air. However, everyone wanted more breeze. On the fifth day, they encountered a small shark and, with a hook baited with bacon, brought it aboard. With superstition at hand and old whaling tales to rely upon, they removed the shark's tail and fixed it

Across the Pond Home

to the stem-head for luck. Pratt noted, "Immediately a little SW breeze sprung up," and they were off into the west.

Albert Pratt's journal faithfully reports each day at sea, the changing weather and sea conditions, and the performance of the yacht and her crew. In the November issue of *Yachting*, he wrote of his concerns prior to joining the crew:

'You're thinking of sailing home in Dorade*?' The tone in which this question was asked implied that I ought not to be at large. 'Why, she's nothing but a racing machine! She has an Eight-Metre hull with a flimsy yawl rig. She goes under the water more than on top of it: there's not room enough in her to turn around, and her cook will give you pancakes all the way home. She's a racer, not a cruising boat. You'd be crazy to put to sea in her.' This was the sort of opinion I heard in England this summer. Having sailed for the most part in beamy, full bodied schooners, it confirmed my own impressions. But Sherman Hoyt, who had sailed over from Norway in* Dorade *and who had seen her make a hundred miles to windward in the North Sea against a week of westerly gales, had a far different story to tell. 'I'd go anywhere in her, any time,' he said. So inwardly dubious, I applied to Rod Stephens for a berth in* Dorade.

Pratt's worries were quickly allayed. He found the yacht comfortable and swift, somewhat to his surprise. He wrote in his journal:

*"*Dorade *is a lovely little boat: she sure can go in light air." "You don't have to watch the sail really for the feel of the boat underneath is enough. She balances well and by dickering with the headsail and mizzen sheets one can secure a balance under any conditions." "*Dorade *surely does go like a witch in light air and slop. Chop and swell does not seem to stop her at all, and she* **never** *has a* **trace** *of pounding." "*Dorade *just scoots along, with a very easy helm and a far better motion than I thought possible. She is a little quick (due to her narrowness and lump of lead) compared to an Alden schooner, but the motion is not in the least unpleasant. The seas are quite steep and sharp, and of good size, but we are very dry on deck. Occasional flecks of spray is all, and our dodger in the weather rail keeps this out of the cockpit. Once every half hour or so a big slop comes over her, but this is to be expected. The boat is very easy to get around on forward of the cockpit: one has no sense of insecurity." "She rolls quite badly sometimes and this is the hitch." "Little* Dorade *still does her steady nine and whooshes down each wave like a kid sliding down a bank, splashes at the bottom and then eagerly runs up the next wave to do it all over again."*

Pratt's observations of Rod Stephens are also interesting. Although Rod was only a year or so older than Pratt, he had already developed a worldwide reputation as a yachtsman, and sailors old and young alike looked up to him. He was seen as hard-driving, physical and competitive. Pratt wrote:

"Rod is a great talker—almost notoriously so: in fact, this was one of the things I was a bit afraid of: but I have no fear now. He may wag his tongue and deal with the topic under consideration from every side but by and large everything he says is interesting, to the point and backed by definite knowledge or experience."

"The wind increased gradually all morning and afternoon. In the middle of the morning we substituted the #2 for the #1 jib topsail, the skipper going forward absolutely naked as is his wont when there is any chance of getting wet."

Samuel Lane's delightful, youthful writing in *The Sportsman* (October 1933) offered his perspective on many parts of the journey and, importantly, on the food for the crew.

Rod Stephens Jr., the 22-year-old skipper, veteran of two Bermuda Races, holder of two Fastnet victories, now heading across the Atlantic for the third time.

ALBERT PRATT'S 1933 JOURNALS

Breakfast-fruit, cereal, bacon and eggs, and Swedish bread- was served at seven-thirty:— general swill—at eleven thirty; supper—canned meat, vegetables, and fruit—at five–thirty. After supper the off watch would blend their dulcet vocals with Cookie's musical banjo and Rod's cheery accordion, and render the most ribald of ditties with such fervor and emotion as to bring tears to the eyes of their confreres. Every night at seven bells Cookie extracted himself from that eighteen-inch trough on the port side of the main cabin which served as his downy couch, but more closely resembled a coffin than a bed, and regaled the crew with a dose of "Doctor Leeson's famous hot beef injection." Whether Bovril, Leibig's, Marmite, or a combination of the three, this excellent brew was known by no other name than "Doctor Leeson's famous hot beef injection." Specialite de la maison, however, was not soup but pancakes. So thin and tasty were Cookie's pancakes that they were ravenously devoured, not, as is customary, merely as a base for maple syrup, but for their own sake. Long after the syrup was exhausted the crew continued to demand more pancakes, and ate them with honey or brown sugar. Only item on the bill of fare that proved truly obnoxious was canned Irish stew. Than that stew nothing could have been more disgusting. On the outside of the can a rosy-cheeked chef indulged in a belly laugh at the expense of the world. We couldn't decide whether he was laughing at the misguided individuals who bought the stew, or whether it simply delighted his sense of the ridiculous to see the foul mixture masquerading under an assumed name, and we all wondered, as we picked over the bones, whether he backed the horse into the pot, or simply pushed him in headfirst.

Left—Rod, up the forestay, characteristically climbing aloft to look for breeze.

Right—Rod Stephens at sea, returning home from the 1933 Fastnet Race. This image, by Albert Pratt, was widely reproduced and hung in Olin's den until 2008. (Bear in mind, photographs of seas generally understate their actual size.)

ALBERT PRATT'S 1933 JOURNAL

Westward they sailed, principally to windward through winds both heavy and light. In addition to entertainment, with singing and music as the evening watches changed, P. G. Wodehouse and his tales of "Jeeves the Butler," no doubt discovered in England, gave opportunities for reading aloud. Rod had banned smoking aboard, but a periodic "stiff hooker" of scotch whiskey was meted out. Despite a small deck leak forward, the vessel was dry for the most part. Young Sam Lane and Albert Pratt joined Joe Appleton and "round-faced" Porter Buck in managing the sailing of the yacht in alternating two-man watches of four hours, but Rod spelled each of them regularly for the evening's eight-to-twelve trick to shake up the order and to give each man an eight hour rest every few days. The cook got the meals out on time, nearly every time. The boat was driven hard, resulting in a record passage of 22d, 15 h from the Scillys to Pollock Rip, off of Cape Cod. The total passage from Cowes to Larchmont was 26d, 15h. No boat of *Dorade*'s size had ever completed the trip westward in so short a time.

The Cruising Club of America had, in 1923, established the Blue Water Medal, its first and arguably most prestigious award, to recognize "a most meritorious example of seamanship." In 1933, the club presented the award to Roderick Stephens Jr, citing, "A three-month, 8,000-mile trans-Atlantic crossing from New York to Norway and return, including victory in the Fastnet Race. Returning home from England by the northern route in the remarkable time of 26 days." More remarkable yet was the fact that the Blue Water Medal had been awarded just seven years earlier to Frederick Ames for his similar westbound voyage in *Primrose IV*, a 50-foot Alden schooner, but that notable voyage had taken 58 days. Rod had proven his skill as a great sailor, and *Dorade* had again proven to be a fast and able wee vessel at sea.

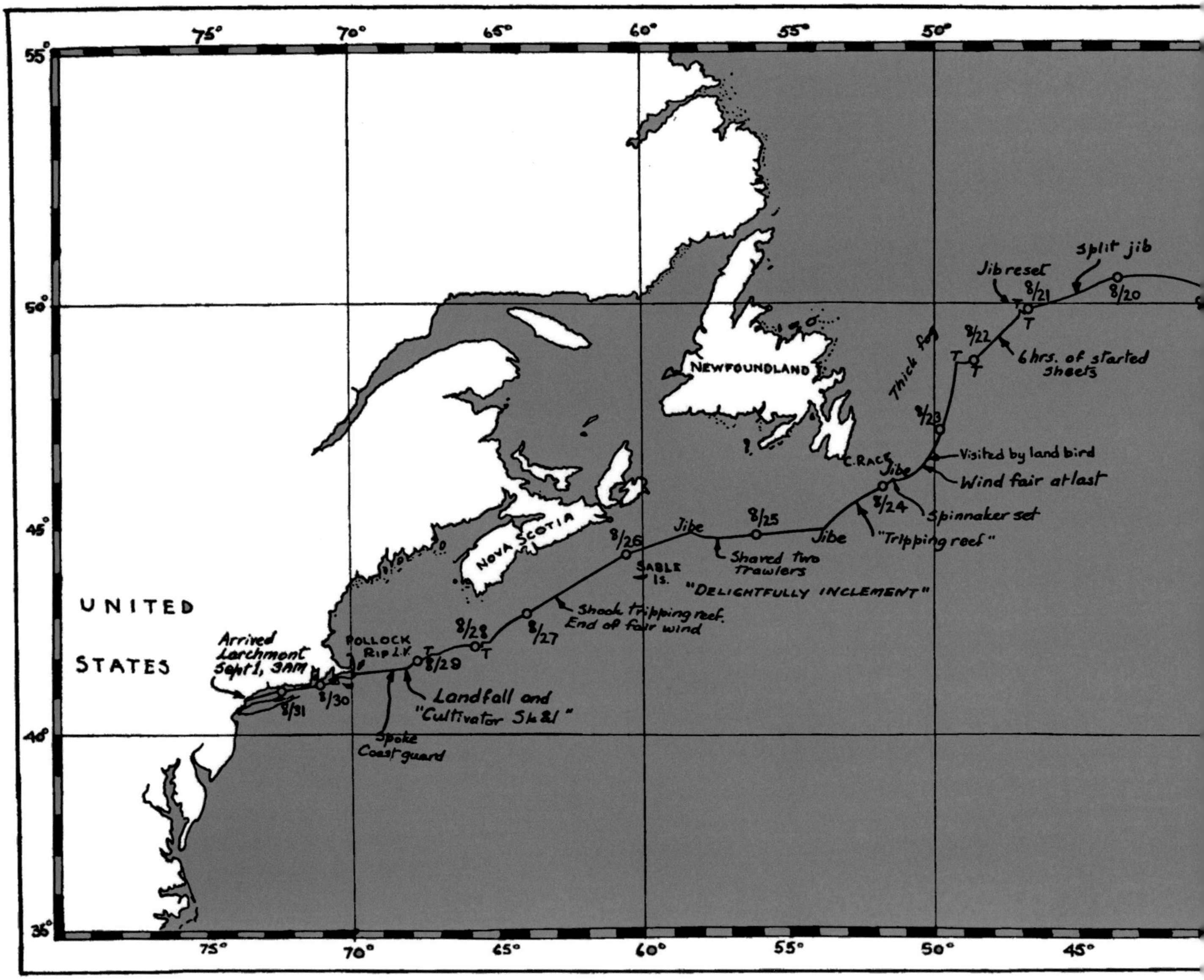
UNITED
STATES
NEWFOUNDLAND
NOVA SCOTIA
SABLE IS.
C. RACE
POLLOCK RIP L.V.
Arrived Larchmont Sept 1, 3AM
8/31
8/30
Spoke Coastguard
8/29
Landfall and "Cultivator Sh&l"
8/28
8/27
Shook tripping reef. End of fair wind
"DELIGHTFULLY INCLEMENT"
8/26
Jibe
8/25
Shaved two Trawlers
Jibe
"Tripping reef"
8/24
Spinnaker set
Wind fair at last
Visited by land bird
8/23
Thick fog
8/22
6 hrs. of started sheets
Jib reset
8/21
Split jib
8/20
75°
70°
65°
60°
55°
50°
45°
55°
50°
45°
40°
35°

Dorade's westward passage shows her following the 50th parallel for most of the voyage, sticking on tacks as long as possible.

COURTESY *YACHTING*

In his book *An Eye for a Yacht*, published in the 1950s, British writer Douglas Phillips-Birt describes *Dorade*'s westward voyage in 1933:

> *A remarkable yacht, the* Dorade, *not only succeeded in winning the Bermuda, Fastnet and Transatlantic races in quick succession, but sailed back across the North Atlantic against headwinds, of great weight when she was reduced to trysail, and taking twenty-six days from Cowes to Larchmont. This passage, made in August 1933, is a significant date in the history of sail. Such speed, in relation to her size, made under sail to windward across the Atlantic, was a new achievement in the long story of the wind driven craft, impossible in the days when sail was the prime*

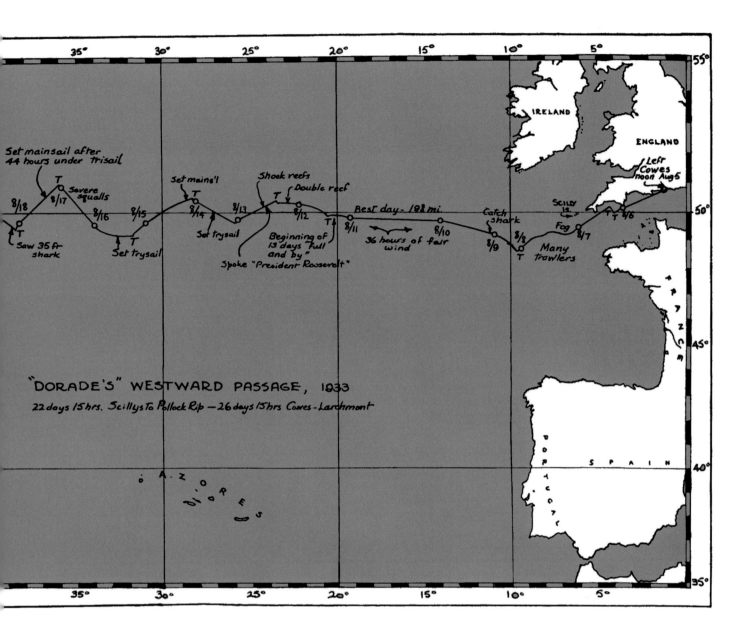

mover of all shipping, and achieved too late in history to have utilitarian value. It was the achievement of that highest development of sailing craft, the modern yacht, evolved by the designer and owing little to the traditional allegiance to the former working craft of sail.

The last entry in Albert Pratt's aging journal was just a hand-written note on a piece of hotel stationery, inserted by him many years later, which read: "Sam Lane—Singled to Bermuda and was never seen again."

Porter Buck, Rod, Sam Lane and Pratt, with Joe Appleton in front.

The 1933 Transatlantic crew in Larchmont (from left): Sam Lane, Albie Pratt, Rod, Dave Leeson, Joe Appleton and Porter Buck

Dorade's Song

Yachting doggerel was all the rage, and with many hours to polish their creation,
the westbound crew composed the following, their *"Dorade Song,"* which was included as the last page
of Albert Pratt's photo album.

From Cowes Roads we're sailing,
With fair winds prevailing,
Down the Channel to the sea.
We're damned glad we're leaving
But we'll soon be grieving
When we catch a Westerly!
Onward! Onward! Thru the spray and foam,
Onward! It's three thousand miles from home—
Drive her rail under,
Split the waves asunder,
And to hell with Westerlies!

While the charger wheezes
In the lightest breezes,
We sail on merrily:
Trawlers' foghorns blowing;
Steamers' lights not showing
'Till they're close upon our lee.
Onward, onward, ghosting thru the fog-
Chalk up every mile upon the log-
Tho head winds delay us
They cannot dismay us
While we sing so lustily

Crew showed predilection
For hot beef injection
Served at midnight by the cook.
In his galley toiling
With hot water boiling,
Cook his nightly dozen took.
Leibig's, Marmite, every kind of soup,
Did he proffer to our weary group:
But the best, no question,
Was the hot beef injection,
So the rest we all forsook.

Sam and Joe the tinker
Rigged hook line and sinker,
Brought a shark up from the sea.
His tail, amputated,
Our bow decorated
For good luck and wind that's free.
Onward! Onward! Now the wind is fair!
Onward! Onward! See our vessel tear!
Drive her bow under,
Split the waves asunder,
And to HELL with Westerlies!

Water Traps & Tiller Locks

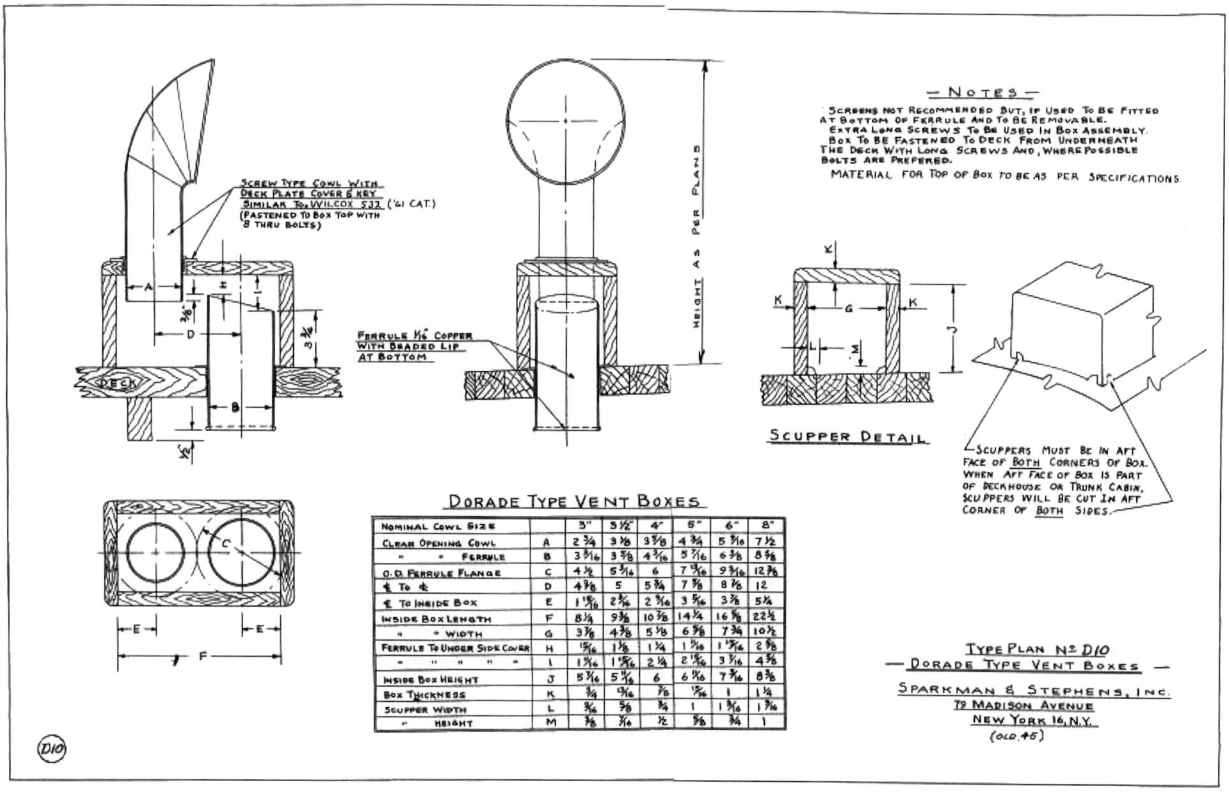

SCREW TYPE COWL WITH DECK PLATE COVER & KEY SIMILAR TO WILCOX 532 ('61 CAT.) (FASTENED TO BOX TOP WITH 8 THRU BOLTS)
DECK
FERRULE 1/16" COPPER WITH BEADED LIP AT BOTTOM
HEIGHT AS PER PLANS
— NOTES —
SCREENS NOT RECOMMENDED BUT, IF USED TO BE FITTED AT BOTTOM OF FERRULE AND TO BE REMOVABLE.
EXTRA LONG SCREWS TO BE USED IN BOX ASSEMBLY.
BOX TO BE FASTENED TO DECK FROM UNDERNEATH THE DECK WITH LONG SCREWS AND, WHERE POSSIBLE BOLTS ARE PREFERED.
MATERIAL FOR TOP OF BOX TO BE AS PER SPECIFICATIONS
SCUPPER DETAIL
SCUPPERS MUST BE IN AFT FACE OF BOTH CORNERS OF BOX. WHEN AFT FACE OF BOX IS PART OF DECKHOUSE OR TRUNK CABIN, SCUPPERS WILL BE CUT IN AFT CORNER OF BOTH SIDES.
TYPE PLAN Nº D10
— DORADE TYPE VENT BOXES —
SPARKMAN & STEPHENS, INC.
79 MADISON AVENUE
NEW YORK 16, N.Y.
(OLD 45)
D10

DORADE TYPE VENT BOXES

NOMINAL COWL SIZE		3"	3 1/2"	4"	5"	6"	8"
CLEAR OPENING COWL	A	2 3/4	3 1/8	3 5/8	4 3/4	5 9/16	7 1/2
" " FERRULE	B	3 3/16	3 5/8	4 3/16	5 7/16	6 3/8	8 5/8
O.D. FERRULE FLANGE	C	4 1/2	5 3/16	6	7 13/16	9 3/16	12 7/8
℄ TO ℄	D	4 3/8	5	5 3/4	7 5/8	8 7/8	12
℄ TO INSIDE BOX	E	1 15/16	2 3/16	2 9/16	3 5/16	3 7/8	5 1/4
INSIDE BOX LENGTH	F	8 1/4	9 3/8	10 7/8	14 1/4	16 5/8	22 1/2
" " WIDTH	G	3 7/8	4 3/8	5 1/8	6 5/8	7 3/4	10 1/2
FERRULE TO UNDER SIDE COVER	H	15/16	1 1/8	1 1/4	1 7/16	1 15/16	2 5/8
" " " " "	I	1 5/16	1 15/16	2 1/4	2 15/16	3 7/16	4 5/8
INSIDE BOX HEIGHT	J	5 7/16	5 11/16	6	6 11/16	7 3/16	8 3/8
BOX THICKNESS	K	3/4	13/16	7/8	15/16	1	1 1/4
SCUPPER WIDTH	L	9/16	5/8	3/4	1	1 3/16	1 5/16
" HEIGHT	M	3/8	7/16	1/2	5/8	3/4	1

Rod Stephens was renowned as a famously practical yacht fitment engineer. After crossing the Atlantic once in *Dorade* and sailing her to Bermuda and back twice, he had an idea. She had been originally fitted with four tall ventilators—two just aft of the mainmast and a second pair just forward of the house, mounted at the outboard corners—to provide fresh air down below. With cowls attached to standpipes rising 23 inches high, it took quite a sea for water to make its way into the ventilators and down below. Nevertheless, sometimes it did. The bells at the top were constructed to swivel away from the seas, and if that didn't do the job, the entire ventilator could be removed and the deck capped with a threaded plate.

Rod tried various approaches to make the vents work more efficiently. One was to weld a baffle with a drain hole to the lower lip of the cowl, thereby decreasing the exposed mouth of the cowls without reducing its air-intake capacity. This approach didn't work very well, so Rod tinkered with other modifications, finally settling on an indirect venting apparatus comprised of a six-inch-tall, deck-mounted box that held the ventilator at one end and vented below through a separate, offset tube extending up into the box.

Drain holes were cut at the deck line of the box to draw water away and out. When properly positioned, the vent allowed only air through the inlet pipe.

Her vents could be left on in most conditions, and the interior remained dry. Sherman Hoyt commented, "Rod's contraptions for mounting cowl ventilators on small boxes on deck with separate standpipe underneath to quarters below have worked to perfection. Shall never go to sea without similar gear again if it can be helped, and don't see why they have never been thought of before." Many who sailed on the boat marveled at the vents' efficiency, and, over the years, Dorade Vents became commonplace on yachts, both power and sail. They are, in some ways, even more famous than the boat itself. According to a common yarn, a passer-by saw *Dorade* and asked, "Why would anyone name a boat after a vent?" *Dorade*'s legendary original ventilators have survived aboard her to this day. Because they are tall, they have provided crews an inviting, if somewhat fragile, handhold on a pitching deck. They are a bit battered, but they still show the baffle that Rod first experimented with, as well as the two, screw-in, bronze plates employed in the experimental stages. They are remarkable artifacts of yacht design.

Opposite—Drawing from Uffa Fox's *Sailing, Seamanship and Yacht Construction*.

Above left—*Dorade*'s original starboard forward water trap vent, showing the 1932 baffle at the lower edge of the bell and the box of 1933. The second bronze plate is a remnant of design experimentation.

Below left—Drawing of the tiller lock, from *Sailing, Seamanship and Yacht Construction*.

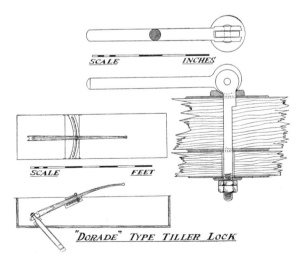

Dorade, Edlu and *Stormy Weather* tune up for the 1934 Bermuda Race. *Dorade* had the highest rating of the three.

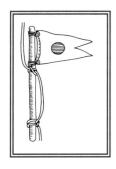

The Rules Change

A fundamental aspect of competition in racing yachts of different sizes and types is the use of handicapping. The objective is to evaluate the performance of the boat in relationship to its theoretical potential. Because larger boats with greater waterlines and sail areas are inherently faster than smaller vessels, a time allowance per course mile is given to the slower craft to equalize the speed differences. As designs develop and speeds are tested, the rules and resultant handicaps change. If a design or size of boat consistently dominates the fleet and makes winning for all other well-sailed boats unlikely, the rules get a makeover.

In the summer of 1933, as the next year's Bermuda Race loomed on the horizon, the Cruising Club of America worked on the formulation of a handicapping change. A number of factors were at work. First, little *Dorade* had dominated long-distance racing for three years running and, although she had not won the Bermuda Trophy, she had won nearly everything else and had been overwhelmingly victorious in the smaller class of the 1932 race. Further, there were those within the fraternity who felt that she was "unwholesome," in the sense that she was too narrow, rolled a great deal and was not ideal as both a racing and cruising yacht, in keeping with the objectives of the CCA. Even her designer, Olin, admitted that boats with greater beam could be more stable and potentially faster on most points of sail. Although he knew that a redrawing of the rating rules would hurt the competitiveness of his first ocean racing creation, he wanted to support the idea of better yachts at sea. It would not be the last time he would lend a shoulder to such progress in advancing stronger or better design ideas.

So the new season dawned with a new rule that introduced a "narrow beam penalty" and reduced *Dorade*'s rating advantage. Olin served on the CCA Measurement Committee. The new rule set a theoretically ideal ratio of beam to waterline and applied a formula that increased ratings for boats that were too narrow and reduced rating for boats beamier than the theoretical target. The penalty had the effect of increasing *Dorade*'s rating, from the 38.26 feet that she carried for the 1932 race to 44.99 feet, an almost unimaginable increase. She was simply classified as a much bigger and faster boat because of her potential for speed despite her size. Further, the CCA and Royal Bermuda Yacht Club instituted a change in classes by dividing the fleet at a rating of 40 feet, with all yachts above that threshold racing in Class A and all beneath it in Class B. Even the *New York Times* commented that the new rules had been influenced by *Dorade*'s dominance and that she would now have to sail against the larger class.

Olin Stephens had been busy with new commissions for ocean racers; in 1934, 16 sailboats between 29 and 79 feet were built to his designs. Forty-seven design num-

This Clove Hitch on a signal halyard shows the method for securing a pigstick or nighthawk staff.

ASHLEY KNOT 2040

bers were allocated at S&S that year, and it was clear that the firm was a premier design resource for racing sailors. Two of the 1934 designs, both built by Nevins, emerged early in the year with the Bermuda Race and the new rule clearly in their sights. The first was *Stormy Weather* (Design No. 27), a 53-foot 11-inch yawl built for Philip LeBoutillier, who headed Best Department Stores. The second was *Edlu* (Design No. 35), a 56-foot 2-inch sloop built for R.J. Schaefer, of the Schaefer Brewing family. These two differed from one another in the sense that *Edlu* was more heavily appointed with cruising comforts and *Stormy* was purposefully designed for racing. There is no doubt that both of these boats were influenced by *Dorade*, but they were importantly different from her nonetheless. While *Dorade* was not designed to any particular rating rule, both of the later boats were.

Added beam satisfied the new Bermuda Race rule's objective of greater stability. Comparing the boats' waterline to beam ratios reveals the change. While *Dorade* carried a ratio of 3.8 as drawn, and in actuality was even slightly higher as she sat lower and lower in the water, *Edlu's* nearly two extra feet of beam gave her a ratio of 3.1, and *Stormy Weather's* design gave a ratio of 3.2. All three boats' waterlines are within a few inches of one another, when *Dorade's* actual floating dimension of 39 feet, 3 inches is taken into account, but both new boats were larger, with greater displacements and significantly greater sail areas. *Edlu's* rig carried 1,449 square feet, and *Stormy Weather* was drawn to carry 1,300 square feet. *Dorade's* sail plan, after being cut down in 1930, called for 1,079 square feet. *Edlu*, the largest of the three, displaced 46,225 pounds, *Stormy Weather* 42,990 pounds, and *Dorade* came in at 37,720 pounds as drawn and weighed in at 1,000 pounds more. Despite her smaller size, *Dorade* gave time to both larger boats and indeed to many in the fleet. Uffa Fox observed in his *Second Book*, "That the rule is unduly hard on narrow beamed boats most will agree, for the little *Dorade*, though the smallest in Class A for the 1934 Bermuda Race, had by this rule to give time to no less than eight vessels (all of them larger) (she gave 50 minutes by the rule to *Grenadier*, a vessel much bigger than herself). This, however, is natural, for no human being is well and truly balanced, and like a pendulum, if we swing far in one direction, we swing just as far in the other immediately after, just as immediately after a war we want peace, for in the past the Bermuda Race has been too tolerant to narrow boats." However, Uffa also acknowledged that, in certain conditions, *Dorade* held an advantage over the larger boats. He observed that her sail-carrying ability was unique for her size, and "we must remember that the little and narrow *Dorade* can be driven harder without slowing up, than can her beamier sisters *Edlu* and *Stormy Weather*."

And so, with two newly defined classes and a fleet of 29, the race began in very light winds on June 24 from Sarah's Ledge, off New London, Connecticut, following the 650-mile course last sailed in 1930. Suffering through the nerve-wracking fetch to Montauk Point, the smaller and lighter boats scampered away from the heavier schooners as the fleet turned south/southwest toward the warm, blue waters of the Gulf Stream on a starboard tack. The light winds did not last long, and the larger competitors caught up. For most, the race would be one, long tack, not unlike the record-setting 1932 contest. By the first evening, the fleet had entered the Gulf Stream and was plunging into seas kicked up by winds of 30 to 35 knots. Nearly all shortened sail that night, and *Dorade* did so as well, but only with the lowering of her mizzen for balance. The competitiveness of the contest was importantly determined on many boats by the number of crewmembers who could complete "one way meals." Some crews were so stricken by seasickness in the heavy going that they lowered all sails and simply coasted along without enough able hands to handle a canvassed ship.

The schooners should have had the best of it in such conditions, but several yawls and sloops held in at the lead, sailed courses that kept the wind fuller and finished well in both classes. While *Vamarie*, a big staysail wishbone ketch, was first to finish, in slightly over three days, *Edlu* and *Dorade* dueled toward St. David's Head and finished within 20 minutes of one another. The legendary yawl beat the sloop, but could not save her time. An allowance of 3h, 45m was given to *Edlu*, a boat launched only three weeks prior to the race and skippered for Rudy Schaefer by Bob Bavier, one of the greatest racers of the day. *Edlu* finished first in Class A and won the Bermuda Trophy, the first of many S&S designs to do so. It was also the first time a sloop had triumphed in the "Thrash to the Onion Patch." *Dorade* beat *Stormy Weather* across the line by five hours and eighteen minutes and, in giving her less than five hours allowance, corrected out ahead by 40 minutes.

Dorade and *Stormy Weather* would meet again in less important races on Long Island Sound later that summer, but it would then be nearly 60 years before they would again compete against one another. Despite the handicapping, the smaller *Dorade* had beaten many newer and larger boats through the water. She was sailed well enough to finish fifth in both Class A and overall. Olin, with Rod aboard, had skippered the now veteran ocean racer brilliantly despite her handicap burden. The Stephens brothers were sailing together again after several years where their schedules had prevented it. No one could have known as they celebrated in the Royal Bermuda Yacht Club's brand-new clubhouse on Hamilton Harbor that this would be *Dorade*'s last ocean race with the Stephens men at the helm. *Stormy Weather* finished seventh in that year's Bermuda Race, and, skippered by Rod in the years that followed, she would ascend to the pinnacle of ocean racing. Olin would find less time to be away from his drafting board, and the sailing that he did would be in support of clients for whom he designed newer yachts. *Dorade* would begin a new chapter in her long life.

Stormy Weather

Much has been written about the similarities between *Dorade* and *Stormy Weather*, a good deal of it relating to the ancestral linkage between the smaller, breakthrough first design and the larger, successful later one. Certainly they both derive from the board of Olin Stephens, are almost equivalent in overall length, waterline length and draft, and both carry yawl rigs. They are both fitted with short houses, although *Stormy*'s is longer. Both are essentially flush-decked and carry similar skylights and venting. A distant glance could produce confusion between them were it not for *Stormy Weather*'s distinctive boomkin, rigged to support the mizzen sheet, and running backstays. In reality, however, they are very different designs, and while it may seem disloyal to the boat that afforded Olin so much early success, *Stormy Weather* is an improvement over *Dorade*. Olin often said so, and there are important reasons why. The first is the pursuit of greater stability. Certainly both yawls are narrow, but the 1934 design is materially beamier, and this adds initial stability. She also is drawn with tumblehome, that wonderful term which describes topsides which are beamier in their center portion than at either the waterline or the rail, a rounding that adds stability when heeled. Righting moment, the measurement of resistance to heeling in foot-pounds, tells the tale. To take *Stormy Weather* to an angle of 30 degrees requires over 53,000 foot pounds of effort. The same test on *Dorade* requires only 27,400 foot pounds. This difference is not primarily the result of greater ballast, although *Stormy* does have approximately 1,400-pounds more lead, carried with slightly less draft. Instead, the reason for the significant difference is hull form because with greater beam and a harder turn to the bilge comes a need for greater effort to make the hull heel. That greater effort allows for a larger rig, and *Stormy Weather* can, in all conditions but driving to weather in a heavy chop, carry more sail and travel faster. She is stiffer and therefore drier, and she rolls less than her predecessor. *Stormy*'s slightly cut-away forefoot may add somewhat to maneuverability by reducing her lateral plane. This reduces proportional wetted area, and although *Stormy* has more in absolute square feet, the total area is proportionally less for her overall greater size. They are both fast and wonderful sea boats, but the improvements made to the newer design produced a better all-around racing and cruising platform. The lines plans on page 101 show the differences in hull form between *Dorade, Stormy Weather,* and the Six Metre *Nancy* (S&S Design No. 17, 1932).

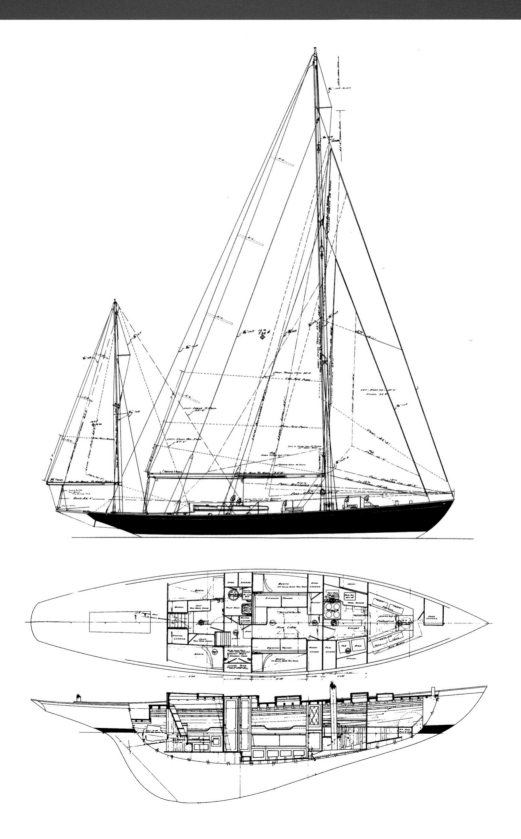

	Dorade	*Stormy Weather*
Displacement	38,720 lbs.	42,240 lbs.
Length Overall	52'	53' 11"
Length Waterline	39' 2"	39' 8"
Maximum Beam	10' 3"	12' 6"
Beam at Waterline	9' 3"	11' 5"
Draft	8' 0"	7' 11"
Sail Area	1079 sq. ft.	1300 sq. ft.
Wetted Surface	492 sq. ft.	527 sq. ft.

Accommodations below provide a comparison that is also noteworthy. *Stormy Weather*'s greater breadth makes her seem commodious in comparison to *Dorade*. Her galley is forward, her saloon is amidship and her head and navigation station are next aft. On about approximately the same waterline as *Dorade*, she is able to fit a separate aft cabin, entered at the base of the aftermost companionway, which leads from the cockpit. A separate companionway through the housetop allows the aft cabin to be separated from the remainder of the yacht. All in all, except for a galley far removed from the cockpit, she is more comfortable, and her bunks are not coffin-like! The watchword of the day in 1934 was "wholesome," a code word for a new and more sea-kindly design. *Stormy Weather* would go on to establish a record as great as *Dorade*'s, and she did so in an increasingly competitive environment. No design could have had the personal importance of *Dorade* to the Stephens family, but Olin always mentioned *Stormy Weather* first when he called out his favorite designs.

Statistical sources for *Dorade* include the S&S technical file, with figures given as built rather than as drawn. For *Stormy Weather*, data is taken from Paul Adamthwaite, based upon calculations he has done from S&S drawings. Interestingly, *Dorade*'s wetted surface as drawn was a mere 468 square feet.

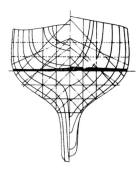
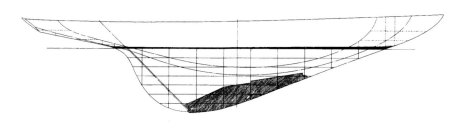

SIX METRE *NANCY*

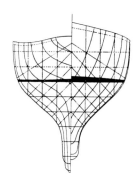
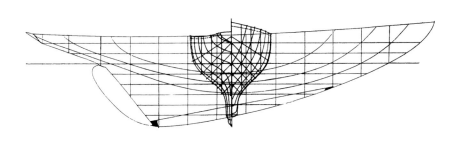

DORADE

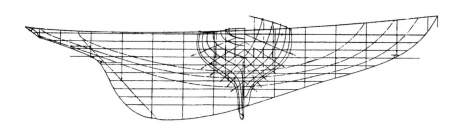

STORMY WEATHER

COURTESY SPARKMAN & STEPHENS

Yacht Dorade, Sold by Stephens Brothers, Will Be Entered in Races on the Pacific

Dorade, most famous of all small deep-sea yachts, is going to leave the Atlantic Ocean, over which her fame has spread for seven years. She was sold yesterday by her brother owners, Olin J. Stephens 2d, and Roderick Stephens Jr., to James Flood of San Francisco.

Within a week she will be shipped to the West Coast on the deck of a steamship. Once there her new owner will enter her in contests on the Pacific, and her first race there will be the one to Honolulu.

On her record, Dorade even surpassed Gauntlet and Duckling, other small ocean rovers, in blue-water performances. Twice she crossed the Atlantic and back, although only 52 feet 3 inches long on deck and but 38 feet 6 inches on the water.

The first time, in 1931, she won the transatlantic race from Newport to Plymouth, England, making the crossing of 2,950 miles in 17 days and 14 hours. She waited there for the Fastnet race of 615 miles and won that with an elapsed time of 4 days, 6 hours.

Two years later she made a cruise to Norway, and while on the other side went to England, where she again won the Fastnet contest. After returning here she entered the Bermuda race in 1934, the last one held, and was the winner in her division, Class B.

———

A radio message received at 1 A. M. yesterday from Gerard B. Lambert's America's Cup class yacht Yankee, which is returning from England under sail, stated that she had headed south out of a storm but then was back on her course to Boston, which she was due east of.

THE *NEW YORK TIMES*, APRIL 25, 1936

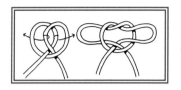

An Altered Course

As the 1935 season began, a number of currents intersected to alter *Dorade*'s course. First, another Transatlantic Race was planned, this time from Newport to Bergen, Norway. Rod was asked by Philip LeBoutillier to skipper *Stormy Weather* in that race and in the Fastnet to follow. There would be six competitors in the Norway race. Olin could see little prospect for sailing his own boat that summer, as his design work and his clients demanded his attention. And so *Dorade* was chartered to Robert Meyer for the summer, and it was not an active one. The *New York Times* reported Meyer's withdrawal from entry in the 394-mile New Rochelle Yacht Club Nantucket Lightship Race in June because he was unable to "find a crew."

Darrell McClure's cartoon in *Yachting* underscores Rod's reputation.

COURTESY *YACHTING*

There is no doubt that economic strain was felt in many quarters by the ravages of the Depression. Yacht yards such as Nevins were building smaller boats at lower prices than ever. *Stormy Weather* and *Edlu*, both larger and more complex than *Dorade*, had cost less to build. The ample available labor allowed *Stormy* to be completed in only four months. Fewer competitors were entered in ocean races, although England's Fastnet, which many had predicted to die after only six boats turned out for the 1933 race, grew to 17 participants in 1935. Nevertheless, economic times were not good.

At the end of the season, Olin and Rod decided that the attention and time required to keep *Dorade* were more than they wished and that they would sell the boat. It is only to be expected that, as young yacht designers, they would find improvements in design to be attractive for their own sailing experiences. Rod was prominently astride a new mount, *Stormy Weather*, and had won the Bergen Race and the Fastnet in her. *Dorade* presented a significant financial responsibility to the brothers, and they considered the idea of selling her to buy something less expensive. One option was Olin's Design No. 27, *Aweigh*. She was smaller overall at 47 feet, roomier with greater freeboard and had been very beautifully built by M.M. Davis & Sons in Maryland. She had won the Miami-Nassau Race and the Key West Race, and so she was fast. She was available for purchase, but, in the end, they gave Drake Sparkman the single task of finding *Dorade* a new home, not replacing her.

Dorade would be the first and last yacht that Olin Stephens would ever own. Drake Sparkman did a good selling job, and advertisements in *Yachting* produced

The Handcuff Knot begins with a Clove Hitch and can be rendered secure if each end is hitch around one of the loops.

ASHLEY KNOT 1140

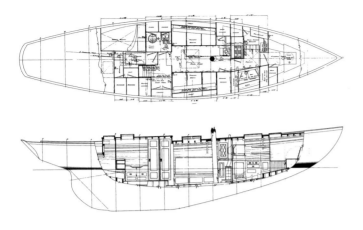

results. On April 25, 1936, the *New York Times* announced that she had been sold the day before to James Flood of San Francisco and was headed to the Pacific to compete in that summer's Transpacific Yacht Race from Los Angeles to Honolulu. Flood wanted a thoroughbred, and he got one. The arrival of the famous yawl on May 26, 1936, was heralded by the *San Francisco Chronicle* in their "Sporting Green" column with great fanfare. *Time* reported that Flood had paid $15,000 for the boat, although that figure has been disputed. Her proud new owner reveled in having the most famous ocean racer in the world at his doorstep on San Francisco Bay.

During the same month that the boat's sale took place, *The Rudder* published an article by Olin Stephens entitled, "The Influence of Ocean Racing on Cruising Yacht Design." In it, he described the evolution of changes in the types of yachts taken to sea to race and the impact on hull shape, rigs, scantlings and rules since the re-inauguration of the Bermuda Race 15 years earlier. He found all of these areas important, and he placed *Dorade* within the march of those changes, offering the following observations of her:

Dorade's design was extreme and even her success had little direct result in bringing about the construction of cruising yachts of her exact type, but her many undeniably good qualities furnished an objective to those who saw them. For she was more than fast. I believe it is fair to say that Dorade *stood for several years absolutely alone in her ability to stand hard driving on all points of sailing and in the roughest water, in safety and relative comfort. Also, her small and very handy jib-headed yawl rig made it possible to get one hundred per cent efficiency out of the boat as a unit with remarkably little effort on the part of the crew. With her narrow, easily driven hull she could do well even under a very short rig. Windward work in rough water was her best point of sailing and reaching in moderate weather in smooth water her poorest. Her maximum speed was very high.*

That summer of 1936 saw another important change in yacht ownership. King George V had left instructions that his great yacht *Brittania* be scuttled upon his death. Designed by G. L. Watson and launched in 1893, she had been the most glamorous of the Big Boat Class in Britain, carrying rigs that evolved to her ultimate rating as a J Class sloop. Not willing to allow his beloved yacht to pass to another owner, she was stripped of her fitments and allowed to fill and sink off of Cowes Road. It had been just five years since Roderick Sr., Olin and Rod had been welcomed aboard *Britannia* by the King, and now both monarch and yacht were gone.

The Stephens Men and Higher Education

Olin Stephens receiving an Honorary Master of Science degree from the the Stevens Institute of Technology, February 1945.

COURTESY SPARKMAN & STEPHENS

Much has been made of the fact that Olin Stephens entered the Massachusetts Institute of Technology in 1926 only to leave his studies of naval architecture after a single term. Similarly, his younger brother, Rod, spent only one year at Cornell University as a mechanical engineering student before leaving to learn boatbuilding at Nevins, never to return. Roderick Stephens Sr., attended college and earned "about sixty-five credits" before he left in order to join the family coal business. So, the men had all declined to pursue undergraduate degrees. However, the trio was clearly completely immersed in the technical aspects of the things that interested them. Olin designed and set the stage for the tank testing and mathematical modeling which began soon after *Stormy Weather* as the development of Harold Vanderbilt's J Class masterpiece *Ranger* took shape. All his life, he waded into and provided leadership with rating rules and measurement theory. He was famous late in life for doing recreational mathematics daily to improve his cognition. For his part, Rod was firmly grounded in engineering. His work on rigs and innovative structures may have begun with *Dorade* and her vents but expanded into revolutionary yachting and military designs. In 1947, the *New York Times* reported that Roderick Sr. had returned to study at Colum-

bia University. It is remarkable to think that this news would still be meaningful to the New York public, but the Stephens men were famous and fascinating. Stephens had long been active and interested in labor relations, and had served on the Bronx Board of Trade and the New York State Commission Against Discrimination. He explained his return to college as follows "I wanted to check some of this academic teaching and training against my own practical experience in labor relations." He was still mindful of his sons having left college. "They haven't as many credits as I have. Unless the boys start soon, I'm going to get that degree first."

Roderick Sr., got his degree, and neither of the sons returned to college. However, their relationships with academia were close. In 1947, Olin was awarded an Honorary Master of Science degree from the Stevens Institute of Technology, and, in 1959, Olin and Rod Jr. were both awarded Honorary Master of Science degrees from Brown University for their work in naval architecture. Well into his 90s, Olin was still lecturing to engineering classes at Dartmouth College and aspiring designers at The Landing School. The spirit of study and inquiry never slackened in any of the Stephens men.

Dorade passes beneath the Golden Gate Bridge.

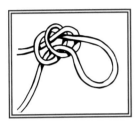

The Other Coast

San Francisco was a city of turmoil and contradiction in the spring of 1936. In some ways alive with progress and in others deeply wounded by the Depression, the City-by-the-Bay was midway through the process of being linked to Marin County on the north and to Oakland on the east by two remarkable bridges. Each represented a unique engineering achievement, but neither was yet finished. Swings in fortune had long been the City's fate, with waves of exuberant expansion alternating with dreadful tragedies. The boom times that had continued through a series of gold and silver bonanzas beginning in the mid-1800s had been punctuated by several panics. San Francisco had grown into a grand metropolis, scattered through its famous sand-dune hills, only to be devastated by the Great Earthquake and fire of 1906. As rebuilding began and continued through the First World War, San Francisco prospered. With the opening of the Panama Canal in 1915, she roared into the 1920s, only to stumble along with the rest of the country with the Crash of 1929. A city elegant and slightly haughty, San Francisco in the 1930s still had good reason to be proud of itself, with its fashionable populace, sophistication, dramatic history and alabaster housing sprinkling its vistas.

San Francisco Bay wraps around the north and eastern edges of The City as it winds through the Golden Gate from the Pacific Ocean. The Bay sometimes glitters, sometimes is smothered in a dense and frigid summertime fog and is always moving vigorously with muscular tides that reward the racing yachtsman who knows them and punish the sailor who does not. The heart of yachting on The City Front in 1936 was the St. Francis Yacht Club, a mere youngster within the yachting fraternity. The St. Francis had erupted in 1927 through the efforts of unsatisfied members of the San Francisco Yacht Club who believed that The City needed a club

Above—The Golden Gate, 1936.

The Poacher's Knot is a noose used for snaring game, tightening as it is tugged from the loop.

Ashley Knot 409

The St. Francis Yacht Club in 1934. Hawaiian Island liners pass, and the Marin Headlands are bare of a bridge.

THE HISTORY OF THE
ST. FRANCIS YACHT CLUB

on the Bay and that the grand economic march of the late 1920s would go on forever. Breaking away from their Sausalito brethren to establish a yachting and social center on land reclaimed from the Panama-Pacific Exposition on The City's northern waterfront, the St. Francis Yacht Club counted among its founding members many of the most influential and wealthy men in San Francisco. Through negotiation with the State of California and the San Francisco city fathers, they secured a lease allowing them to build their clubhouse on pilings over the bay and to expand the small-boat harbor built for the Exposition to allow for the moorage of their yachts.

The clubhouse emerged from the Bay attached to landfill created in 1915 and was completed in 10 months, ready to open in late 1928. An attractive and prominent membership, an accomplished general manager and a capable staff soon made the club a premier social gathering place. But just as the membership expanded and the initiation fee was increased, the economic music stopped. The Crash occurred just 302 days following the club's opening night, and things began to unravel. The membership limit of 400 was almost reached in 1930, and the initiation fee had increased from the founders' fee of $200 to a level of $1,500. By 1932, that fee had fallen to $100. When *Dorade* arrived in 1936, the fee stood at $50 and was routinely waived if you owned a boat or could only afford the $7 monthly dues. The two Bay-

spanning bridges under construction served as a beacon of progress, but times were hard—particularly for a fledgling yacht club. However, there was probably no real doubt about its survival. The wealth of some of the club's important and dedicated founders would have seen to that. Nevertheless, the St. Francis was in a storm and battened down.

James Flood was born on Bastille Day, July 14, 1908, making him younger, by three months, than Olin Stephens. The prominence of his family in the history of California and San Francisco allowed him a remarkable perspective on life. His grandfather, James Clair Flood, and three other Irish investors, had purchased mines in the Comstock Lode midway through the mining life of that famous gold and silver discovery in the Sierra Nevada range to the east and north of San Francisco. Their explorations through the base of Mt. Davidson in Virginia City, Nevada, led them to the greatest silver deposit ever discovered in the United States, and the Flood family fortune was made. He built a spectacular mansion atop Nob Hill, in the best part of the city, with neighbors such as Mark Hopkins and Collis Huntington, builders of the Central Pacific Railroad, which constituted the western portion of the Transcontinental Railroad. Flood's son James Leary built the Flood Building at the corner of Powell and Market streets, in the city's commercial center.

The 1906 quake and fire left very few buildings standing around either of these important properties, but both the Flood Mansion and the Flood Building survive to this day, the former now the elegant and imposing home of the Pacific-Union Club and the latter still held by the Flood family. Jim Flood grew up with the legacy of his father and grandfather all around him. In his youngest years, he lived in the family's mansion on Broadway in the City and in their 44-room country estate, Linden Towers, in Palo Alto. He showed his early love of boats by building,

This photo appeared in the *San Francisco Chronicle's* "Sporting Green" column on May 27, 1936.

with his boyhood friend Gordon McIntosh, a dinghy that they sailed on the sloughs of the South Bay. He was sent east for his education, and attended Exeter Academy and Yale College, graduating in the Class of 1932. *Dorade's* great triumphs in 1930 and 1931 were everywhere in the news, and there can be no doubt that those exciting accounts reached Flood at college in New Haven, Connecticut. After graduation Flood returned west, and purchased a Bird One-Design, again with his pal Gordon McIntosh, for racing on the Bay. Birds are a particular San Francisco Bay yachting institution. The raised-deck, 30-foot sloops were designed by Frederick C. Brewer in the 1920s, and their modest sail plan and weatherly hull form made them a popular and competitive small-boat class on the windy Bay. The Bird was great, but by 1935 Flood was looking for a bigger boat, and the call came from Drake Sparkman of a famous yawl for sale.

Dorade arrived aboard an American Hawaiian freighter and was unloaded at Pier 26 on the City Front. She was towed to Lester Stone's yard in Oakland to receive topsides and bronze bottom paint, and to have her spars stepped. The Farallon Race, an annual contest of 58 miles out the Golden Gate, around the Farallon Islands and back to the City Front, was scheduled to take place in just 10 days. The Honolulu Race would start from Los Angeles on the Fourth of July, just five and a half weeks away. Flood needed to get her ready for both. His first order of business was to assemble a crew, and he turned to one of the most savvy and well respected boat drivers he knew, Myron Spaulding.

Spaulding was a famous helmsman and skipper, highly sought after by racing-boat owners. He was also a first violinist with the San Francisco Symphony Orchestra, a self-taught naval architect and an accomplished boatwright. Flood had raced against and been taught to sail Birds by Myron Spaulding, and he wanted to take no chances. He approached Spaulding in early April, before the purchase of *Dorade* was even complete, to ask whether Spaulding would skipper the boat in the Honolulu Race. Flood admitted later that he cringed at the thought of commanding such a famous and successful yacht and failing to do well with her. He commented that September in *Yachting*, "We won because we didn't dare to lose." Losing would obviously not be the vessel's fault. Spaulding reveled at the prospect of driving the famous yawl. Flood added crewmen with an eye to the long race and included John Katros, Leon Walker, Joe McAleese, Ed Sykes and a very young James Michael. This last crewman, then only 17 years old, would play an important role in the yawl's future.

Flood and his crew had very little time to prepare for their first contest, the Farallon Race. *Dorade* had been launched the day before and had been sailed only a few hours. The start was set for midnight, in order to provide a dramatic, daylight finish for spectators and, for competitors, a nice evening at the bar. Heavy winds were forecast beyond the Golden Gate. With shortened sail, *Dorade* set out into the darkness, giving up distance to those more fully canvassed. But as the winds built, she moved through the fleet, rounded the northern-most of the islands and set sail for home, adding sail along the way. She finished first by over an hour against larger competitors. It was a good thing because she had been uniquely rated by the Race Committee as scratch boat, but she still saved her time. Twenty–seven year old Jim Flood must have been delighted with his new yacht. He and his crew began elaborate preparations to equip the boat for the trip down the coast and the start of the Honolulu Race.

Above—Myron Spaulding takes a sextant sight, braced between the mizzen boom and a shroud.

COURTESY SPAULDING WOODEN BOAT CENTER

Below—Departing for San Pedro and the 1936
Transpacific Race, *Dorade*'s crew waves so
long to San Francisco. Left to right: Joe McAleese,
John Katros (cook), Myron Spaulding (skipper),
James Michael.

PACIFIC SKIPPER MAGAZINE, 1936

The crowd of yachts in the harbor of Santa Monica on the Fourth of July before the start of the race to Honolulu.

ACME

Trade Winds, Leis and Mai Tais

The Transpacific or Honolulu Yacht Race was initiated by King Kalakaua, of the Sandwich Islands, in 1886. From his Iolani Palace, he instructed his chamberlain and private secretary to invite the commodore of San Francisco's Pacific Yacht Club to organize a race to the islands in celebration of his, the king's, 50th birthday the following November. He offered prizes, the first to be a "trophy valued at one thousand dollars, the second valued at five hundred dollars, and the third a cup to be presented by the Hawaiian Boating Association." Also available to any officers and guests of the yachts would be a residence for their use. What an enticing invitation! Inexplicably, it was not taken up. However, it marked the first notion of such a yacht race, and it presaged the kind of "island hospitality" that has characterized the Honolulu Race. The offered trophy re-appeared many years later, finally employed as an elegant reminder of the King's grand gesture. For years, it was awarded to the overall winner of the Transpac Race; it now resides in the Bishop Museum in Honolulu.

It took twenty years, until 1906, for the first race to be held, a year which coincided with the inaugural Bermuda Race and the San Francisco earthquake. That year, a ketch from the New York Yacht Club, a schooner from the South Coast Yacht Club in southern California, and another schooner from the Hawaii Yacht Club set off from San Pedro Light on the 2,225-mile course to Diamond Head. They all arrived safely, in passages of 11 to 15 days, and the race was established. Eight successive races were run before and after the First World War, but there were never more than six participants. By 1932, when the Bermuda Race had drawn 27 competitors, the Depression had reduced the Transpac Race to just a pair of boats. In much the same way that the Fastnet's demise was predicted in 1933, concerns about the Honolulu Race were also aired. By 1934, however, the world looked a bit better, and a record 12 boats entered the race.

Most great ocean races are characterized by some specific guess about weather or ocean current. The Bermuda Race involves never-ending ruminations on the location and course of the Gulf Stream's "meander," as this warm water current snakes its way north and east in the Atlantic. The Swiftsure Race, in the Strait of

The Single Hook Hitch ties and casts off easily and holds well to a large hook so long as a too large line does not overflow. Ashley labels it "probably original."

ASHLEY KNOT 1886

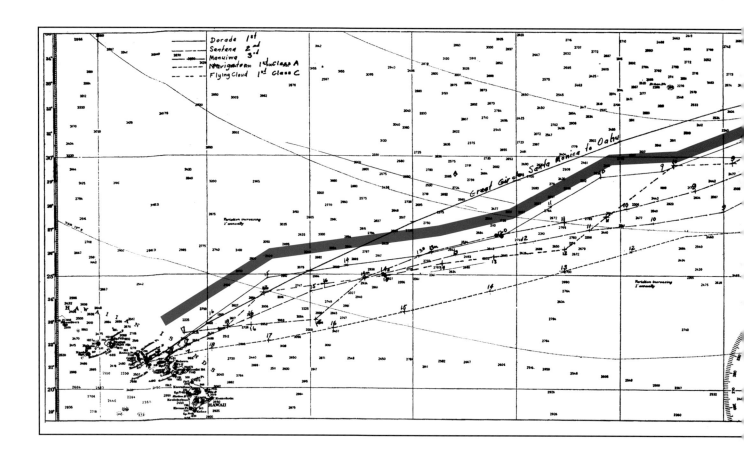

Dorade 1st
Santana 2nd
Manuiwa 3rd
Navigator 1st Class A
Flying Cloud 1st Class C

Great Circle Santa Monica to Oahu

Juan de Fuca between Vancouver Island and Washington's Olympic Peninsula, is often a game of playing the tide and guessing whether the American or Canadian side of the Strait is favored. The Fastnet Race pits the fleet against the strong currents of the English Channel and the Irish Sea. In the Honolulu Race, the issue is the famous Pacific High, a pocket of high pressure, sometimes stretching over a thousand miles, which moves south and north, and expands or contracts in the Pacific, roughly on the course from California to the Hawaiian Islands. It is characterized by heat and calm, and has stymied many a winning effort. Racers have found themselves slatting for days, waiting for the wind to build as the high-pressure pocket smothers them in its calms. A common strategy is to head south to avoid it, but this adds miles to the course. Going high along a great circle route can save miles and is an option if the guess is for a weak high-pressure pocket below one's course or a pocket moving north away from this route. A straight course to Honolulu is sometimes directly into the heart of the windless doldrums. The objective is to head west into the prevailing winds around the islands of Catalina and Santa Cruz, then ease to a course that allows for the northeast trade winds to carry you to the Islands. The winds off of the California coast can be fickle and often die at sunset, leaving the fleet to be swept by the tides in the early hours of the contest. Leaving the lower Channel Islands to port is a longer route, but it often avoids the islands' wind shadow. Tide can push a becalmed yacht onto Catalina's shore if

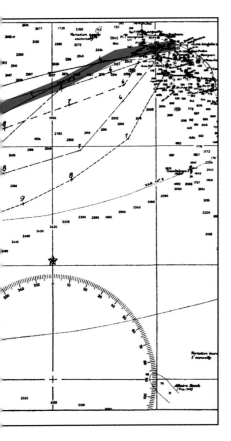

the wind also dies in the channel between Catalina and Santa Barbara Island. It is not an easy choice. In later years, the choice was eliminated by making the Islands a turning mark and forcing all to leave them to port.

The 1936 Honolulu Race began in Santa Monica, outside of that city's newly completed breakwater. Ahead, 2,210 miles away, lay the finish line at Diamond Head Light, off of Honolulu. Thousands of spectators crowded the Santa Monica Pier to see the fleet of 22 yachts start their journey in winds so light that some competitors took two days to lose sight of land. The fleet was broken into three classes, and the keenest competition took place in Class B, a group comprised of *Dorade* as its smallest. *Circe*, a 64-foot cutter from Seattle, carried the highest rating. The duel between these two made history. Twelve of the entrants were schooners, a rig that was still significant in ocean racing, although no longer dominant. There were also five yawls, three ketches, and two cutters. Most of the yachts came from Southern California, although three came from San Francisco, two from Honolulu and two from Seattle. In very light breezes, the fleet set out at noon on the Fourth of July and immediately split into three groups, passing above, through and below the islands that lie just offshore. The group heading above Santa Cruz Island composed about half the fleet and included *Dorade*, *Circe*, and W.L. Stewart Jr.'s schooner *Santana*.

All three of these boats were to gain great fame in West Coast yacht-racing circles through the 1950s. *Circe*, in particular, provided wonderful parallels and contrasts with *Dorade*. Ben Seaborn had drawn her when he was 17 years old, still in high school in Seattle. The boat was launched in 1932. It could not have been complete exuberance that prompted her owner, Ray Cooke, to entrust the work of her design to so young and untrained a yacht architect. Surely, Olin Stephens and his triumphs at a very young age must have provided some of the courage for this decision. Cooke was also famously tight-fisted, and the young designer probably came cheap. Cooke had recently married Seaborn's mother. *Circe* carried a towering cutter rig, was narrow, and had a cut-away forefoot and a very long keel. In many ways, she was more reminiscent of Alden's schooners in underwater shape, but her rig was more advanced.

Santana, at 55 feet, was designed as a schooner by Sparkman & Stephens in 1934 (Design No. 59) and was famously owned by Humphrey Bogart and Lauren Bacall in the '40s and '50s. Although Olin is reported not to have liked schooner rigs, *Santana* was beautifully drawn, and, with greater beam than *Dorade*, she embodied more of the design thinking evident in *Stormy Weather*. Her potent combination of design and crew made her a newly minted favorite.

The fleet scattered quickly, with *Dorade*, *Santana* and *Circe* staying high and pursuing the Great Circle course. The larger entrants, such as the 78-foot schooner *Navigator*, chose to head south in search of the trades, which would drive their longer waterlines faster. Others split the difference, and soon sightlines between the yachts were lost in the expanse of the Pacific. The early days of the race were very slow.

An immense, three-spreader, cutter rig drives *Circe* on Puget Sound.

SEATTLE YACHT CLUB ARCHIVES

Two days out, *Dorade* led the fleet but had made only 225 total miles. It took three days for the entire fleet to clear the Channel Islands. By the third day, the Hawaiian entry *Dolphin* discovered that her water tanks had failed, leaving her with only a very scant supply. She turned around and headed back to San Pedro. *Dorade* stayed above the rhumb line and remained the most northerly of the fleet. She swapped the lead with *Circe* several times, taking it on the ninth day at sea with a best day's run of 224 miles, only to give it back the following day, as the larger *Circe* clipped off 254 miles. They jockeyed back and forth along the Great Circle route, trading positions above and below it, but never in sight of one another. *Santana* was on their heels, and so was the Honolulu schooner *Manuiwa*, owned and skippered by Harold Dillingham.

On July 15, 11 days out, *Circe* was 360-miles northeast of the finish, and *Dorade* trailed her by 35 miles. At this point, *Circe* chose to head further southwest, and *Dorade* kept south, heading for the finish. On the afternoon of the 13th day, spotters saw first one and then another sail heading down Molokai Channel to Diamond Head, *Dorade* in the lead, and *Circe* closing on her rapidly. The boats closed to within a mile and roared under spinnakers to the finish to the delight of the Hawaiian onlookers. At 4:50 p.m., little *Dorade* passed Diamond Head Light to finish first. In an astonishing result after so many miles at sea, *Circe* crossed a scant 13m, 55s later. Next to cross the line—after midnight, with searchlights trained on her from shore—was *Santana*. Time allowances left *Dorade* with a clean sweep, the first in the history of the race: first overall, first in class and first on elapsed time. She had recorded the first ocean racing victory for the St. Francis Yacht Club. Jim Flood's worries over his performance with her were over.

Dorade's fame, established in the Atlantic, had now reached the Pacific. It is interesting to think of that moment in 1936 within the context of a sailboat's racing record. *Dorade* was a six-year-old yacht and had won the Transatlantic Race, the

An artist's rendering of the 1936 Transpac finish, derived from a photograph that appeared in *The Honolulu Advertiser* and *Yachting*.

Fastnet Race, the Honolulu Race and had finished first in class in the Bermuda Race. Although sailed under differing rules, she had distinguished herself against newer competitors and, despite concerns regarding her size, had never been considered to be in danger despite over 15,000 miles at sea. Nothing of note had broken, and no one had been injured. As she crossed the line in the Molokai Channel that July of 1936 she had established herself as the most successful and influential yacht of her time. Further, West Coast society had been taken by storm in a flurry of yachting interest. Articles about the 1936 Honolulu Race appeared not only in *Yachting*, *Rudder*, and *Pacific Skipper*, but also in *Time*, *The Sportsman* (along with articles on steeplechase racing and hunts to the hounds) and San Francisco's *Women's City Club Magazine*. If the great horse Seabiscuit was the American darling of the racetrack in the 1930s, *Dorade* was certainly the darling of the sea.

One of the wonderful things about the Honolulu Race is arriving on a Pacific island that is beautiful and famously welcoming. The start of the celebration commences with landing and the draping of massive flowered leis around the necks of the crew. Wives and girlfriends, over on the liner *Lurline*, greeted the warriors of the deep. Hosts are assigned and the parties begin, sometimes at such a pace

117

The Honolulu Advertiser

Hawaii's Territorial Newspaper

INCOMING MAIL
FROM THE COAST
Tatuta Maru, Mon., 7 a.m. (S. F.)
FROM THE ORIENT
Asama Maru, today, 6 a. m.
FROM THE SOUTH SEAS
Niagara, July 24.

OUTGOING MAIL
FOR THE COAST
Malolo, today, noon (L.A.)
Asama Maru, today, 3 p. m. (S.F.)
FOR THE ORIENT
Tatuta Maru, Monday, 3 p. m.
FOR THE SOUTH SEAS
Aorangi, July 24.

81ST. YEAR, NO. 17,871.— 14 PAGES.   To Reach All Departments TELEPHONE 3311   HONOLULU, TERRITORY OF HAWAII, U.S.A., SATURDAY MORNING, JULY 18, 1936.   Weather: New York, 66; Chicago, 70; San Francisco, 32; Vancouver, 32.   PRICE FIVE CENTS.

DORADE FIRST TO FINISH YACHT RACE

Fleet's Chief Sees Return To Principle Of Limitation

World Naval Race Not to Continue Indefinitely, Says Hepburn

SURE OF LOYALTY

Believes Island Japanese True as Rest of U.S. Citizens

By ALEXANDER MacDONALD

Jingos may bellow and the world nervously watch while nations plan bigger and bigger navies, but the man who is commander-in-chief of the U. S. fleet refuses to believe that only chaos waits at the end of the race.

"The principle of limitation," in the reassuring words of Admiral Arthur J. Hepburn, "will serve to halt nations from plunging on in an endless world naval race. Limitation, though now at a low ebb, is by no means a dead issue and is on the map to stay. Nations, I believe, have a spirit of reasonableness that will mean a return to the principle of limitation."

End of the Pacific Trail ∻ ∻ The Dorade Sweeps Past Diamond Head

Circe Next Across Line In Dramatic Sea Contest

Leader Ends Transpacific Jaunt After 13 Days, 7 Hours on Ocean

APPEARS WINNER

Seattle College Crew Only 13 Minutes Behind Rival

Commodore Harold Dillingham estimated he would bring the Manuiwa, his defending champion in the transpacific yacht race, across the finish line at 4 a. m., he informed Earl Thacker, rear commodore of the Pearl Harbor Yacht club, by radio early this morning. Thacker and members of the Dillingham family left Pier 5 in a launch at 1:30 a. m. to meet the Manuiwa off Diamond Head. Globe Wireless received the same message.

By MACK MATHEWS

Driven by a ballooning cloud of all the canvas she could carry, the 51-foot yawl Dorade came storming down the northeast trades to cross the line at Diamond

---

Above—On July 18, 1936, the front page told Honolulu the winner. The *Honolulu Advertiser* crowned *Dorade*'s crew "knights of the whitecaps," while the *New York Times* had labeled them, "youthful Vikings."

Right—Jim Flood being "lei'ed" at the awards banquet. A t-shirt clad Myron Spaulding looks on.

The Transpac Governor's
Trophy held proudly by a
beaming Jim Flood.

that the sailors yell uncle in the hope of a little quiet time. In 1936, the two most elegant and prominent hotels on Waikiki Beach declared a free and open bar to all Transpac participants. Mai tais all around. Months later, in the September issue of *The Rudder* ("The Magazine for Yachtsmen"), the editor complained that the final results had not yet been sent. He hypothesized "that our seagoing correspondents partook of too much of that famed Hawaiian Hospitality and forgot such prosaic things as press deadlines." Despite the slow reporting, the clean sweep and St. Francis victory had been *Dorade's*. What a grand way for Jim Flood to celebrate his 28th birthday.

In recognition of *Dorade's* overall victory in the race, Hawaii's Territorial Governor Joseph Poindexter presented Jim Flood with a fully rigged outrigger sailing canoe, appropriately fashioned in silver.

HONOLULU RACERS FETED AT SAN FRANCISCO

Both Northern and Southern California yachting enthusiasts admired the trophy presented by Pacific Skipper to "Dorade" for winning the race to Honolulu. (Standing, port to starboard) Marsh Duffield, Arvid Norman, Chris Jenks, Myron Spaulding, Capt. Jack Polkinghorn and (kneeling, port to starboard) Dick Erlin and James Flood, owner of "Dorade."—Haas-Schreiner Photo.

Top left—The skipper's telegram to his mother fails to mention winning the race.

Top right—*Pacific Skipper* covered the crew in its October 1936 issue.

Left—The lovely plate, showing the boat and engraved, "The Pacific Skipper Trophy, Trans Pacific Yacht Race, 1936, Won by Yawl *Dorade*," hangs in the St. Francis Yacht Club behind a model of the ocean racer.

AUTHOR'S COLLECTION

Opposite—The October 1936 issue of *The Rudder* featured *Dorade*'s remarkable racing record.

Outstanding Yachts of America

DORADE

ROSENFELD PHOTO

THE YAWL DORADE is unquestionably one of the outstanding yachts of all time. Designed to be a success at ocean racing she has entered every major offshore contest in the calendar of the sport and has rolled up a string of victories which has never been equalled by any yacht in deep water.

Extreme in model and with a moderate yawl rig of what was originally regarded as "freak" proportions, she has demonstrated an ability to stand any amount of hard driving in rough water on all points of sailing, with perfect safety and great efficiency. Her best point of sailing is to windward in rough water and her maximum speed is very high.

Narrow, fine lined, sharp-ended, she is a radical departure from the accepted idea of an offshore cruising yacht. She was frankly designed for speed at sea with the sacrifice of comfort—if need be—and to take fullest advantage of the Bermuda Race rule as it stood at the time. She was designed to the rules of the New York Yacht Club by Olin J. Stephens, II, of Sparkman & Stephens, Inc., New York, and has been sailed during most of her career by either Olin or Rod (his hard driving brother). She was built by Minneford Yacht Yard in 1930. She measures 52 feet overall, 39.17 feet on the waterline, by 10 feet 3 inches beam by 8 feet 2 inches draft. Displacement is 38,720 pounds. Sail area with four lowers is 1,079 square feet.

When she first came out she carried a bowsprit and somewhat larger sail plan and it was not until this was reduced and refined in certain respects that she really began to make history.

In her first year she showed that she was going to be a yacht to reckon with in the future, taking second place in her class (B).

The following year she sailed the Transatlantic race from Newport to Plymouth, England, really starting off her winning career by beating a fleet of ten first class yachts by two whole days boat for boat, completing the 3,000 mile course in the record time of 17 days 1 hour and 14 minutes.

She followed this victory with a decisive win in the stormy Fastnet race of that year, to confound the critics who said it was all luck.

Next summer she again sailed to Bermuda and took first place in her class and in 1933 once more sailed across (cruising) to Bergen, Norway, took in the Fastnet and won again and capped the season's work with a record westward passage from Cowes to her home port of City Island, New York, of 26 days, 15 hours. From land to land —the Scillys to Pollock Rip —she took 22 days.

The next Bermuda Race saw her considerably handicapped by a revision of the rating rule and this partly contributed to a rather poor showing.

After that she was chartered out and didn't figure in the public prints again until her sale last fall to James Flood of the St. Francis Yacht Club, San Francisco, California. Flood took her in the Farallon race almost as soon as she arrived and she won hands down, which would seem to prove that it hasn't been just the skill of Rod and Olin Stephens which has put Dorade on top all these years.

Then just to show that this wasn't any flash in the pan she whipped a fleet of twenty-one yachts in the Honolulu Race just recently, leading them all to Diamond Head in thirteen days without any need of her fifty-two hour allowance. This victory gives Dorade the unique distinction of having won every major ocean race in the yachting world today.

33

Basking in Success

With *Dorade* as his yachting platform and his prominence in San Francisco as his birthright, Jim Flood was an imposing young bachelor. He and the boat were constantly featured in the yachting press and occasionally in the society pages. He was photographed sailing with beautiful women on San Francisco Bay, and the crews he gathered to sail the boat were competent and committed. Flood had relied on the expertise and navigating skill of Myron Spaulding to take him to Hawaii, but in the spring of 1937 he concluded that he needed those skills himself and enrolled in Marine Navigation 775C with the University of California Extension Division. The two-month course earned him one unit of credit, and he was awarded an "A" for his study.

By 1938, Flood's bachelor days had come to an end with his meeting of the lovely Elizabeth Dresser, whom he married that summer after a whirlwind romance. Betty Flood took to *Dorade* as a willing young bride without great sailing experience but with enthusiasm. She found it exciting. She recalled sailing the boat without an engine and of the "unspeakable language" overheard during landings at the St. Francis. She even found herself the only member of the crew not afflicted by *mal de mer* during a passage south to Monterey Bay, and she was pressed into service as skipper because no one else was up to it. Flood's family had demolished Linden Towers in 1936, and his parents lived primarily in the mansion at 2222 Broadway in Pacific Heights. Because the ballroom was large enough, Flood would take his cotton sails there for drying after races, and his salty crew would invade the elegant household until the senior Floods had had enough and concluded that it might be better to have their cook and staff deliver meals to the sailors on the boat in the Marina.

———opposite———

With Hollywood actress Kay Aldridge taking in the sun off of Catalina, an attractive starlet takes the helm as dashing Jim Flood gives directions in this photograph for the society pages of 1938. Miss Aldridge was famous for her roles in such serial films as "The Perils of Nyoka" and "Phantom of 42nd Street."

JOHN SWOPE / COURTESY JOHN SWOPE TRUST

The Shroud Knot based on the Diamond Knot provides a quickly tied splice using minimal material for a repair.

ASHLEY KNOT 1583

Flood also addressed the boat's rig. With guidance from Rod Stephens, a new mainmast was built for the boat that featured a hollow, rectangular (not round) section and three spreaders. The rake of her masts was retained, and the new spar made her less tender by reducing weight aloft. The sailplan was increased from 1,079 square feet to 1,137 square feet, still 55-square-feet less than the original, 1930 rig. She would carry the same sailplan into the next century, and with it she was made into an even better racer and was probably sailed with less strain. *Dorade* had landed in a fortunate circumstance with James Flood, her capable second owner. The mizzen retained the remnants of *Natka*'s spar.

The late 1930s found *Dorade* racing prominently on San Francisco Bay. In June 1937, she set a new record (9h, 27m, 28s) for the 56-mile Farallon Race, but she did not win on corrected time. (It is interesting to note that, in 1954, the 72-foot yawl *Baruna*, a maxi ocean racer, took nearly 12 hours to complete the same course in

Jim Flood is at the helm with
the hills of Pacific Heights
in the background.
COURTESY ELIZABETH D. FLOOD

The Flood "Sail Loft" at
2222 Broadway in San
Francisco's Pacific Heights.
AUTHOR'S COLLECTION

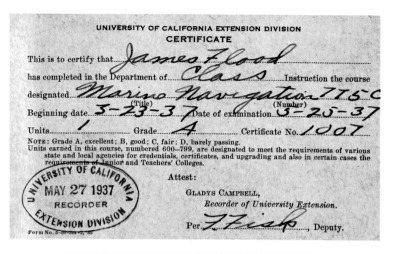

DIMAGGIO HITS THREE HOMERS IN GAME

Cracks Record

TRACK STARS ARRIVE TODAY

NINE CIRCUIT BLOWS IN NINE DAYS FOR NEW KING OF SWAT

UMPS LED OFF FIELD; SEALS LOSE TWO

TOWNS, OTHER ACES DUE AT BERKELEY

PLAN DRILLS

San Francisco Examiner Sports

MONDAY, JUNE 14, 1937

YACHT MARILEN WINS

Yawl Dorade Sets Farallon Record

Top—Jim Flood completed his course in navigation in the spring following his Transpac win.

COURTESY ELIZABETH D. FLOOD

Above—*Dorade* shares the front of the *San Francisco Examiner* sports pages with "Joltin' Joe" in 1937.

---

the heavy weather which suited her.) The 1937 Farallon Race was boosted in the Monday *San Francisco Examiner* Sports section with a picture of the yacht and the title, "Cracks Record." The lead head-line on the page read, "Dimaggio Hits Three Homers in Game."

Dorade competed in the Hearst All Clubs Regatta that year against Cyril To-bin's newly converted 12 Metre *Seaweed*, but did not win. In the spring of 1939, Rod Stephens joined the boat for the Far-allon Race, but they finished down the order. Still, Flood had been bitten by the ocean racing bug, and the next Trans-pac called. It had been agreed that the Bermuda Race would take place on even-numbered years, and the Transpac would be held on odd-numbered years. Because it was felt that a race in 1937 would be too soon after the 1936 contest, the next Transpac was scheduled for 1939, and the jockeying for the starting venue be-gan in earnest. The Golden Gate Inter-national Exposition, or "San Francisco World's Fair," as it came to be called, was scheduled to take place in 1939 to coin-cide with the completion of the Golden Gate and Bay bridges. Jim Flood, ever a staunch San Franciscan, was intent on seeing the start of the Transpac take place from San Francisco Bay to add to the festivities. Along with William Stewart, he led in the effort to convince the Transpacific Yacht Club to approve of the course from the Bay. Both men were in good positions to have some influence, with Stewart as a stalwart of Southern California yachting and Flood as the 1936 winner. Many other venues weighed in for the starting site, but with all of the drama and preparation for the Exposition bolstering the case, San Francisco was finally chosen. The course was 120-miles shorter than the one from Los Angeles, but it was not to be a faster race.

A Toy *Dorade*

By 1934, Dorade had become so well known that she was seen as the archetype for a sailboat, even in the minds of toy manufacturers. The Boucher Playthings Manufacturing Corporation, located at 126 Lafayette Street in New York, introduced a wooden kit for a toy model based upon the now famous yawl. With a hull that needed to be whittled from a roughly shaped plug, the kit included blocks for house and deck furniture, strips for rail caps, a selection of cast metal fittings and a rig. The plans were drawn by John Williams and dated January 29, 1934. The little yawl had become a miniature icon to children wanting a real ocean racer.

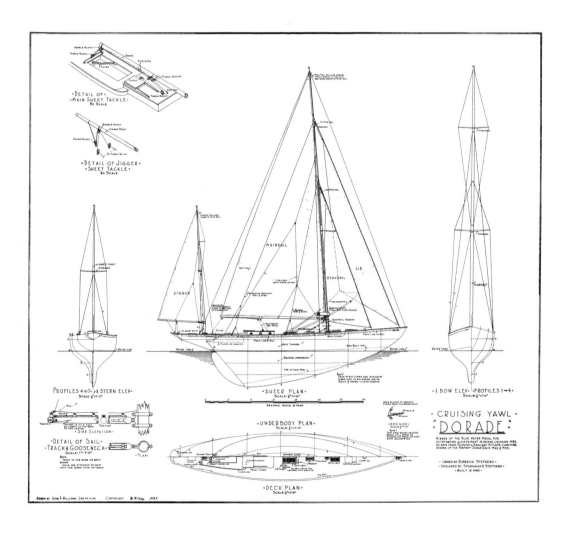

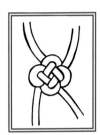

Back to Diamond Head

The yachting participants of the East and West coasts certainly paid attention to one another and their respective racing, but not many boats from either coast ventured into the others' contests. Certainly boats like *Dorade* had migrated from one coast to the other, but the connections were few and far between. William L. Stewart Jr. of the Los Angeles Yacht Club had raced his new *Santana* to Hawaii in 1936 and, at the urging of his friend and former MIT roommate Pierre duPont, agreed to enter the 1938 Bermuda Race with the promise of duPont reciprocating by bringing his yacht *Barlovento* west for the 1939 Transpac. Stewart won the schooner class in the 1938 race to the Onion Patch, but as the Transpac approached, duPont found himself in Washington DC, engaged as one of Franklin Roosevelt's "Dollar a Year" advisors. He could not make the trip. duPont prevailed upon his friend Richard J. Reynolds to carry the banner of the eastern yachting fraternity. Reynolds had commissioned a 55-foot cutter, *Blitzen*, from the design boards of Sparkman & Stephens in 1938, and she had dominated the racing scene in the east with her masthead rig. She was fitted with a race-oriented interior that was open and efficient, and her fore-triangle was large to accommodate powerful headsails. She was shipped to San Francisco in preparation for the race but sat unloaded on the decks of her freighter in the days just before the start, caught in a longshoremen's strike. Flood worked hard to help Reynolds organize her unloading in Alameda, and she was hurriedly rigged for the race.

Also arriving for the race was William Stewart's new, 67-foot yawl *Chubasco*, built that spring in Southern California and designed by Sparkman and Stephens. With *Dorade* and *Blitzen* also from the boards of S&S, it was clear that the East Coast design firm was sending their successful racers west. The fleet of 26 included 13 entries from Southern California, nine from the Bay Area, *Circe* from Seattle and the Hawaiian entry *Lady Jo. Odyssey*, a 58-foot Los Angeles entry, had Myron Spaulding aboard as navigator and Jim Michael, still a teenager, along for his second Transpac. The entire fleet rafted up side by side at the Exposition Port of the Tradewinds at Treasure Island and attracted huge crowds. Specially built pavilions—including the Court of Pacifica, the Chinese Village, the Towers of the East and the Court of the Seven Seas—provided the backdrop for the Transpac fleet, all

The Chinese Butterfly Two-Strand is an effective lanyard knot with separate bights.

ASHLEY KNOT 812

——opposite——

Richard J. Reynolds' powerful S&S cutter *Blitzen* showing her big fore-triangle with spinnaker set. She was brought west for the 1939 Transpac.

© MYSTIC SEAPORT

129

The Court of Pacifica at the
1939 Golden Gate International
Exposition.

assembled together in the days prior to the start for the first time in the race's history.

It is hard to imagine a better venue anywhere in the world for shoreside viewing of a yacht race than San Francisco Bay. Treasure Island had been man-made to serve the Exposition, with its attractions and exhibition spaces as the center of it all. The race organizers and the public looked forward to the spectacle of the Transpac fleet starting at the Exposition and heading out the Golden Gate in the typically strong winds of a July afternoon. The start was scheduled for 3:00 p.m. on July 4, to take advantage of a strong ebb tide that would speed the fleet on its way against the prevailing westerly. But instead of a sparkling and dramatic spectacle, the crowds—sinking the finger piers at the Exposition, and the thousands who stood watching from the Marina shore, the Marin headlands and the deck of the Golden Gate Bridge—were served uncharacteristic grey fog and light winds. As the fleet split, *Dorade* hugged the Marin shore to the north, and the larger boats headed down the Bay's center to find a fair tide. Most of the yachts were lost to the spectators in the gloom. The slow going was to continue out the Gate and into the evening fog.

Along for the race was the 107-foot scratch boat, *Contender*, and for the first time in ocean racing, it was arranged that *Contender*, equipped with a powerful receiver/transmitter, would receive daily position radio reports from the fleet and relay them to shore for a broadcast update of the race. The first broadcast, picked up on stations as far away as New York, was transmitted from the start. Such an open and public approach raised eyebrows, because the tradition of ocean racing had fostered secrecy of position even to the point of competitors dousing their running lights for stealth at night. But the fleet, at least the majority of it, participated and found that the positions were enormously interesting as weather and speed were called out. They also realized that the positions were only as accurate as the navigators aboard.

The fleet sailed for over eight days in light to moderate air, and the larger boats worked south in hopes of finding the trades. *Blitzen* held to a generally rhumb-line course, and *Dorade* stood more northerly, hoping to save miles. It proved to be the wrong choice. By the ninth day, *Blitzen* and others had scalloped their way to the south and began to pick up the trade winds, which pushed them at times to hull speed. With her ample fore-triangle and a set of spinnakers unlimited by the rating rules (actually longer on the foot than the boat itself), *Blitzen* raced toward Molakai Channel with the big boats and finished two hours after *Contender* and second overall, beating the 84-foot schooner, Class A *Fandango* by a scant 51 seconds. *Blitzen* corrected out first in fleet. *Dorade*'s northerly route took her another day and a half

Zoe H, the eventual winner in *Dorade*'s Class B, moored with the assembled Honolulu Race fleet in front of the Golden Gate International Exposition grounds on Treasure Island in 1939. The Tower of the Sun is seen to the right.

TRANSPAC 1906-1979

to complete the course, and she finished fourth in Class B and ninth overall. Her rating again penalized her, as she gave 9½ hours to the larger *Blitzen.* But that difference would not account for the relative order. The race was excruciatingly slow for the smaller, Class C boats. The last of them, *Viking Childe,* finally finished in over 23 days, over 9½ days after the first boat crossed, setting a record for the slowest passage in the Race's history. Sailboat racing is always a gamble. Nevertheless, *Dorade* had taken her crew the 2085 nautical miles with pride and in safety. It would take a decade and a half and a world war before she would race to Honolulu again.

War and Change

The Pacific Coast is a long way from Western Europe, but by the sailing season of 1940, it seemed a lot closer than ever before. With Britain under attack and American industrial might ramping up to provide for her support, the preoccupation with the military was omnipresent. Nevertheless, yachting continued and the Hearst All Clubs Regatta included 250 competitors that year. Jim Flood continued to campaign *Dorade*, but by early 1941 he had become more involved in the war buildup, with a growing family and with his work within the family businesses. Young James Michael had raced *Dorade* as a crew member in the victorious 1936 Transpac and he loved her. Still a teenager, he had sailed his second Tranpac aboard *Odyssey* in 1939. A remarkable scholar whose father had helped to found one of San Francisco's preeminent law firms, Jim Michael had been raised in an intellectually vigorous family, where only French was spoken at home in order to add to linguistic breadth. Imposing in height, he had completed high school at 17, finished college at the University of California at Berkeley in three years and was intent on a career in law. He was considered a brilliant young man. On the occasion of his 21st birthday in March 1941, he received an interitance. With it, he bought *Dorade* from Jim Flood. Despite the war concerns, a Honolulu Race was tentatively planned, and the Transpacific Yacht Club was taking entries.

Radio reporting had come with the prior race in 1939. The 1941 race brought a requirement that each competing yacht be equipped with an engine. It did not need to be much of one, and it did not need to be supplied with more than 25 gallons of fuel, but it was a new requirement. While the vast majority of yachts built during the 1930s had been fitted with an auxiliary, *Dorade* remained as originally fitted, without power. Michael installed a small, four-cylinder Graymarine gas engine and modified the boat's rudder with an aperture to accommodate a propeller. It was not uncommon for sailboats to install an offset shaft, thereby avoiding the turbulence and construction complexity of a rudder aperture, but the disadvantage of an offset shaft was that the non-direct alignment caused steering issues, particularly when backing down. The engine installation with an aperture in *Dorade* ended over a decade of pleasant relief from the weight, odors, space taking, noise and mechanical aggravation of the "iron jib." *Dorade*'s history with power was not to be an easy one. Michael also ordered a new suit of sails for the race from well-known West Coast sailmaker Kenneth Watts in Los Angeles and began to assemble a crew.

——opposite——

Dorade lies next to the famous yacht *Yankee* of 1906, in front of the St. Francis Yacht Club in the San Francisco Marina. This photograph by John Kabel appeared full page in *Yachting*, December 1941. By the time it hit newsstands, the nation was at war.

COURTESY *YACHTING*

A Selvage Strap and Toggle provides the rigger with a fast, easy to untie but temporary lashing although it is subject to capsize if without a load.

ASHLEY KNOT 1896

133

A short list of entrants emerged for the Honolulu Race, but the continuing calling of men to the military made commitment to the race increasingly difficult. It was to be so for Jim Michael. He had accepted a commission in the Navy Reserve while he was a student at Berkeley, and, as the race loomed, he realized that he would not be able to compete. That summer, seven boats—the largest of them 54 feet—left from San Pedro for the Hawaiian Islands. *Dorade* was not among them.

Five months later, the entire calculus changed with the bombing of Pearl Harbor. Quickly, the concerns of an enemy attack on the West Coast altered the Bay and its yacht racing scene. The shelling of an oil rig near Santa Barbara by a Japanese submarine hastened the building of fortifications. By the spring of 1942, the Navy had asked that the racing buoys be removed from in front of the St. Francis, and a submarine net was installed to the west of the club and north across the Bay. Pairs of constantly steaming tugs operated two gates that opened for authorized traffic only; recreational yachting was prohibited seaward of the net. Private yachts were required to paint identifying numbers on their hulls and decks that could be read from the air. Binoculars, field glasses and firearms were prohibited aboard, and sailing on the Bay and its estuaries was limited to daylight hours. That spring, Jim Michael sailed *Dorade* to victory in the Vallejo Race—up the Sacramento River—but he, along with Jim Flood, was called to active duty very soon thereafter. By mid-1942, Jim Michael was headed for the Pacific Theater and had left his yacht in the hands of his friend and St. Francis Yacht Club companion Stan Natcher. Both men would later serve as commodore of the St. Francis, but that would have to wait. Michael found himself at war, and his boat would be sold before he returned.

Many private sailing yachts were enlisted as lookout vessels off of the coast. They were very lightly armed, if at all, for any confrontation. On the Pacific coast, private yachts were assigned to stations 50 miles from one another and clustered off of Point Arena in Northern California and Point Conception in Southern California. They waited for the Japanese fleet to appear until the Battle of Midway confirmed their location far out in the Pacific—not off the West Coast. Motor yachts could not carry enough fuel to stay on station for more than a few days, and so sailing yachts were dispatched for zones as far offshore as 300 miles to report any enemy sightings. Jim Flood found himself at sea on Templeton Crocker's globe-girdling schooner *Zaca* for weeks on end. These privately-enlisted and skippered vessels were well manned, but, despite their vigilance, no sightings were ever made. Other yachts were requisitioned by the War Department and purchased for the effort to be manned by Navy personnel. Many of these yachts did less well as a result of neglect during the conflict. *Dorade* was considered too small for such an assignment, and she sat at her berth on the City Front until 1943, when Jim Michael by mail directed Stan Natcher, his trusted sailing friend and an executive at Standard Oil Company of California, to sell her. Very soon a new owner, Ralph James, emerged into her life. James was in the industrial distribution business in Seattle and loved sailing. A member of the Seattle Yacht Club, he was friendly, optimistic and, like so many others, he was also in

The sloop *Volante* in San Francisco Bay during 1942. Her identification numbers appear on the housetop, and one of the submarine net tenders appears to the left, steaming forward in place and keeping the net taut.

THE HISTORY OF THE ST. FRANCIS YACHT CLUB

love with the yawl. She was about to head to the Pacific Northwest, where she would spend nearly four decades.

Having sold *Dorade* prior to the war, Jim Flood also brought a famous S&S yawl to the Bay from the East Coast two decades later. Thomas Watson Jr. had, in 1957, gone to the New York design firm and to Abeking and Rasmussen in Lemwerder, Germany, to build *Palawan*, his second yacht of five that would bear that name. Watson had risen to head IBM, a company founded by his father. The second *Palawan* was a beautiful, bright-hulled, 55-foot, centerboard sloop, designed as a racer/cruiser to the CCA Rule. She was a successful, larger development of the centerboarders like Carleton Mitchell's *Finisterre*, which had been so dominant in the 1950s. She was very comfortable and grand but also proved to be fast enough, winning her class in the 1960 Bermuda Race and placing well in races along the Eastern Seaboard. As Watson made plans for his third *Palawan*, the second was sold, and Jim Flood brought her to the West Coast, where she sailed—rigged as a yawl—until joining *Dorade* in the northwest in the 1990s.

Palawan II

COURTESY
SPARKMAN & STEPHENS

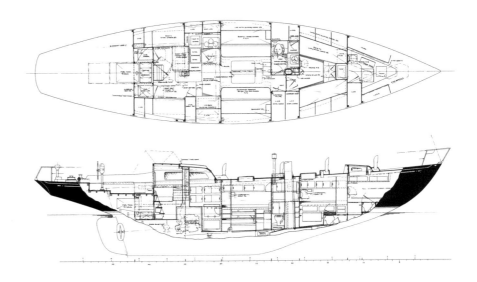

Baruna, with all flying, drives down the Bay in front of Alcatraz and The City.

THE HISTORY OF THE ST. FRANCIS YACHT CLUB

Despite being in San Francisco for only seven years, *Dorade* was fortunate to be owned by two very good young sailors who took grand care of her. Both Jim Flood and Jim Michael played important roles in yachting in San Francisco. Flood was an early leader and supporter of the St. Francis Yacht Club, and Jim Michael served two terms as the club's commodore. *Dorade* was each man's first large sailboat, but they both were to go on to own other famous and prominent yachts in later years. In 1953, Michael bought the great Sparkman & Stephens yawl *Baruna* (shown above to windward, sailing with *Bolero* under the Golden Gate Bridge) from Henry Taylor and brought her to the Bay from the East Coast. The 72-footer, built by Nevins in 1938, had amassed a remarkable racing record, with three Bermuda Race victories. She became the queen of the Bay. In *Nowhere Is Too Far*, a history of the Cruising Club of America, John Parkinson declares that *Baruna* was the greatest big yacht of all time. And she made news racing her great, S&S rival, *Bolero*, during the 1950s and 1960s, putting San Francisco at the center of big yacht, around-the-buoys sailing.

The enthusiastic and affable Ralph James brought *Dorade* to the Pacific Northwest and the Seattle Yacht Club in 1943.

The Waters of Puget and Vancouver

The northwest corner of the continental United States is notched by a large, geographically spectacular inlet and sound. Named for both its Spanish and British discoverers, the waters are sheltered to the northwest by Vancouver Island, that British Columbian gem that stretches nearly 300 miles northwest from the head of Admiralty Inlet and Puget Sound all the way to Cape Scott. The passage between Canada and the United States at the island's southern end is the Strait of Juan de Fuca. At the western end of the strait is Cape Flattery, off of which lies Tatoosh Island. The Olympic Mountains tower, snowcapped and craggy, on Washington's Olympic Peninsula, and they dominate the sailor's view to starboard, in clear weather of course, all the way up the Pacific coast of Washington, down the Strait of Juan de Fuca, south down Admiralty Inlet and into Puget Sound, far to the south of Seattle. The strait was purportedly discovered by a Greek explorer named Apostolos Valerianos, who was also known by the name Juan de Fuca as he traveled through Italy attempting to raise financing for his expeditions. His explorations in the Pacific caused him to claim the existence of a large passage with "devers islands" which he recorded on charts of 1592, and named after himself, exactly a century after Columbus. His claims have been questioned because of errors in location and description, but his name stuck.

Dorade's new owner, Ralph James, faced a big challenge; how he was able to solve it remains a mystery. It was nearly impossible to move yachts up and down the coast during wartime. Security concerns as well as shoreside armaments and fortifications made it dangerous and illegal. San Francisco was even guarded with mines outside the Golden Gate. Yachts on both coasts stayed put for years. However, through arrangements not explained, Ralph James was able to get *Dorade* out the submarine nets and mines of San Francisco, up the coast with its lookouts, into Puget Sound with its fortifications and guards, to the Strait of Juan de Fuca, past the gun emplacements at Joyce, Port Townsend and Marrowstone Island at the head of Admiralty Inlet, and into Seattle. The man to do this was none other than Myron Spaulding. He, with a shorthanded crew of Sausalito and San Francisco stalwarts, made the trip in November 1943 without incident, spending 120 hours motoring up the coast into the prevailing northerly. They spent the 25th off the coast of

The Monkey's Fist is a multi-styled single line terminal knot for a heaving line and often covered a ball of stone, iron, lead, marble or glass.

ASHLEY KNOT 2200

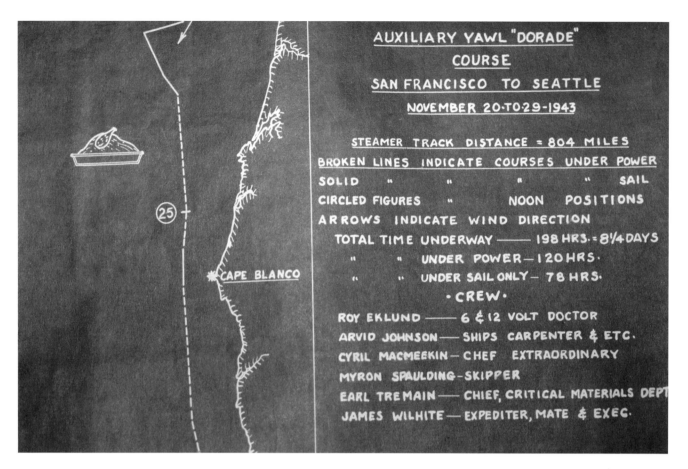

AUXILIARY YAWL "DORADE"
COURSE
SAN FRANCISCO TO SEATTLE
NOVEMBER 20·TO·29-1943

STEAMER TRACK DISTANCE = 804 MILES
BROKEN LINES INDICATE COURSES UNDER POWER
SOLID   "   "   "   "   SAIL
CIRCLED FIGURES   "   NOON   POSITIONS
ARROWS INDICATE WIND DIRECTION
TOTAL TIME UNDERWAY ——— 198 HRS. = 8¼ DAYS
    "   "   UNDER POWER — 120 HRS.
    "   "   UNDER SAIL ONLY — 78 HRS.
·CREW·
ROY EKLUND ——— 6 & 12 VOLT DOCTOR
ARVID JOHNSON —— SHIPS CARPENTER & ETC.
CYRIL MACMEEKIN — CHEF EXTRAORDINARY
MYRON SPAULDING-SKIPPER
EARL TREMAIN —— CHIEF, CRITICAL MATERIALS DEPT
JAMES WILHITE — EXPEDITER, MATE & EXEC.

A section of Myron Spaulding's hand-lettered chart of the voyage north in November 1943. The crew is noted, and a turkey marks the Thanksgiving feast on the 25th.

COURTESY SPAULDING WOODEN BOAT CENTER

Cape Blanco and celebrated Thanksgiving with an improvised turkey dinner. The boat was taken all the way into Portage Bay and presented at the Seattle Yacht Club on November 29. Spaulding and his crew were quietly returned by military transport to Alameda Naval Air Station. Such special treatment may have been the result of Spaulding's military connections. Possibly, James had a way to get permission. It is certain the trip north had some form of clearance, for, without it, *Dorade* would have been blown out of the water at some point along the way. The yawl had found its third important port.

The arrival of *Dorade* was an important event in the northwest, certainly no less important than her coming to the West Coast with Jim Flood in 1936. However, the war was still on, and yachting activities were limited by security concerns and material shortages. Ralph James had joined the Seattle Yacht Club in 1939, but by the time he bought *Dorade*, he had moved from active to furloughed membership, due to his military service status. He had sold his 42-foot, Ben Seaborn-designed *Nautilus*, built by the Blanchard Boat Company, in order to buy *Dorade*. He sailed his new charge on Puget Sound and day-sailed on Lake Washington. In 1944, he won Class A in the Vashon Island Race and took second in the Hat and Protection Island races, but the circumstances of the war limited her use.

At war's end, racing resumed. James finished with the best corrected time in the 1946 Vashon Island Race but was disqualified for fouling *Cirrus II* at the start. Ralph James loved and delighted in *Dorade*, and, in an aesthetic choice that altered her look for the next five decades, he proudly carved her name on either side of her bow and on her stern with "Seattle" below as her hailing port. He tackled her ownership with the same fun and enthusiasm that he exhibited in his varied and successful business endeavors, but, as the early postwar years engaged him more actively in business and family matters, he concluded that he needed a less aggressive racer, one better suited to his growing brood of five daughters. In February 1947, Ralph James sold *Dorade* to John Franklin Eddy. Roy W. Corbett of Marina Mart brokered the transaction. Having had three different owners in the decade since leaving New York, she was about to embark on her longest continuous ownership and make her history in the Pacific Northwest.

A Long and Caring Ownership

John Franklin Eddy was a son of privilege. Born in 1909 and raised in Seattle, he was scion of one of the great lumber and commercial families of the Pacific Northwest. The Eddy family had come to Puget Sound in 1902 from San Francisco to acquire the Port Blakely Mill Company on Bainbridge Island and to found the Skinner and Eddy Company. Port Blakely, situated across Puget Sound from Seattle's Elliot Bay, was the largest lumber shipping port in the world in the 1890s. The high-quality Douglas fir and cedar from the Olympic Peninsula on Washington's verdant west coast supplied the mills and fed the holds of lumber vessels bound for markets throughout the world.

—opposite—

A stunning portrait of
Dorade in light air, heading up
Admiralty Inlet in the 1950s.
The painted burgee of the Seattle
Yacht Club is permanently
affixed to her masthead as
a wind vane.

PHOTO BY KEN OLLAR /
© GUY HOPPEN

Left— Port Blakely, Puget Sound
in 1905. Seattle lies shrouded
in the distant fog as the lumber
fleet loads in the snow.

WILHELM HESTER COURTESY SAN
FRANCISCO MARITIME NATIONAL
HISTORICAL PARK

The Double Sheet Bend connects two
lines and is designated as 'Strong" by
Ashley, although not as secure as the
Double Bend.

ASHLEY KNOT 1424

143

Aquilo at anchor in front of Chatterbox Falls in Princess Louisa Inlet in British Columbia.

© MUSEUM OF HISTORY AND INDUSTRY

The Eddy family had interests in shipping, shipbuilding, fishing and banking. Franklin Eddy was educated at The Thacher School in Ojai, California, and Harvard College and The Harvard Business School. He then entered the Navy, ultimately rising to the rank of commander. He served in the South Pacific and was awarded the Bronze Star. Following war service, he returned to Seattle to begin a career in banking at People's National Bank, at that time a privately held institution where he and his family held alliances. His family had owned a series of yachts throughout the 1920s and 1930s, and Eddy had been introduced to yachting on his father's 128-foot steam yacht *Aquilo*.

When Ralph James decided to sell *Dorade*, 38-year-old Franklin Eddy leapt at the opportunity to own a racer of such pedigree and racing fame. He had saved all of his pay from his years in the Navy, never cashing his checks, with just such a chance in mind. It was to mark the beginning of the yawl's longest continuous ownership, for she was cherished by her new owner for the next 32 years.

Eddy's father had joined the Seattle Yacht Club in 1909, the same year his son was born, and Franklin became a member at about the time he became *Dorade's* owner. As has always been the case, *Dorade's* fame made every owner somewhat famous, and Franklin Eddy was no exception. Beginning in 1947 and continuing through the mid-1960s, Eddy campaigned the racer actively and attended to her requirements. The major regattas of those years on Puget Sound were the Tri-Island Series, the annual Swiftsure Race and the Pacific International Yacht Association

144

A Long and Caring Ownership

Regatta. Active and growing participation by the Seattle Yacht Club and the Royal Vancouver, Royal Victoria, Tacoma and later the Corinthian Yacht Clubs made yacht racing popular and the participants numerous. *Dorade* competed in the so-called Big Boat or AA class, although she was certainly not as large as John Graham's great Philip Rhodes-designed yawl *Maruffa*, Max Wyman's *L'Apache* or Dr. Carl Jensen's beautiful S&S yawl *Adios*, all keen racers of the day. They all gave *Dorade* time, and she took advantage of it. During these years, she completed 13 Swiftsure Races and won its AA Class six times, in 1947, 1948, 1951, 1952, 1954 and 1964. Frustratingly, the overall prize always eluded her. The Tri-Island Series consisted of races around Vashon Island, Smith or Protection Island, and Hat (Gedney) Island, contests covering distances of between 48 and 88 miles. *Dorade* took a fourth in her first season under Eddy and won the Tri- Island Series in 1950. He won the Pacific Coast Yachting Championship Regatta in Class AA in 1950 and 1952.

There was no doubt that *Dorade* was fast, and Franklin Eddy worked to assemble crews who could sail her. He took good care of them. Many of the crewmen in the early-1950s were physicians, and she became known as "the Doctors' boat." Ray Rairdon, who became important in Franklin Eddy's racing activities in both boats and cars, recalled that some of the doctors complained about the roughness of the manila lines. Dr. James Y. Phillips, a neurosurgeon in Seattle who frequently raced with Eddy, worried that the weekend's yacht racing could impact his hands for Monday's surgeries. So Eddy fitted the boat with cotton and linen running rigging to keep his crew happy and their hands soft.

He had the boat maintained by the best yards in the area, including the Jensen Motorboat Company, owned by the famous and accomplished Anchor Jensen. Jensen had built the successful hydroplanes *Slo-Mo-Shun IV* and *Slo-Mo-Shun V,* which set world speed records and won the Gold Cup in the 1950s. Though self-taught, Jensen was an expert mechanical engineer, and he understood speed. *Dorade* was his cup of tea. Vic Franck's yard did structural and refinishing work on *Dorade.* Franklin Eddy encouraged all the Seattle yards he worked with to contact Sparkman & Stephens in New York for advice on repairs and modifications. Rod Stephens was important in these interchanges and there was no doubt that the boat remained very important to him, and to Olin throughout Eddy's ownership. Olin stopped by the Seattle Yacht Club during the late 1940's and wandered alone down the dock to see his first important ocean racing design. Harold Ben had served the boat for Ralph James and now Franklin Eddy. He had engaged Miles McCoy to help him on the boat, and, one evening, they saw a small, elegant man staring at the boat and saying, rather to himself, "Well, there she is…" Ben asked him if he knew the boat. The visitor smiled and modestly introduced himself as Olin Stephens. Enough said.

Dorade's 1953 Honolulu crew, wearing pineapple-frond hats and leis. From left: Miles McCoy, Franklin Eddy, Peter Holst, Steven Chadwick, Talcott Ostrander, James Cain, Dr. James Y. Phillips and Dr. Walter Ricker.

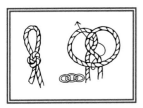

Pacific High

In 1953, Franklin Eddy decided that *Dorade* should enter the Honolulu Race again. His friends and competitors from Puget Sound were joining in, and it seemed only reasonable to take the great racer back to the contest that had brought such glory in 1936. The race had been cancelled during the war years, but was revived in 1947, first with 34 participants and then with fleets of 23 and 27 in 1949 and 1951, respectively. The 1953 race would be from San Pedro; preparations were made to assemble *Dorade*'s crew and get her south. True to tradition and with an eye to speed, Eddy decided to remove the engine and close up the shaft log for the race. Once the boat arrived in Southern California to prepare for the race, the engine was removed, crated and shipped back to Seattle. They would not benefit from the small time allowance given for dragging a prop, but the tradeoff seemed a good one.

The space where the engine sat could be used to store food and water for the long race. It was a bit like old times, and, certainly, Eddy was a traditionalist. With a race of over 2,250 miles and a crew of eight to manage the relatively complex rig, lots of supplies were needed. Eddy had the provisions carefully pre-packed according to dates at sea and organized in crates; the supplies were delivered dockside for loading. As always, he took good care of those who raced his boat. Among the crew was neurosurgeon Dr. James Y. Phillips, a fine sailor, grand companion and, with his medical training, a handy man to have along. He had been a merchant mariner and part-time prize fighter in his years before medical school. Those skills were potentially useful, too. A 23-year-old sailor named Miles McCoy had written Eddy asking to join the race. While they had never met, McCoy had sailed on some of the most respected racers in the Northwest, including Ray Cooke's *Circe*, the cutter that had nearly taken line honors from *Dorade* in the 1936 race. McCoy had a captain's license and was stationed at Kaneohe Bay keeping Corsairs in the air at the Marine Corps Air Station. When he was a teenager, he had worked briefly on *Dorade* for Harold Ben. After doing a little checking, Eddy realized from those who knew him that this young man was a real find. He invited McCoy to join as a deckhand. McCoy persuaded his kindly commanding officer into an unspecified "emergency leave," and he jumped a plane to Alameda and made his way by car to Southern

The Angler's Loop or True Lovers Knot is a pair or "couple" of overhand knots. It is secure but a bit bulky in the water tied as such. Ashley designates it "strong."

Ashley Knot 1038

Boxed supplies dockside
awaiting storage in the space
vacated by the engine.

COURTESY
MILES McCOY

California. The crew also included navigator Talcott Ostrander, Dr. Walter Ricker, James Cain, Steve Chadwick Jr. and Peter Holst.

The fleet set off at noon on the Fourth of July in very light air. The 32 entrants included Max Wyman's *L'Apache* and Dr. Carl Jensen's *Adios*, from Seattle, and California racers *Chubasco, Queen Mab, Yo Ho Ho, Atorrante, Altamar, Tasco* and *Chiriqui*. It also included the 161-foot *Goodwill*, the 10th-largest commissioned yacht in the world, able to fly up to 30,000 square feet of sail. Owned by Ralph Larrabee of the Newport Harbor Yacht Club, she carried a crew of 36 and dwarfed even *Morning Star*, Richard Rheems' 97-foot ketch from Los Angeles. But, for boats large or small, it was to be the "Race of the Big Calm."

And so the fleet chose their strategies, with the largest competitors, *Goodwill* and *Morning Star*, taking the southern route. Eddy chose to take the route above and sailed the most northerly path in the entire fleet, closest to a great circle route. Maybe he was banking on the yawl's past success with northerly routes in the Atlantic. Maybe he thought his aging racing yacht needed to take a flier. In any event, it was to be a hot and slow race working downwind to the Hawaiian Islands. Photographs and films of the race show spinnakers set, a wind scoop permanently fitted and special chafing gear designed to keep the spinnaker sheet from destroying itself when rubbing against the underside of the boom for endless hours. They show a crew attired in bathing suits.

The big boats found better wind on their southerly course, and their lead widened as they worked southwest. An unusual addition to the 1953 Transpac was a chaperone for the fleet. The Coast Guard cutter *Yocona* proceeded across the Pacific in company with the yachts and received daily position reports from the competitors. As had been the tradition since 1939, positions were broadcast to the fleet, and *Yocona* broadcast weather information as well, sometimes with reports of no wind. There were no surprises as to where boats were, but there were still plenty of changes in the standings. The corrected time standings were calculated and broadcast for all to hear and for the race's progress to be reported on shore. Six boats, including *Goodwill, Chubasco, Chiriqui, Atorrante, Altamar* and *Staghound*, jockeyed for the corrected-time lead. *Dorade* was never in the hunt. As expected, *Goodwill* took line honors, with a time of 11d, 2h. The performance proved her ability in light air despite her great size. With a bit more wind, she might have broken the record of 10d, 10h. She crossed the line at Diamond Head with all 30,000 square feet of sail flying in a fresh breeze. Observers were surprised to see the boat cross the line and continue sailing down the Molokai Channel. Later, reports emerged that there had been a bit of a mutiny at the finish, and the crew had informed the owner that they were done with being mistreated and that, with the race over, he could reduce sail

The wind scoop provided much needed ventilation below in the heat of the Pacific high pressure hole.

on his own. With a 10,000-square-foot spinakker flying on a 75-foot-long pole, the owner realized he needed to make ammends. As *Goodwill* disappeared from view, negotiations and apologies ultimately brought the sails down. The great schooner made her way into Kewalo Basin, where congratulations were waiting for the first to finish.

The breeze was light for those still sailing, and boats straggled in over the next several days. *Staghound* finished nearly 4½ days later but won Class C and first overall on corrected time. *Dorade* finished seventh in the 10-boat Class B and 18th overall. The passage took 15 days, at an average speed of only 6.27 knots. To top things off, in the last miles of the race, a bronze masthead eyebolt gave way and *Dorade* lost her headstay. As her crew watched in pain, several boats passed her, and she finished without a spinnaker under two staysails. The final competitor, *Blue-jacket*, finished the race 10½ days after *Goodwill* had crossed the line, long after the first and then a second awards ceremony had been completed. For *Dorade*, Franklin Eddy and the crew, it had still been a grand experience, one they would treasure for the rest of their lives. As they landed, they were greeted by wives and girlfriends bringing them traditional Hawaiian hats and leis. They enjoyed the lush and friend-

Goodwill, with 30,000
square feet of sail flying, takes
line honors in the 1953
Transpac Race.

TRANSPAC 1906-1979

ly islands, and *Dorade* was scheduled to be sailed back to Seattle, having completed her third Transpac. However, the race had been slow and too time-consuming for those who had planned to make the return delivery trip. Miles McCoy considered going AWOL but thought better of it. Arrangements were made to ship the boat home, but a shipping strike slowed things down. Eddy camped out at the Moana Hotel until *Dorade* finally left for her ultimate return to Seattle. She arrived dirty and streaked from her trip on the cargo deck. Her boxed-up engine was waiting to be reinstalled, keeping her motorless record to Hawaii intact.

In his submission to the compendium *Racing At Sea*, Richard Terkel, former commodore of the Transpacific Yacht Club and member of the Cruising Club of America, wrote regarding the unique radio reporting practiced in the Honolulu Race:

Dorade's crew is greeted in Honolulu. Matching shirts complete the ensemble.

COURTESY
MILES MCCOY

"The Honolulu race communications plan of daily radio muster and weather information dissemination has sometimes been criticized by eastern sailors and writers. Those who have sailed to Honolulu have a different point of view. Not only does the check-in add a safety factor but there is a daily peak of excitement as crews listen and plot the positions of every boat. The race starts again every morning with navigator, weatherman and skipper over the chart to debate tactics and plan future strategy. Weather information is not a forecast, but simply the terse report by the Coast Guard of barometric pressure at reported points, so each boat must make its isometric weather map each day, study this against the performance in other races, and make its own forecast. The TransPacific sponsors feel that this is as essential training for amateur yachtsmen as navigation."

Racecars and Wrestlers

Franklin Eddy loved *Dorade*. He sailed her well and cared for her passionately. His car carried the Washington vanity plate *DORADE*. Despite the many hands who served the boat on a paid or amateur basis, Eddy was always engaged and in charge when he was aboard, taking his bunk forward to port and steering when he wished. He was famous for driving the boat on Swiftsure Races from the start in late morning until midnight and then, exhausted, turning in to his bunk to allow his crew to carry on into the night. He was mindful of the perennially balky nature of her various engines and anticipated their failures, having at times fitted a sea anchor ready to deploy as she entered the Hiram M. Chittenden Locks connecting Lake Washington to Puget Sound or her slip at the Seattle Yacht Club. When the transmission failed to respond to a shift to neutral or reverse, he would simply deploy the sea anchor, avoiding a catastrophe and he did this with a studied nonchalance.

Eddy did not cruise the yawl extensively in Admiralty Inlet and up the Inside Passage of British Columbia but preferred to enter races and other yachting events with plenty of guests aboard. He shocked the Northwest yachting establishment by ordering a pale-blue spinnaker rather than the all-white norm of the early 1950s. Eddy was generous and wanted to have others enjoy his yacht. He was also daring and, to some, overly aggressive at the tiller. In the 1963 Swiftsure Race, the fleet started in a near dead calm. A foul tide made the passage around Race Rocks, a challenge, and various strategies were employed by the fleet, including anchoring. Eddy kept *Dorade* moving in the light air and attempted to slip to the east of the lighthouse, between the rocks, rather than down the channel to the west, with its stronger tides. The area is a rock garden, and Eddy's paid hand at the bow warned the skipper that they could not safely negotiate the passage. Eddy yelled back from the helm, "you take care of your end, and I'll take care of mine." No other competitors were around to join in their folly. Suddenly and inevitably, *Dorade* struck "hard water" and bounced over the top of the rocks. From the bow came the call "Well, at least my end is through!" The rising tide soon floated them off, and *Dorade* finished her next to last ocean race under Eddy's ownership third in class and in the middle of the fleet overall. The final Swiftsure for Eddy came in 1964, when he finished with a bang, winning Class AA for his sixth and final time.

A Loop Knot or Department Store Knot is common and easily untied.

ASHLEY KNOT 1018

153

Franklin Eddy receiving rally
instructions in his Mercedes
Benz 300SL coupe

Through the 1950s and 1960s, Eddy's crew took an active interest in the boat and sometimes even sailed it without him. Eddy was also interested in sports cars, and, in 1956, he acquired a Mercedes Benz 300SL Coupe, the famous "Gullwing" sports racer that had been adapted from the successful Mercedes W194 Grand Prix racers of the early 1950s. The cars had competed in the Carrera Pan-Americana Mexican Road Races and in Europe in events such as the 24 Hours of Le Mans. Mercedes thought that a production version suitable for the road, as well as for amateur racing, would find an audience. It did with Eddy. Introduced in 1954, the Gullwing was equipped with the first production fuel-injection system, which was fitted to a straight, six-cyliner, three-liter engine and generated speeds of 155 mph. During a production run of 1,400 cars, the coupe, with its distinctive, fold-up, winged doors, was the pinnacle of its type, owned by royalty and celebrities, including King Hussien of Jordan, Sophia Loren, Zsa Zsa Gabor, The Duke of Edinburgh, William Randolph Hearst Jr. and the great photographer David Douglas Duncan. Franklin Eddy joined this group with an intention to race. Through this interest, he met Ray Rairdon, a tall, gregarious, red-haired sports-car driver of great talent and charm, who was later to win the Sports Car Club of America Championship in the early 1960s in a Corvette. Auto racing also led Eddy to Myron Doxon, a Mercedes Benz dealer and crack mechanic, who was the only engine tuner Eddy could find who was able to keep his thoroughbred running right. With Rairdon at the wheel and Doxon tuning the car, Eddy had a team around him that enjoyed some success and had great fun.

By the 1960s, *Dorade*'s mainmast had been girdled in a bronze fitting, which gave strength to the area at the gooseneck and provided strong mountings for the halyard winches. It also added lots of weight.

AUTHOR'S COLLECTION

Right—Wrestler and *Dorade* crewman Frank Townsend, aka "Killer X" and "Farmer Boy Townsend."

ONLINE WORLD OF WRESTLING

Given his success in sports car racing, it was only natural that Eddy invite Rairdon and Doxon for a sail, and as the years went by they all raced and enjoyed *Dorade*. Rairdon, particularly, became an advisor to Eddy with respect to the boat, not as a paid hand, but as someone who was able to oversee improvements and could also manage the foredeck with his quick reflexes and six-foot, five-inch frame. When repairs were needed at the masthead, it was Rairdon who helped in the design and installation of a large bronze cap that received the shrouds, headstay and permanent backstay. Deterioration had allowed the mast tangs to fail, and Rairdon made certain the cap was muscular enough to take the loads. The cap was a large and heavy fitment. He also advised Eddy about yard bills and attempted to oversee the quality and cost of the work being done. Now in her fourth decade, *Dorade* was getting older, and things needed attention and rebuilding.

Rairdon recalled an incident from those days on the foredeck when the spinnaker-pole fitting at the mast failed, and the heavy, solid pole crashed on top of his head, gashing his scalp. Eddy, always impeccable in his care for the ship, reflexively hollered forward, "Don't bleed on that deck!", his first reaction being to keep blood stains from the vulnerable, and now venerable pine deck planking. Seeing that Rairdon was badly injured, he realized the absurdity of his exclamation and rushed to aid him, with profuse apologies. Rairdon forgave Eddy, but, in response, designed a second bronze mast reinforcement, this time a massive girdle around the mainmast above and below the gooseneck. To this were attached the halyard winches and spinnaker-pole gear. Things wouldn't come adrift again.

Another crewmember was Frank Townsend, a professional wrestler who battled in the United States and Japan under the *nom de guerre* "Killer X" or "Farmer Boy Townsend." Eddy thought Townsend's strength might be an asset, even though the wrestler knew very little about racing sailboats. Myron Doxon had warned Townsend, "You may be strong, but you're not stronger than the wind." The words proved all too prophetic. On the night of May 15, 1965, *Dorade* made her way swiftly up Colvos Passage, the channel to the west of Vashon Island in South Puget Sound, as she competed in that year's Tri-Island contest, the Vashon Island Race. While the waters are not broadly open, the weather in late spring in the Northwest

Dorade's original transom was removed in the 1960s and hung for years over the lunchroom door at Vic Franck's boatyard.

can be treacherous. Running under spinnakers as midnight approached, the fleet was struck with a powerful squall from the southwest. One 33-foot yacht was sunk off Magnolia Bluff, on the Seattle side, and shredding spinnakers could be heard, if not seen, across the racecourse. Accounts differ as to what caused the accident. It was reported that Townsend fell overboard trying to retrieve *Dorade*'s mangled chute. Others said he was hit by the mizzen boom and was dead from the blow before he hit the water. In either event, Townsend disappeared over the lifelines into the darkness without flotation. The search in the inky blackness and howling wind produced no sign of him, and it was not until the next day that his body was found. Eddy had been below when the storm hit. Doxon had been at the helm with Rairdon on deck forward. The next day, they delivered the tragic news to Townsend's widow and two-year-old son. Ironically, the next month, *Motor Boating* magazine featured *Dorade* under the caption, "Great American Sailboats."

Townsend's widow knew something of Franklin Eddy's wealth, and Eddy was horrified that his sailing and racing had left a two-year-old without a father. He approached Sonia Townsend with an offer to establish a large college endowment for her son, but she rebuffed him and sued. A nasty legal battle followed, and, reportedly, the final settlement, made before final court action, enriched the lawyers and left the Townsends with far less than Eddy had first offered. But Eddy had lost more than the settlement. His taste for racing had been crushed. He continued to direct the maintenance of his yawl, but it wasn't the same. Some said that his heart was broken over the Townsend tragedy, and his health began to turn downward.

Dorade was showing her age as well. Her frames were old, and her fastenings were tired after over four decades of racing. Her original, pine decks were split and leaking. In the late 1960s, a number of major repairs were effected. Her decks were replaced with a plywood underlayment, and cedar was laid over, although teak had been recommended. The gas engine was replaced with a Perkins 4-107 diesel. Areas of her stern as well as the rail cap were showing rot. Her transom ended up being removed and replaced. The original transom hung for years over the door to the employee's lunchroom at Franck's. Her topside seams were showing, and, to solve the problem, they were routed out and made visible in a fashion seen in boats by Blanchard and Kettenberg. In 1974, she had planks replaced and substantial refastening done by Donato & Sons' yard in Seattle. In this refit, nearly 600 feet of Honduras mahogany appeared on the material list, along with 620 bronze fasteners. Despite the care she had been given by knowledgeable owners, time was marching on.

Franklin Eddy never married. In the early 1950s, he dated prominent sailor and Seattle Yacht Club regular Hortense Harley, who raced Stars, Geary 18s and on the

well-known cutter *Circe*. She loved to sail and was competent at it. She occasionally took the tiller and planned strategy, and she managed the galley with ease. She was even allowed to bring her monkey, Mo, aboard. Her diary recorded her role with Eddy on the boat. "Together we helped plan our strategy as to how the tides could help us to the finish line. One time in racing through the San Juan Islands to Victoria I dared him to take a shallow short cut where we could have gone aground had the tide been a bit lower. It worked! We won in the middle of a dense fog when we couldn't even see the finishing boat."

Their relationship ended in the summer of 1953 when, after her assistance in Seattle in provisioning the boat for the Transpac, Eddy simply neglected to invite Harley to join the other women heading to Hawaii to

The social life of the time included elaborate costume parties, and Hortense Harley and Franklin Eddy were often in the center of things. Above, they are at the "Shipwrecked in Space" party at the Seattle Yacht Club, 1953.

COURTESY
LOUISE DALEY

welcome the crew at the finish. Despite their long courtship, she was done. Within months, Harley had married her old high-school beau.

The late 1960s and 1970s saw Eddy's health decline, and he became more and more reclusive and immobile. He lived in a corner of the library of his mansion on Capital Hill. Late in his life, he was lifted in a wheelchair by four men, placed in the cockpit of his *Dorade* and off they went for a sail.

J. Franklin Eddy died on April 11, 1978, at the age of 68. He had owned *Dorade* for over 31 years. He knew how important she was to the history of American yachting, some of which he himself had made. His will was simple, only 2 ½ pages in length and its Third Article read as follows:

"I do give and bequeath all of my right, title and interest in and to my yacht *Dorade*, Registry No. 245019, to Mystic Seaport, Inc., of Mystic, Connecticut, for its charitable, scientific and educational purposes. I do authorize my executor and executrix, hereinafter named, to make provision and pay for the transport of *Dorade* to Mystic Seaport, Inc., Mystic, Connecticut, from the assets of my estate."

The announcement of the gift must have surprised Mystic Seaport. It surprised a few others, as well. Mystic had owned the S&S schooner *Brilliant* for nearly three decades and had used her as a sail-training and educational platform. Briggs Cunningham had made a gift of the yacht to Mystic in 1952 and had continued to pro-

157

Franklin Eddy's Seattle home, with his beloved Mercedes 300SL "Gullwing" Coupe in front.

© THE MUSEUM OF HISTORY AND INDUSTRY

vide funds for her upkeep and programs since donating her. *Brilliant* is sturdily built and is still seen as one of the great masterpieces of Henry Nevins' boatbuilding art. She is a sea boat, more able than *Dorade* to take youngsters and adults sailing. *Dorade's* slender ends and narrow beam afford fewer opportunities for safety and comfort. Eddy, as the owner of a famous yacht and a sports-car racer to boot, must have been influenced by Cunningham's example of donation, and he certainly knew that his yacht was an American treasure.

His gift was a generous and thoughtful one, but Mystic, upon learning of it, immediately decided to sell her, sight unseen. Eddy specifically provided for her transportation and could easily have left an endowment for the boat, but had not thought to do so. Mystic could not keep her unless she had prepackaged financial support. They called yacht broker Bates McKee in Seattle and engaged him to auction the boat to the highest bidder. Eddy would have been devastated. Also claiming ownership on a debt of $150,000 by an undocumented agreement with Eddy was his longtime boat hand, Leon McIntire. The claim was easily trumped by Eddy's will.

By December 1978, Mystic had in hand an offer in the amount of $50,000. They petitioned the court to be allowed to accept it despite the fact that Eddy's competency, and thus his will, were being contested by one of his heirs. Mystic's counsel stated in their petition to the court that "Mystic Seaport is desirous of selling the yacht… in order to protect itself should the will… be set aside for whatever reason. Mystic Seaport would have to incur substantial costs in the maintenance and repair of the yacht *Dorade* if it is not allowed to sell such yacht until a final determination is made as to the competency of J. Franklin Eddy." The court agreed that the sale could go through, with the understanding that, if the will was set aside, Mystic would return the sale proceeds, less any expenses, to the estate. The estate was not finally closed for another 5½ years. And so, in early 1979, Mystic honored the highest bid, an offer submitted by Antonio D. Gomez, a retired airline pilot from Seattle and Sonoma, California. Like so many before him, Gomez had loved the boat for decades, was enchanted by *Dorade's* beauty and fame, by tales of her races and her owners. It was a romantic purchase, and it was to be a bumpy romance.

Racecars and Wrestlers

Above—With *Dorade* aground off Appletree Point, her crew tries to heel her free and watches the small classes sail past her to the finish.

PHOTO BY KEN OLLAR /
© GUY HOPPEN

Left—Opening Day in the Lake Washington Ship Canal, all hands sporting sweaters embroidered with "*Dorade*."

PHOTO BY KEN OLLAR /
© GUY HOPPEN

Dorade in Race Passage at the start of the 1979 Swiftsure Race.

© ROY MONTGOMERY

One Last Swiftsure

Tony Gomez had dreams of returning *Dorade* to racing. More than a decade had passed since Franklin Eddy had actively raced the boat, a logical outcome given his advancing age and declining health. But it is also likely that the loss of crewman Frank Townsend in the 1965 Vashon Island Race, and the sad fallout from that tragedy, had dampened his racing resolve. But Gomez was convinced that *Dorade*'s days of glory could be repeated, and Charlie Ross fed those notions. Ross was famous in yachting circles in the Northwest. He had won the Star North Americans in 1948, a significant accomplishment, and had actively sailed Six Metres in the 1950s and 1960s and raced in the Swiftsure Race and Tri-Island Series. In *Gossip*, a great Pacific Cruising Class sloop, Ross had won the 1953 Swiftsure Race, and, in an Owens Cutter, he had been the victor in the 1947 race. He and his brother Bob were involved in a yacht yard on Lake Washington in Seattle and in the building of small powerboats. He had raced to Honolulu in 1951 and was a very experienced man on a boat. Ross convinced Gomez that there could be no greater adventure than to return *Dorade* to the circuit, first with a tune-up in the 1979 Swiftsure Race and then an entry in the Honolulu Race, now called the Transpac, from Long Beach to Honolulu.

Under Ross's direction, a number of changes took place, including, most importantly, removing the tiller from the cockpit well and replacing it with a wheel. Ross felt that the narrow footwell in the cockpit was constricting the arch of the tiller and not allowing the rudder to swing the boat as tightly as possible. Ross was probably correct at some level, but, with a ballast keel which spanned a distance about equal to one-half her waterline length, *Dorade* had clearly not been designed for around-the-buoys racing. Further changes included a large saloon table, which could be lowered on two stainless shafts to extend the port settee berth inboard and add more sleeping room. A microwave oven was installed to port, above and outboard of the engine. Finally, *Dorade* was fitted with a roller-furling foil, and Ross ordered a large, overlapping genoa, a modern approach to the headsail question on a rig still sporting remnants of its original, 1930 fittings. These changes were made to outfit the boat more comfortably for the transpacific trip.

By Opening Day of the yachting season, celebrated in Seattle on the first Saturday in May, *Dorade* was ready. Tony Gomez drove her proudly in the traditional

A Rolling Hitch attached a block for a light load to a stay. A more weighty requirement would utilize a lashing about the stay.

Ashley Knot 1999

Antonio Gomez at the helm on
Opening Day, 1979.

yacht parade through the Ship Canal from Portage Bay to Lake Washington, past the Seattle Yacht Club and the dignitaries' reviewing stand. As the boats returned after the parade, *Dorade* was struck amidships by another boat, scraping her freshly painted topsides. It was not a good omen. Charlie Ross assembled a crew for the shakedown Swiftsure Race to be held, as always, over the Memorial Day Weekend in late May. The boat was delivered to Victoria by Ross, Gomez and three others and rafted up in front of the Empress Hotel in the dramatic Victoria Inner Harbor facing the elegant British Columbia Parliament buildings. The return of *Dorade* after so many years caused a stir within the fleet. Many were delighted to see the old racer again. Moored next to Henry Kotkins' great, 73-foot yawl *Diamond Head,* the two boats made an impressive sight. Other famous names assembled included *Weatherly,* the Phil Rhodes-designed, 1962 America's Cup defender. *Dorade*'s crew had arrived, one member coming from as far off as San Francisco. The boat was short-handed and included only a couple of experienced sailors. A grand dinner was held at the Union Club of British Columbia, a tradition for prominent Northwest yachts like *Diamond Head, Dorade, Adios, Maruffa* and Ned Skinner's *Kate II* during the 1950s and 1960s. Gomez and Ross were included. It was like old times. Ever the hot-blooded and romantic Spaniard, Antonio Gomez celebrated the nostalgic event by gleefully dancing on the foredeck in the nude after dinner, swilling sangria from a bota bag. The rest of the crew hustled him below quickly, for fear of being thrown out of the race by the conservative Royal Victoria Yacht Club. The next morning found him feeling the effects of the prior evening's consumption and the day also arrived with a fierce westerly that was forecast to increase to a gale. It was to prove all of that.

As the fleet left the Inner Harbour, an elderly lady walking in front of The Empress was helped to her feet after the wind tipped her over. Out into the starting area and a building westerly, the fleet milled about under shortened sail, but not *Dorade.* Under full main and mizzen with a reef in the new roller-furling headsail, she jockeyed for position.

Not everyone was excited to see *Dorade* return. Some felt that she was past the point of entering the Swiftsure, a race considered by some to be the toughest overnight contest in the world. Ray Rairdon had cautioned Charlie Ross, urging him not to go, saying that her days of long distance ocean racing were over. The Transpac committee had doubts as well. Charlie Ross sought to allay them by successfully

One Last Swiftsure

completing the Canadian race, being admitted to race to Honolulu and then heading south for the Transpac in early July.

The Swiftsure Race begins at Brotchie Ledge, off Dallas Bank, outside of the breakwater of Victoria Harbour, and heads out through Race Passage into the Strait of Juan de Fuca. Swiftsure Bank lies 68 miles away in the open-ocean entrance to the strait, between Carmanah Point on the Canadian side and Cape Flattery on the American. Now marked by a racon buoy positioned in deeper water slightly to the east, the bank had kept the lightship's *Swiftsure* and *Relief* on station until 1962 to assist mariners in entering the strait from the North Pacific. The bank is shallow and notoriously lumpy, as the Pacific Ocean hurls its rollers incessantly against the North American shore. The timing of the race dictates that almost all but the very fast in heavy conditions—or the very slow in most conditions—must pass this weather mark during the darkness of night.

The starting time approached, and the fleet separated into shorter and longer courses, with the larger boats, including *Dorade*, heading off first. The starting line was not square, and a port tack was clearly favored. Accordingly, the big guns in IOR Class 1 began charging on port, but not past Charlie Ross. Calling for his advantage, he starboard-tacked the fleet, forcing them in turn to tack away, and, with so much commotion in so much breeze, prompted a general recall. A second start saw *Dorade* repeat the starboard-tack maneuver, this time forcing the famous 12 Metre *Weatherly* to tack away. But this time the start was clean, and the fleet headed to Race Rocks, the passage from Victoria into the body of the strait. The wind built, and the anemometer hit 50 knots. *Dorade*'s main was slack and rattling, in order to keep the boat on its feet. Only a staysail was rigged, and the mizzen was furled. Ross called for a reef, and a good portion of the short-handed crew looked back in confusion. Several experienced crewmembers assembled the others to tuck in the reef. One man was told to lower the main. Lacking experience with the drum-brake main-halyard winch, he put in the handle and quickly opened the brake. The handle spun violently and hit the most forward crewman, who was calling the reefing, in the right hand, breaking a finger in two places and splitting the wooden winch handle roller, which flew into the sea. The injured sailor thought for a second that the flying pieces were his hand. Upon inspection, he found all fingers accounted for, but the little one badly broken. One less hand on deck. Below he went to try to bandage his wound with the only available supplies, rigging tape and a plastic knife for a splint. Another crewman trimmed off the excess plastic from the knife blades and asked how he felt. It was decided to press on despite the injury. The tide was flooding strongly, which kept the seas down, but *Dorade* struggled out through Race Passage with her staysail partly raised and her reefed main eased and flapping. Gomez sat in the cockpit, clutching a little "hair of the dog that had bitten him." The rest of the crew hung on uncomfortably.

Charlie Ross wearing a Longacres Racetrack cap, sails the broken yawl back down the sound after withdrawing from the Swiftsure Race of 1979.

AUTHOR'S COLLECTION

Ross called for crossing to the American shore to avoid the current. He planned a good, long tack and then a beat up the far coast, staying close inshore until the tide became favorable later in the day. The winds remained strong, and reports of gusts up to 60 knots were received. Others in the fleet joined *Dorade* on the American side. By mid-afternoon, she was 30 miles from the starting line, in the exposed bay to the east of Pillar Point, on the Washington side, about halfway to Swiftsure Bank, hugging the shoreline. The beach was near aboard, and Ross had the boat on a starboard tack. The seas were building as the water became shallower, and the hulls of competitors completely disappeared in the troughs of the waves. Suddenly, *Dorade* grounded, hitting the sandy bottom as she came off of a wave. She stopped and then hit again, still heading for the beach as the waves lifted her and dropped her on the sand. The engine controls did not include an ignition switch in the cockpit, and Ross struggled to turn the boat back out into open water. He had no headway. Without asking, the injured crewman down below started the engine and yelled to Ross to gun it at the top of each wave and try to turn the boat away from the beach. Gomez hung ashen in the galley and asked the crewman below, "Are we going to die?"

"No," came the reply. "But we may have to swim."

"I can't swim," yelled Gomez.

"Well then," said the crewman, "you might die."

The pounding on the sand continued for maybe eight blows, but Ross was able to rev the engine at the tops of the crests. *Dorade* turned in small increments to escape the clutches of the beach and headed out to sea. Several crewmen immediately checked the bilge to see if the boat was taking on water. She seemed fine, and the engine was turned off. The crew decided that they would declare that it was started to avoid disaster and ask the Race Committee for a penalty instead of a disqualification. The race would go on.

So, off the beach they came on port tack, through the long, deep swells. The crew was all shaken by the grounding experience, but there was plenty of activity demanding their attention. As they re-entered the strait, some of the fleet was heading along the shore on starboard tack. They had been less concerned with avoiding the flood than with the depth of water further inshore. Boats would disappear beneath the swells showing only their sails. *Dorade* would sometimes disappear from them as well, and her heading was difficult to discern as she drove north, away from the American shore. Crossing ahead of her on starboard was *Zubin Ubi II*, a 44-foot sloop with an experienced skipper. Ross did not dare cross her on his burdened port

One Last Swiftsure

tack, and the winds made the calculation of speed difficult. Ross called for the main to be eased, but the boat only gained speed as it came off the wind. Assuming that *Zubin Ubi II* would hold her course, Ross aimed to take her stern. The crew of *Zubin Ubi II* signaled its concern about the crossing. *Dorade's* crew hailed them to hold their course, but certainly no one could hear the voices, lost on the roar of wind and waves.

Dorade continued to fall off as the boats converged, but the crew of *Zubin Ubi II* concluded that *Dorade* was not going to pass clear astern. Instead of tacking away, *Zubin Ubi II* fell off to take *Dorade's* stern. The boats drove straight at one another with a combined speed approaching 20 knots. For a few seconds, things seemed to freeze in motion. Then, suddenly, explosively, *Dorade* and *Zubin Ubi II* crashed headlong into one another, *Dorade* plowing into the fiberglass boat at the port bow, driving her slender but powerful wooden bow through the fiberglass hull and under its deck. The deck of the 44-footer sliced into the new headfoil of the great ocean racer, pulling her mast forward, splitting it in two and breaking off the masthead at the uppermost of her three spreaders. The backstay was ripped from the deck, its insulator scattering ceramic shrapnel through the cockpit, missing the skipper and two crewmen. The mainsail was pulled forward through the center of the split mainmast and became tightly wedged there.

The boats hung together in forlorn embrace for a moment and then came apart. A massive hole the shape of an inverted triangle could be seen in the bow of *Zubin Ubi II*, but it was not seen for long. Accusations and hollering between the crews over rights, burdens and courses commenced. Scott Rohrer, a well-known Six Meter sailor who was aboard a nearby boat and later testified regarding the accident, commented, "It was astounding to watch the two crews beefing the rules with the boat sinking beneath them." The argument didn't last long. The sloop's skipper announced on the radio that they had been damaged and were retiring from the race. Seconds later, he announced that they were returning to port. Again, within seconds, he hailed that they were abandoning ship. The crew of *Dorade* watched in horror as the bow of *Zubin Ubi II* began to dip. The sloop's crew, all in the cockpit, pulled the lanyard on the emergency life raft, which unfolded and inflated on demand. The eight crewmen stepped off the sinking racer onto the raft without a wet deck slipper or a chance to recover a single item from down below. Mortally wounded, *Zubin Ubi II*

The crew of *Zubin Ubi II* pile into a life raft between *Dorade's* bow and their sinking racer. *Blue Marlin*, in the background, took them all aboard.

hung for long minutes, kept afloat by the air trapped in her stern, and finally sank into the Strait of Juan de Fuca off Pillar Point in American waters.

As the crew floated in the crowded raft, other racers responded. *Hagar*, an able, fast, small, IOR design with Rohrer aboard, offered assistance, but *Blue Marlin*, a Cal 40, picked them up. The crew declined an offer to board *Dorade*. The mess aboard could not have given them confidence. The masthead, with Ray Rairdon's massive, bronze cap, swung wildly as the boat pitched and rolled. The crew tried and finally succeeded in capturing it without any decapitations and lashed it to the mast. The upper spreaders were broken off with the rig, the stubs remaining all akimbo on the remaining mast. The mainsail could not be lowered because it was clamped between the broken sides of the shattered mast, which had split down the middle. The mast stood, but with neither a forestay nor a permanent backstay. A staysail halyard and the running backstays were rigged to keep the remaining mainmast section in the boat, and the mainsail, trapped high on the stub of the main mast, was run forward on the boom and wrapped around the base of the mast to keep it from flying. The mizzen was set, and *Dorade* turned east down the strait to go home. The Coast Guard had heard all the reports and asked the boats involved to report regularly. The westerly eased somewhat, and a quiet fell over Ross and his crew. Gomez was angry at the shambles of his beloved boat but also relieved not to have had to learn how to swim. The less-experienced crew wondered if this kind of thing happened often in sailboat racing, and the crewman with the broken finger called ahead on the radio to Port Townsend to alert the Emergency Room there to expect him late that evening.

Dorade made her way under power and mizzen into Admiralty Inlet for Port Townsend, but not without going aground again on the shoal just around Point Wilson after dark had fallen and the cognac had been passed around to ease the strain. The Coast Guard was again notified, and the local police shined the head-lights of their squad car from the beach onto the broken yawl as she waited for the rising tide to free her. The wind that had lashed the fleet in the afternoon had died, and the Northwest skies gave up their famous drizzle. A Port Townsend policeman was waiting as the boat arrived to take the injured crewman and his mangled finger to a bleary-eyed doctor. X-rays were taken, and the doctor fished what he thought was the image from an X-ray vat, slapping it wet onto a screen for diagnosis. "That little finger isn't broken" he exclaimed. "It's your index finger with the fracture. I had a break exactly like yours earlier this week from a basketball game. Oops, wrong X-ray!" The finger was ultimately set in San Francisco. When he returned to the boat with some pain pills, every bunk and floorboard was taken by the sleeping crew. He slept in the rain under a sail in the cockpit. Chastened by this experience but sustained by the affection he held for *Dorade*, the wounded crewman went on to become the author of *Dorade: The History of an Ocean Racing Yacht*.

Dorade motored to Seattle the next day, a Sunday, with the wind on her nose. She arrived at Shilshole Marina to off-load part of the crew and then made her

The last remaining fiberglass shards of *Zubin Ubi II* are still implanted in the bow.

way through the Hiram Crittenden Locks connecting Puget Sound to Lake Union. She offered a sad spectacle to Sunday sightseers at the Locks. She lay at Cadranell's Boatyard on Lake Union awaiting repairs, her pulpit crushed, forward starboard bulwark missing, mainsail still trapped in her splintered mast and the scars of the hull of the *Zubin Ubi II* stretching six feet back from her bow to the point where the fatal piercing finally stopped. The last floating piece of *Zubin Ubi II*, a shard of ragged fiberglass, was wedged into her starboard bulwark. Knowledgeable gawkers assembled to see the famous racer. Her final Swiftsure was done.

It is ironic to note that, on the other side of the Atlantic, the Fastnet Race was sailed that same summer. While *Dorade* changed much about yacht design in 1930, the Fastnet Race of 1979 further changed all thinking about yacht design and safety. As a violent storm swept through that fleet of 303 racers, most devastated were the smaller boats, which lagged behind the bigger, faster competitors, which had rounded Fastnet Rock earlier and outran the most savage aspects of the storm. A total of 15 sailors lost their lives. Five boats (all under 38 feet) sank, 19 boats were abandoned and recovered and only 85 competitors finished the race. Much blame was attributed to the extreme, full forms prompted by the IOR Rule and to a lack of strict safety preparedness. Yet sailing at sea, as always, embodies a certain danger.

The effects of the aftermath of the Swiftsure collision emerged in Victoria with an inquiry by the race committee. *Dorade* was found responsible for the accident based upon her burden as the boat on port tack. There was dispute over whether she fell off to leeward to allow *Zubin Ubi II* to pass ahead. The fact that *Zubin Ubi II* altered course into *Dorade* did not affect the outcome. An expensive insurance settlement was made. The wreck of the *Zubin Ubi II* was found rolling across the seafloor off Pillar Point but was not raised. Aside from one permanently crooked little finger, no one was hurt, a miraculous piece of good fortune.

Dorade lies at Cadranell's dock on Lake Union, her mainsail still wrapped around the remnants of her mast.

Back to the Bay

Dorade was repaired with the insurance proceeds over the next several months at Cadranell's, her bow restored and her mainmast rebuilt. By mid-August, she was ready to go again. Gomez had returned to Sonoma and his vineyard, and he chartered her to the Swiftsure crewman from San Francisco. Early into the charter, her engine, without an oil pressure alarm fitted, broke an oil line and pumped the contents of her lubricating system into the bilge. The engine seized. There seemed no end to her difficulties—maybe she was telling the world that she was a sailboat and didn't really want an engine. It was a message given repeatedly. The charterers sat at the Canadian Customs Dock on South Pender Island trying to decide how best to handle the problem and confront a ruined cruise. She could certainly be sailed home, but it was a risk that didn't seem worth taking. They were approached by friendly and sympathetic Canadian yachtsman Dennis Ashby and his wife, Dorothy. The couple offered to tow *Dorade* to the well-known Philbrook's Shipyard in nearby Tsusum Harbor for repairs. Their vessel was a jaunty, Bill Garden-designed, 32-foot powerboat, *Maishlemani.* The name is Zulu for "Four-Eyes," and it was given to Ashby's bespectacled grandfather during the Boer War. So *Dorade* was carefully towed over a rippled sea into Sidney, British Columbia, from Bedwell Harbour, and given over to Philbrook's to have her engine looked at.

The charterer and his guests licked their wounds ashore and made plans to fly home. Gomez was informed that the damage had occurred and immediately flew north to inspect but changed his mind in disgust when he landed in Seattle and called to say that he was not taking the final leg of the trip to Sidney. "Fix it yourself" he said. The Perkins diesel was rebuilt and *Dorade* was returned to Seattle.

Gomez concluded that he wanted *Dorade* to be closer at hand, so, in the spring of 1980, he and a crew sailed her down the coast to San Francisco. As has always been the case, the arrival of the great racer was heralded as a wonderful event by those who had known her in the Bay from her great days under Jim Flood and Jim Michael. The sailing cognoscenti of the St. Francis Yacht Club were eager to see

In late summer of 1979, the powerboat *Maishlemani* (shown to right) towed *Dorade* to Sidney, British Columbia, to repair her broken engine. The charter crew looks jolly, nonetheless.

AUTHOR'S COLLECTION

Single Carrick Bends without seizings were worthless and sometimes fatal. There is little between this knot and Eternity save the seizings. Dangerous.

ASHLEY KNOT 1445

169

her and be aboard, none less so than R.C. Keefe, the Staff Commodore of the St. Francis. Keefe is a San Francisco sailing institution, having raced on the Bay all his life, crewing on such legendary yachts as *Baruna*. He has kept the vivid yacht-racing history of the 1930s, 1940s and 1950s alive on the West Coast. His racing experience put him aboard the boats and alongside the owners who made that history, and he is a St. Francis member through and through, serving as staff commodore and in many other flag positions. When he heard that *Dorade* had been spotted in Sausalito, he was tantalized by the opportunity to race the great yawl. Gomez needed a sailing master for the boat; Keefe was his man.

The return to San Francisco went well, at first. Keefe directed the fitting of new sails, built by Kenny Watts and suitable for the Bay. He assembled crews to sail her and occasionally race her in regattas such as the Master Mariners. Jim Flood and Jim Michael joined him for a sail in 1981. He took her to Tinsley Island, the famous St. Francis Yacht Club outstation up the Sacramento River, near Stockton. Her engine was perennially non-functioning, but the steady westerlies through the Golden Gate made it possible for a capable crew to sail her in and out of her berth in the City Front yacht basin, just south of the St. Francis. It was an exciting and grand sight, entirely consistent with the way she had sailed the Bay in the 1930s. That sense of nostalgia was about to move to an even higher level.

Dorade and longtime rival *Adios* race in Class AA on Puget Sound in the 1950s. Both made their way to San Francisco Bay in the 1980s. *Adios* was renamed *Oruna* and fitted with a forest of winches by the Barient Company.

PHOTO BY KEN OLLAR / © GUY HOPPEN

by Sarah Pileggi

Two grand dames at sea

Santana and Dorade met in a match race of oldies but very goodies

This wasn't a boat race," said Tom Conroy, commodore of the St. Francis Yacht Club, on Saturday afternoon, May 22. "This was a yachting event." And so saying, Conroy presented to Ted and Tom Eden, owners of *Santana*, a 91-year-old silver loving cup with curvaceous *fin-de-siècle* sirens engraved on its sides. Earlier that afternoon on wind-whipped San Francisco Bay, the Edens' Olin Stephens-designed yawl, built in 1935, had defeated another famous Stephens yawl, the 52-year-old *Dorade*, in a match race, an event as anachronistic as the boats themselves.

The whole idea of such a match—one wealthy sporting gent challenging another with nothing at stake except pride—is romantic enough in this age of George Steinbrenner, but when you throw in two renowned beauties like *Santana* and *Dorade*, you have the stuff of legend.

The 55-foot *Santana* was built for cruising and racing by W.L. Stewart Jr., son of the founder of the Union Oil Co. After the 1938 Bermuda Race, in which *Santana* won her class, Stewart sold her and she passed into the hands of a series of owners, one of them Humphrey Bogart. *Santana* eventually ended up in the care of Tom and Ted Eden, twins, architects, yachtsmen, *bons vivants*.

Whereas *Santana's* fame grew with the passing years, *Dorade* had hers from the beginning. *Dorade* was the boat that made Olin Stephens' reputation as a designer and changed the face of ocean racing. Until *Dorade*, successful racing yachts were usually big, gaff-rigged schooners, longer, wider and heavier than the 52-foot, 40,000-pound *Dorade*. In 1931, Olin, then 23, and his younger brother, Roderick Jr., entered *Dorade* in the Trans-Atlantic race from New York to Plymouth, England and finished so early that there wasn't a committee boat to greet them when they entered the harbor A month or so later, *Dorade* again astounded the yachting world by winning England's Fastnet race, and when the crew returned to New York, it was given a ticker tape parade.

After *Dorade*, some of the most famous boats of the century came from Stephens' drawing board: *Edlu, Stormy Weather, Baruna, Bolero, Ranger, Vim, Courageous, Finisterre.* But *Dorade* was both the first of that line and the only boat Olin Stephens ever owned. In the 1938 Bermuda race, seven of the first 10 finishers, including *Santana*, were Stephens designs. By that time *Dorade* had gone west to San Francisco

continued

Blackaller (left) had Santana narrowly ahead of Keefe and Dorade on a windward leg that carried them in front of the city on the Bay.

Dueling Dowagers

R.C. Keefe's father had always told him to "make something happen." In December 1981, he had discussed chartering *Dorade* from Tony Gomez. But for various reasons, he continued as her sailing master. Gomez was tiring of the boat and its burden and was considering selling her. For his part, Keefe had a plan to draw attention to her and maybe attract a new owner: a match race with her old Honolulu Race competitor *Santana*. Originally schooner-rigged, *Santana* was now a yawl and had become an important classic fixture on the Bay. Her history included ownership by Humphrey Bogart, Ray Milland and Dick Powell. San Francisco is a little bit uppity about Hollywood and the whole Southern California movie business, but deep down inside there is a real appreciation for glamour and star quality. *Santana* has that. The thought of these two great S&S yawls from the 1930s match racing on the Bay kindled excitement. Keefe made his challenge, and the news media pounced on the nostalgic meeting. The nostalgic meeting was picked up in the press. *Santana* had dominated the Master Mariner's Regatta for years, so it only seem right for the contest between the great yachts to take place in May, before the Master Mariner's Regatta. In many ways, it was really just a fun exhibition.

Santana, drawn in 1935, incorporated Olin Stephens' more advanced design thinking in the mode of *Stormy Weather*. She is beamier and is longer on her waterline. She should theoretically be faster. The Eden brothers, Tom and Ted, had owned and loved her. They dramatically and capably sailed the boat on the Bay. Twins and architects, they were entirely up to the challenge that Keefe proposed and they even raised the ante. When the bragging about speed and the haggling about handicapping grew louder, the Edens brought aboard one of the great sailors on the bay, Tom Blackaller, to steer *Santana*. Blackaller, a Star world champion, was slated to drive *Defender* in the following year's America's Cup eliminations. He was a larger-than-life personality, with a booming voice, broad smile and shock of white hair. Blackaller had sailed the Bay for years, had raced Six Metres, built sails for North Sails and raced sports cars when not driving boats. If you thought about the term "rock star" as it came to be used in sailing, Blackaller certainly helped to define the label. Keefe was rumored to be lining up the great helmsman John Bertrand to drive *Dorade*, and he gathered a group of very experienced Six Metre sailors to pull all of the strings. Bertrand could not make the date, so Keefe drove the boat himself, festooned in a starched white shirt and St. Francis tie.

The ubiquitous and important Bowline finds many uses, this with a hooked block.

ASHLEY KNOT 1016

————opposite————

The June 7, 1982 issue of *Sports Illustrated* included an article written by Sarah Pileggi. Skippers Blackaller and Keefe led the duel.

© SPORTS ILLUSTRATED

The press called it the race of the "Dowagers" and the battle of the "Grand Dames." *Santana* owed *Dorade* 84 seconds over the 12.5-mile course. Under grey skies on May 21, 1982, the boats began to jockey with one another off of the St. Francis Yacht Club. They were watched by a throng pressing against the windows in the bar, and by many others outside, lining the seawall. *Santana* immediately encountered problems with her mizzen and was unable to hoist it. In a gesture of competitive gallantry, Keefe lowered his so as not to appear the opportunist. When Rod Stephens later saw pictures of the race in *Sports Illustrated*, he was very critical of the notion of sailing *Dorade* to weather without her jigger. He felt that it spoiled her balance and speed, and wrote to her owner, Mike Douglas, in later years, "I strongly suggest that she never be sailed without using the mizzen. Keep the mizzen set under any and all conditions, as there is no harm if it luffs a little bit when you get a little too close to the wind." There was no doubt that he still wanted to see her sailed properly and do well, even though she was now over 50.

The windward-leeward course passed back and fourth on the bay in front of the club. In the lighter breeze, *Dorade* took the lead, flying an assortment of sails—including a spinnaker from someone else's boat—from her mizzen. But as the wind freshened to the mid twenty knot range, the more powerful *Santana* passed her and pulled away. The lead grew, as *Dorade* held her spinnaker longer and sailed a lower and longer course, rather than change headsails.

The old differences in righting moment could be clearly seen in the comparative heel of the two designs. What had been true of *Stormy Weather* was evident in *Santana*, with her similarly beamy design. The Bay produces strong winds but serves them up without the big seas that allow *Dorade*, wet and on her ear, to slice through them effectively. Standing up to the breeze, *Santana* drove more swiftly across the course. In the end, *Santana* crossed the line more than seven minutes ahead, easily saving her handicap burden. The skippers were both tossed into the Bay at the dock, an elegant silver cup was presented to the Edens and the cocktails were served well into the night. It had been a grand afternoon and a notable classic yachting spectacle. But just as the Great Race of the Grand Dames finished, *Dorade* was about to change hands. Antonio Gomez, who had owned the boat for two and a half very eventful years, was shooting birds in Napa while the race was under way. He had been approached by a syndicate of investors who had ideas about how to capitalize on the boat's fame. The sale was made, and *Dorade* was about to sail into a very difficult period.

The 1982 Master Mariner's Race was held in late May, and *Dorade* participated, finishing well but not winning her class. Across from the racecourse in Sausalito, plans were afoot for a new real estate development. Her new owner was Gerard Bosco, and his syndicate of investors was seeking $15 million in financing to build a restaurant/condominium development on the water in Sausalito. The facility would be called the Dorade Yacht Club, and *Dorade* would be moored in front to attract attention and validate the "Club's" connection to the famous yawl. It wasn't quite

the same approach taken with the *Queen Mary* in Long Beach, but the general idea was similar. The syndicate needed someone to mind the boat as the project and its financing proceeded. R.C. Keefe, as the most knowledgeable skipper around, was engaged again as the master of the vessel. His job was to keep her prominently active on the Bay and to direct expenditures for her upkeep and improvement. In return, he was allowed to sail her. And *Dorade* needed improvements after some years of cosmetic attention but very little in the way of structural work. Frames, floors, mechanical systems and some planking called out for repair. Keefe began to address the deficiencies, and the syndicate paid the bills. The boat was pledged to the bank as part of the security for the loans advanced against the project. As time went by, Keefe inquired about how fundraising was going. He was advancing funds himself and was concerned about being made whole. Assurances were given that things were on track, but he kept a watchful eye so as not to get too far ahead of the reimbursements for the charges incurred. By the end of 1983, there was increasing evidence that the project was in trouble and *Dorade* was caught in its midst. In late 1983, Keefe declined to renew his agreement as master; shortly therafter, the Dorade Yacht Club came acropper. The lawyer for the syndicate was Charles Chalmers, who also saw the storm coming. Through maneuverings to protect his legal fees, he was able to secure title to the boat. She had fallen out of Coast Guard documentation, and Chalmers obtained a California title for the boat in his name. The syndicate declared bankruptcy, and Chalmers served up a slightly forlorn *Dorade* up for sale in early 1984.

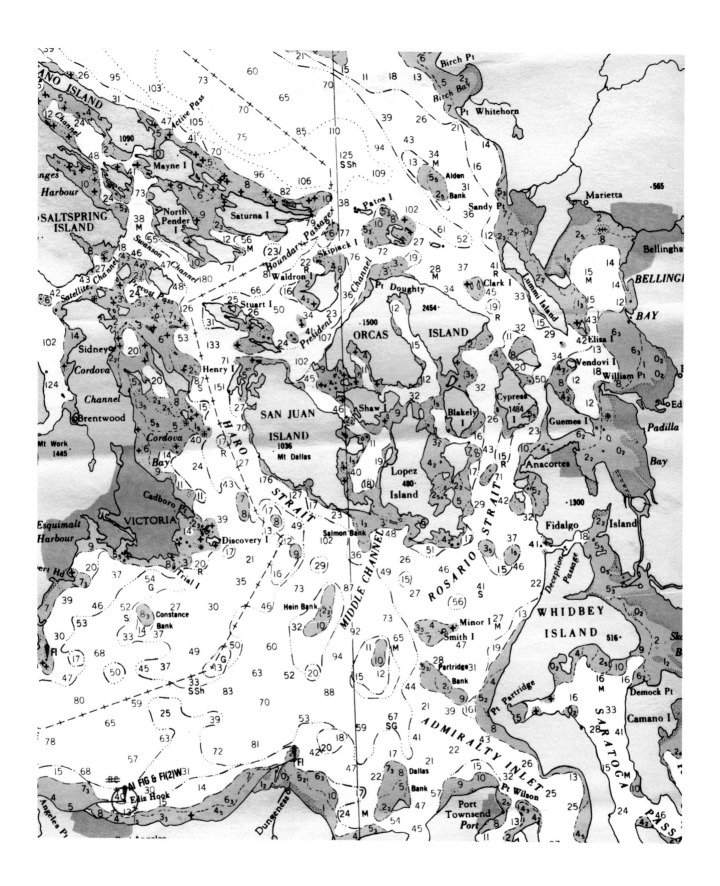

176

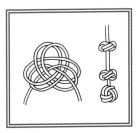

In the Shadow of Turtleback Mountain

The San Juan Archipelago consists of two groups of islands nestled between the southeast coast of Vancouver Island and the British Columbia and Washington mainland to the east. One group, now in Canadian waters, is called the Gulf Islands; the American group is known as the San Juans. Together, they total more than 400 islands, large and small, created by glaciers carving through volcanic rock in a southeasterly direction, leaving a series of small mountaintops, around which the seas filled. The islands are covered with salal, various mosses, Douglas fir, maple, arbutus and cedar. Their tidal range is high, their waters deep and their history long. The North Salish Tribes, including the Lummi Indians and their offshoots, have inhabited the Vancouver Island region for over 9,000 years. They wintered in their cedar longhouses within the protected islands of the archipelago and ventured to the outer western coast to encamp for summer fishing and hunting. Western influence began in 1791 with the Spanish explorer Francisco de Eliza's charting of the region under the authority of the Viceroy of Mexico, he of the imposing name Juan Vicente de Guemes Pidilla Horcasitas y Aquayo, Second Count of Revillagigedo. The names Juan, Pidilla, Guemes and Horcasitas made their way into the names given to various islands and bays, the latter being shortened and given to the horseshoe-shaped and mountainous Orcas Island. The British followed the Spaniards the very next year with the first of several expeditions to the region led by George Vancouver. In classic style, he renamed a substantial part of the area. To this day, the islands carry Indian, Spanish, British and even a few American names. The Spanish, the English and even the Russians have laid claim to the group. The Oregon Treaty, signed by President Polk in 1846, intended to settle the matter by defining the American/Canadian border along the 49th parallel. While Vancouver Island, which extends to the south of that line, was explicitly defined as Canadian territory, the language of the treaty was not clear regarding the San Juans. Skirmishes and forts arose on San Juan Island between the English and the American camps and, in 1859, escalated into what became known as the Pig War, the last armed confrontation between America and Britain. Although the "war" was signifi-

The Lanyard Knot in series is referred to in ancient texts and variants are used for climbing.

Ashley Knot 581

cant in island lore, its sole casualty was a pig. The dispute about ownership of the islands was not settled until 1872, when Kaiser Wilhelm I of Germany decided it through arbitration, drawing a meandering border through the islands, awarding most, but not all, to the United States.

The San Juans have evolved from first people's cultures thriving on a bountiful land to more modern economies based upon commercial fishing, forestry and farming to, finally, all of these in mix with recreation. They resemble so many island regions, such as those in Maine, on the Carolinian coast and even the Sandwich Islands. Squarely in the center of the San Juan Group is Orcas Island, the largest of the American islands in the group, boasting Mount Constitution and the islands' longest bays, East Sound and West Sound. Orcas' western half is dominated by the Turtleback Mountain Range, so named because it looks exactly like a massive turtle in profile, a sight marking the island from 50 miles away. Turtleback wraps around West Sound, an inlet of about four miles, dotted with small islands like Skull Island in Massacre Bay, Victim Island, Double Island and Skull Rock. Smuggling and piracy were important ingredients of island activity until the end of the nineteenth century.

In the shadow of Turtleback on West Sound's western shore is Four Winds-Westward Ho, a unique and delightful children's summer camp. Founded by the creative and independent Ruth Brown in 1927, the Four Winds Camp is firmly cemented in the childhood memories of four generations of boys and girls from all over the United States and the world. With strong traditions of singing, sailing, canoeing, horses, archery, poetry, pottery, woodcarving and swimming, the voices of the campers ring across West Sound all summer long. The girls still wear blue bloomers and middy blouses; the boys wear blue polo shirts and Bermuda shorts. It is in some ways a throwback to an earlier time and in other ways a progressive, diverse experiential learning environment, supported by a growing endowment and a farsighted board of trustees. By 1984, Mike Douglas was executive director of Four Winds-Westward Ho, and he was hunting for a boat.

Through a loose arrangement and some creative cajoling, the camp had always had a big sailboat at its disposal. At various times, the boat had been the schooners *Red Jacket* and *Westward Ho* or the S&S sloop *Courageous*, thanks to the generosity of the Helsell family and others. The camp was supported by its neighbor to the south, the industrialist Edgar Kaiser Sr., who gave generously of his time and resources for decades.

Charles Chalmers' for-sale listing for *Dorade* was given to Joseph Rinehart of David Fraser Yacht and Ship Brokers in Sausalito. Knowing generally of the legendary background of the yawl, he wrote to Olin Stephens, requesting a history of the boat and her racing record. Upon learning more of the significance of *Dorade* and understanding that Sparkman & Stephens remained in the yacht-brokerage business, Mr. Rinehart offered to step away from transacting the sale and allow S&S the listing. He wrote "my desire to see *Dorade* fall into loving hands <u>far</u> outweighs any

Mike Douglas watches over a
Four Winds camper at the helm.

© NEIL RABINOWITZ

need or wish I might have to realize financial gain from participating in her sale." Olin and Rod both entered into a cordial correspondence with Rinehart, assuring him that he should keep the listing and providing him with a summary of important races. The listing remained active as the Master Mariner's Race was held in May, but there were no buyers as the summer came and went. Other brokers around the country became aware of the opportunity, but she was still a 55-year-old racing yacht with significant needs in a world dominated by fiberglass and more comfortable, modern offerings. As the fall approached, the boat had been on the market for over six months. Sparkman & Stephens and Cannell, Payne and Page—a well-known classic yacht brokerage in Camden, Maine—were both introducing *Dorade* to buyers. One of the interested parties was Mike Douglas.

Douglas had sailed all of his life in the Northwest. He was sailing at the age of eight in a dinghy launched from his family's powerboat. He had owned a Blanchard Senior Knockabout, a Thunderbird, a Stonehorse, a Dragon, a Lightning, and a BB 11. He had become a teacher after finishing graduate school and spent over a decade with The Bush School, a long-standing and prominent kindergarten through twelfth grade private school in Seattle. Douglas came to Orcas Island and Four Winds to become its director in 1979. By 1984, he was looking for a Sparkman & Stephens yawl, both for his family of three children and for use in the camp's sailing program.

Douglas's hunt for a yawl had brought him to submit an offer on an S&S boat called *Egret*, which was for sale in Seattle, and he had given the broker a generous 30 days to respond. Without an answer to his offer, he watched the calendar carefully. During the final week, he received a call from Jim Payne at Cannell, Payne and Page. Douglas had met Payne on a cross-country trip years before and shared his interest in a boat. "If you want an S&S yawl, I have one for you," said Payne. "*Dorade* is for sale."

In 1979, Douglas had seen the broken spar and crumpled bow of Dorade after the ill-fated Swiftsure Race. Despite her bruises, he had joined the throngs of admirers. When he heard Payne's news, he immediately wired funds to secure her.

Mike and Carina Douglas.

Douglas knew that, if his offer on *Egret* were accepted, he would have a big problem on his hands. But he knew he wanted to own *Dorade*. For one, very long weekend, he had offers out on about 100 feet of S&S yawl. It just happened to be in two pieces. Sunday, the deadline passed and his offer expired on *Egret*. On Monday, *Egret*'s broker called to accept Douglas's offer. He was shocked when told that it had expired. Douglas arranged to have *Dorade* surveyed, and headed to San Francisco for a sea trial.

Charles Chalmers, lawyer/owner, dressed in a dark suit and carrying a briefcase, met Mike Douglas at the boat in Sausalito. Chalmers suggested that he might like to go for a sail but changed his mind when he looked at the Bay and realized that he would be accompanied only by Douglas and one other crewman. The typical westerlies piped through the Golden Gate, and as Douglas and his crewman left the dock under sail and headed out past the shelter of the Marin Headlands, the breeze caught the yawl and sent it flying down the Bay. The engine still didn't run. They sailed her down to the lee of Alcatraz and tucked in a reef. Back they went, up the City Front and into the basin at the St. Francis, where they moored.

Douglas was delighted at how *Dorade* handled. She was a dream come true, and she was his. The survey and his observations made it clear that the yawl was in no condition to go to sea, so, for help getting the boat packed up and trucked to Seattle, Douglas called the most knowledgeable man he knew—Miles McCoy, the same Miles McCoy who had taken *Dorade* to Honolulu as a 22-year-old, with Franklin Eddy. Now living on West Sound, Miles came down, packed up the boat and her spars in Sausalito, put her on a truck and, with Mike Douglas, chaperoned her in their car up the coast. Launched at Anacortes on the edge of the San Juans, *Dorade* was back in familiar waters, with her engine miraculously revived. She was on her way to Four Winds-Westward Ho and the care of Mike Douglas, his family and his campers for the next 12 years. She had entered into a very different period in her

In the Shadow of Turtleback Mountain

life, one dominated by an owner who understood how precious and important she was, but who also understood that she must survive within the context of a teacher's budget and the spirit of her times.

Large, wooden boats may be romantic and beautiful, but the undertaking of their restoration had not yet blossomed in 1984, particularly in the United States. Many wooden boats younger than *Dorade* had fallen into disuse and were lost. Difficult and expensive to rebuild, they had been patched up and put to sea with some trepidation, or they had been cut up or abandoned. In his book, *The Great Classic Yacht Revival,* Nic Compton makes the case that the great movement to significant worldwide yacht restoration began in America with the establishment of Dick Wagner's Center for Wooden Boats in Seattle in 1974 and the founding by Jon Wilson of *The Wooden Boat* magazine in 1977. There is also important credit to be given to Mystic Seaport Museum and the fundamental work of Maynard Bray in leading important conservation and restoration in the shipyard there. These events, along with the extraordinary development of the Clayton Antique Boat Museum in the Thousand Islands and the inaugural Port Townsend Wooden Boat Festival, pioneered an astonishing renaissance of interest, spending and fascination with old boats. But, in the early 1980s, there was not a broadly based cadre of enthusiasts

Dorade's young crew of Four Winds - Westward Ho campers enjoys an easy sail on West Sound.

in America ready and willing to spend large sums on the task of researching and restoring classic yachts. The American enthusiast Elizabeth Meyer would set a lofty new standard with her jaw-dropping restoration of the British, J-Class racer *Endeavour*, but that was several years away.

Dorade's restoration was not a simple problem. She was 30 to 40 years older than other available and attractive examples of wooden yachts with important pedigrees and less structural fatigue. She was an antique in many ways, in her layout and crew-intensive rig. She was always a man's boat. Not overly comfortable, with a cockpit that required creative seating, she delivered wet plunges to weather in a heavy sea and a dark and cramped interior. There had never been and never were to be feminine devotees of *Dorade*. She was beautiful and exciting to men, and generally seen as a rival for attention, adulation and resources by women. *Dorade* was a very expensive project for a very narrow audience. The Europeans in the Mediterranean glamour set would need to show the Americans the way in big-budget, classic-yacht restorations. Later, they did just that. But, in 1984, *Dorade* was not yet a candidate.

And so from West Sound, Orcas Island, she was to devote her time and grace to the role of a family boat and a memorable, waterborne carrier of teenaged campers. For the time being, it was a good fit.

Sharon Douglas crafted special
ceramic plates in gratitude for a
winter berth for the yawl.

The program was pretty straightforward. Douglas owned the boat, and the camp paid him a modest amount to use her during the summer camping season. He, in turn, used those funds for her maintenance. That maintenance included bright-work sanding and varnishing by the campers every spring as well as two coats of varnish on the spars, still in place, applied from a bosun's chair. When the boat first arrived from San Francisco, the California sun had, over several seasons in Sausalito, left her masts bare, except for the lowest 10 feet, which fell within easy reach. Douglas stripped, bleached, treated and varnished the spars as well as the rails and deck furniture. His campers helped and he admits that some of the work done by his young helpers may not have been suitable for a gold platter and that quarts of varnish sometimes toppled onto *Dorade*'s decks. Though he certainly cringed at such incidents, he recognized that this was the way she was going to have to be kept and used. The campers loved to contribute and, though they may have known nothing of her fame and pedigree, they knew instinctively that she was special.

Douglas, in a quest to keep the boat as simple as possible, stripped out the non-functioning electronics that had been layered on over the years. He sailed her locally on daysails and some overnight trips as far north as Nanaimo, in British Columbia, and as far west as Victoria. Douglas even accepted an invitation to bring *Dorade* to the Vancouver World's Fair, and the campers joined in the festivities. Sailing included races such as the Round the County Race and the Shaw Island Classic—relaxed, low-key events with mixed and varied fleets. The mizzen staysail was a particular favorite with her young crews, easy to set, dramatic and dubbed, "the funs'l." The Perkins engine continued to give uneven service, which meant crews had to be prepared to sail the boat out of tight spots, and they did. Douglas recalled a landing at nearby Jones Island, a lovely state park crowded with yachts in the summer. Under sail, she entered the North Harbor, sailed through the anchored fleet, came head to wind, dropped her sails and anchored, all done quietly by her crew of blue uniform-clad campers. The entire bay watched and then burst into applause.

During the winter, boats remain in the water in the Northwest. *Dorade* was moored at a number of places on West Sound between seasons, cloaked in a heavy winter canvas cover constructed for her by Miles McCoy. One winter found her moored at Double Island, just south of the camp, where a fierce northerly produced winds upwards of 120 knots. A cyclonic turbulence, unique in the history of Northwest storms, scattered timber on Orcas Island like random matchsticks. The masts of the yawl could be seen gyrating above the sea foam, but her hull was lost in the blown seawater that rose from the sheltered bay. The aftermath presented a broken up dinghy, chafe to the port side caused by a parted bow line, and damage to the stem and bow pulpit. She was repaired and spent subsequent winters on the other side of West Sound, moored to the author's dock. People on West Sound who could offer seasonal moorage did so as a way to help Mike Douglas keep the boat at the camp. Thanks often came in the form of handmade pottery, crafted by Mike's wife, Sharon. Their wedding took place on *Dorade*'s bow in 1988. Over the years, a collection of Sharon's unique and special plates, coffee mugs and sugar creamers was assembled and treasured. Everyone was delighted to have the aging but still stunning yawl carrying campers across West Sound.

As interest in the restoration of great yachts increased throughout the 1990s, Douglas occasionally received inquiries about his yawl. She was not for sale. By 1995, however, as he and Sharon considered the financial burden of sending three children to college, they had a hard time justifying *Dorade*'s expense. Although her maintenance program was working well and posing relatively little financial strain, it was clear that she might command a price in the market that was three or four times what Douglas had paid for the boat a decade earlier. He is arguably the only owner to have profited by her. Furthermore, the camp really needed a bigger boat, as *Dorade* was only able to carry six campers along with Douglas or his competent skipper Philo Lund. She obviously needed structural work to some of her frames and floors, and she periodically needed sails. It was time to send her along to a new home.

The December 1995 issue of *WoodenBoat* carried a page of listing by Cannell, Payne and Page. At the top of the group was a picture of *Dorade* on the Four Winds Camp dock. The caption read, "52' Famous S&S Yawl. A Piece of Yachting History and Unique Opportunity. Offers Wanted." On several occasions, Mitch Gibbons-Neff, president of Sparkman & Stephens, had contacted Mike Douglas to find out about the boat. He had previously mentioned an Italian buyer with an interest in important S&S designs, and he called again. Douglas was very much hoping that the boat would stay in the United States and had made it clear to Jim Payne and to Mitch Neff that the asking price of $200,000 was based importantly on her value as a unique yachting artifact and would be negotiated more freely with an American than a European. There was no doubt that he would ask for a premium if she left the country. While offers were received during the winter and early spring, they were not high enough.

Finally, a price was agreed upon and the offer came from Europe. Federico Nardi owns Cantiere Navale dell'Argentario, and he loves boats designed by Olin Stephens. His yard had completed the restoration of several of them, including *Nyala*, a Twelve Metre built in 1937 (Design No. 217). Nardi was hunting for European buyers who would engage his yard to restore important yachts. In 1995, *Dorade* was the perfect candidate. His buyer was Dr. Giuseppe Gazzoni-Frascara. Nardi is an expert on the myriad details of classic yachts, and his yard has become one of the most highly respected restoration yards in Europe. His office is cluttered with bronze fittings, restoration records, original plan drawings and ancient photographs of classic yachts. His knowledge is encyclopedic. Importantly, he is quite charming, as well as handsome. The author's wife and daughter were certainly taken by his courtly manner, movie-star looks and infectious enthusiasm during a visit to his yard and the luncheon that followed. When asked if he had a family, Nardi shrugged his shoulders and smilingly replied, "I am only a lonely bachelor who lives with a dog."

In the Shadow of Turtleback Mountain

Nardi convinced Gazzoni-Frascara that he should buy *Dorade* if she was what he thought she was, and Gibbons-Neff would broker the deal. An inspection was needed, so Nardi, with his chief of restoration, Pietro Siena, flew to New York to collect Mitch Neff and then carried on to Seattle. Mike Douglas met them as they emerged from a deHaviland DH2 Beaver floatplane at *Dorade*'s dock on West Sound. It must have been quite a meeting. Mike Douglas is a trim and fit Northwesterner who wears the casual garb of a camp director and outdoors teacher. Mitch Neff emerged from the plane in a New York Yacht Club tie and blue blazer, smoking his ubiquitous pipe. Federico Nardi came out of the plane wearing an elegant, open-necked silk shirt, with his dramatic mane of flowing, grey-blond hair and a perfect tan. He was followed by a lovely young American woman, who had decided to join him for the trip. They, in turn, were followed by his chief of construction, Siena. Douglas hadn't expected such an elaborate visit. As Nardi and Douglas visited on the dock, Neff and the Italian boatwright went below. Nardi did not. Douglas was surprised by the brief visit. They had come all the way out to Orcas from halfway around the world, and they stayed less than an hour. In reality, the visit was really a very simple one. They needed to know that the boat was really *Dorade*, and they confirmed that she needed a major rebuild. There was no good way to know how extensive the work would be until she was taken apart. She was in far better shape than many examples of her vintage, in that she was still sailing actively. However, the purchase price was only a small part of the expected cost of putting her back into proper condition. They knew what they were buying, said their goodbyes and headed back to Seattle. The deal was struck. *Dorade* was delivered to Anacortes by Douglas. She was trucked to Portland, Oregon, and then loaded onto a freighter bound for Italy. She had fetched her European premium, but there was no joy on Orcas at seeing her go.

Dorade, from aloft, her beautiful, narrow deck gleaming after the refit.

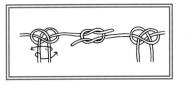

Ciao, Bella

Monte Argentario is a peninsular appendage of the Province of Grosetto on the western coast of Italy. Lying in Tuscany, 150 kilometers southwest of Florence and 100 kilometers northwest of Rome, the mountainous promontory juts into the Tyrrhenian Sea towards distant Corsica. Its history dates from Roman times, when it was awarded to the Domitii Aeronbarbi family in return for monies lent to the Republic to wage the Punic Wars. The name Argentario is purportedly derived from the ancient Roman word *argenterii*, meaning money lender. Two bays pinch the peninsula; Porto Santo Stefano on the north, and Porto Ercole on the south. Its long history has seen occupation by Etruscans, Romans, Spaniards, the Napoleonic French, the Duchy of Tuscany and, finally, the Kingdom of Italy in 1860. Valuable as a military location, with its harbors and outlook from Punta Telagrafo, a 645 meter peak on its seaward side, Monte Argentario was heavily bombed in World War II. During the 1950's the peninsula slowly recovered to become a fishing, yachting and recreational getaway for summer residents escaping to their seaside villas from a steaming Rome.

The What Knot is used in one of the prettiest of rope tricks. Although loose in appearance, two pullers will not budge it.

ASHLEY KNOT 2579

Cantiere Navale dell'Argentario began as a small shipyard on Monte Argentario's northern harbor, Porto Santo Stefano, supporting the local fishing industry. Driven by the charismatic and talented Federico Nardi, the yard has become an icon in the restoration of classic yachts. Nardi joined with four others in a management buyout of the yard in 1991 and began augmenting the yard's commercial boat work with the restoration of important yachts, notably those designed by S&S. His first important project was the Twelve Metre *Nyala*, which he had convinced Patrizio Bertelli to buy and restore. Bertelli is the hard-driving and demanding force behind the famous Italian design house, Prada, founded by his wife's grandfather, Mario Prada, in 1913 and launched into a new and competitive formulation by Bertelli in the 1990s. He had looked at other famous classics, like Fife's *Altair* and *Belle Aventure*, but finally engaged Nardi to restore *Nyala*, a near sister to the famous *Vim*. Nardi found the racer in Rhode Island in 1995; *Nyala* was rebuilt and relaunched in 1996. The yard was also rebuilding *Linnet*, a Herreshoff New York Yacht Club 30.

Dorade was to be the next glamorous project, under the ownership of Giuseppe Gazzoni-Frascara, an Italian industrialist whose business interests include the well known artificial sweetener brand "Dietor" as well as "Bologna", the Italian football

In Portland, Oregon, *Dorade* is loaded aboard, bound for Livorno, Italy.

league powerhouse. Gazzoni had owned a number of modern sailboats and was active with a series of Swans, most recently a Swan 77 named *Dag*, but *Dorade* was his first foray into classic wooden boats. He chose for her captain the man who served as mate on *Dag*, the experienced and well-traveled Englishman, Giles McLoughlin, new to the wooden boat world as well. McLoughlin's resume included five Atlantic crossings as well as work in the Pacific and the Caribbean. He was delighted to have his hands on the great classic yawl.

Dorade was delivered to Nardi's care as deck cargo aboard the rusting freighter *Mediterraneo*. The little yawl was craned off of the deck in Livorno and launched alongside. Her mainmast was stepped, and Nardi, armed with a couple of good pumps just in case, sailed the yawl the 100 miles south to Argentario. Gazzoni and McLoughlin met her at the yard and immediately went for a sail. Certainly, there were many issues to address, but she was in far less dire condition than Nardi's future S&S restoration projects, such as *Stormy Weather* and *Sonny*. She didn't leak excessively, was fair of shear and all of a piece. Everyone at the Cantiere was excited to have a part in her future.

But problems did exist. She was in obvious need of a new deck, and her maststep was wasted. Soft planks at the garboard and above had to go, and some broken frames, refastened and sistered repeatedly over five decades, had to be renewed. Her balky, Perkins diesel needed to be replaced with something more compact and modern. Refinishing needs were basic, and extensive. A return to originality in her rig and steering arrangements was called for and her spars invited, in numerous ways, the replacement or rebuilding of her traditional fitments. Nardi's plan, with the approval of Gazzoni-Frascara, was to retain as much of the original boat as was possible and repair what was needed. Her interior was mostly intact, although it had been altered somewhat over the years. Hanging knees, darkened with age, would remain in place if they were still structurally sound. The work was to be as sympathetic and non-invasive as possible to preserve what Gazzoni and Nardi knew was a yachting treasure.

And so the Cantiere took *Dorade* apart for the first time in almost seventy years, took her down to a place that seemed reasonable in the light of an operating yacht that had some structural needs, but had a precious place as an artifact of yachting history and construction. With almost an archeologist's view, Nardi tried to strike a

The damage wrought by over six decades of hard sailing appeared as Dorade came apart. The bronze strapping so fundamental to her strength had created electrolysis and lignification in her wooden structures.

PHOTOS BY JAMES ROBINSON TAYLOR

balance between replacement and preservation. He went as far as his sensibilities and the constraints of Gazzoni's budget dictated. *Dorade*'s deck and bulwarks came off, along with every piece of deck furniture, from her Dorade boxes and hatches to her deckhouse. Her deck beams were inspected and restored as necessary. Her hanging knees and lodging knees were generally sound and saved. On went new bulwarks and caprails. They laid a new, 1 ¼-inch, single layer teak deck. While the original deck was white pine—a high-maintenance wood that Nardi used in other restorations—the owner decided against it for *Dorade*.

Below the waterline her ballast keel was dropped to inspect and replace keelbolts. Her frames were laid open at the turn of the bilge for inspection and replacement. New planking, a new mast step, renewed garboards, floors, strapping, all needed to be addressed. They relocated the engine to the center of the saloon, beneath new, varnished, teak floorboards, which replaced the original cork. Custom-made, stainless steel floors also served as motor mounts, which helped place the weight of the power plant in the center of the boat. Her original engine placement from 1941 had changed her balance and with so much weight added to her stern, her fuel tank had been positioned in the bow to compensate. *Dorade* is very narrow all over, particularly at the turn of her bilge. But, there was just enough room in the saloon bilge for a modern, four-cylinder Yanmar diesel, with a fuel tank just ahead of it and an hydraulic gearbox behind. Routine maintenance such as oil filter changes and fan belt work were difficult, but not impossible, in this location.

Also hidden under the port bunk was a high capacity watermaker. The boat was to be used for family cruising. Because she carried only 120 litres of tankage, the watermaker allowed her to stay out of crowded harbors and the long lines at the watering dock. It was a sensible, modern approach that extended her usefulness and range.

Top—Ready for launching, Argentario, 1997.

Bottom—Frederico Nardi, Olin Stephens and Giuseppi Gazonni-Frascara at recomissioning, 1997.

The interior was meticulously renewed, with rebuilt cabinets, countertops, painted overheads and quilted leather upholstery. The salt water sink—which Olin and Rod added early on, but was not included in the original drawings—was eliminated. Instruments were hidden behind removable panels to preserve the appearance of 1930. The bearing compass didn't make it back aboard, but the tiller did, fashioned carefully in its somewhat heavy, stout, original configuration. The new tiller was laminated, rather than solid, in construction. Her rig was renewed with strops on the mizzen and a knob at each masthead. The heavy, bronze masthead reinforcement was removed, and seven feet of the mast's upper section rebuilt. However, the bronze girdle which held the winches and spinnaker pole gear at the deck was retained. A new, bronze windlass, appropriate to her age, was added. The restoration was completed in an intensive time frame, and *Dorade* was ready for the 1997 yachting season. Everyone who saw her knew she would be a triumph.

It is interesting to evaluate the state of classic yacht restoration in 1997. In 1930, *Dorade* and Olin Stephens achieved a breakthrough in the field of yacht design. Some 67 years later they were about to create another breakthrough in the field of yacht restoration. Although both of these events were preceded by harbingers of things to come, *Dorade* and her designer provided the tipping point on both occasions. Classic-yacht restoration had been limited to a few, large, outlying projects, such as *Endeavour*, along with a large number of smaller, less expensive rebuilds. In many ways, the restoration of *Dorade* changed all of that for a cadre of important boats in a medium size range. Nardi was instrumental in selling the concept of the value of these yacht-racing artifacts to a group of wealthy Italians who could afford to have them extensively restored. His clients Bertelli and Gazzoni-Frascara were famously demanding, but Federico Nardi, by virtue of knowledge, commitment and personality, could work well with them. Nardi pushed the limits of accepted economics to establish a new level of value and worth for these antiques and while he may have been a bit ahead of the market-value curve, he was on the right track. There were certainly limits to what his buyers would tolerate in terms of cost, perfection and authenticity. Nevertheless, Nardi's work took the boats, their owners and their designers to a new level of recognition and fostered the glamorous rediscovery of great designs.

Federico Nardi accomplished one other very important reunion: the reconnection of Olin Stephens with *Dorade*. Now in his early 90's, Olin had not really been close to the boat since it had gone to San Francisco in 1936. Rod Stephens had played a more active role in the life of the yawl, periodically advising owners on repairs and rigging issues, but, by 1997 Rod had been gone for two years. It is a pity that he didn't live see *Dorade* restored, that he wasn't able to hold her tiller again as he had done over so many miles of ocean. Sparkman & Stephens presented Dr. Gazzoni-Frascara with a bronze plaque, which was affixed to the bulkhead at the top of the companionway ladder. It announced the "Rod Stephens Restoration Award for the Outstanding Restoration of *Dorade*, S&S Design #7, 1997."

Olin Stephens was left as the only survivor of those early years and he commented over and over at the satisfaction he felt at seeing his designs treasured and lavished with restorative care. He, as a yacht design institution, had been able to participate in representing his yachts to old and new audiences alike. It is like seeing the adoration of Picasso or Andrew Wyeth or Enzo Ferrari—luminaries celebrated while they were still living. With yachts it has taken longer but Olin had lasted longer and both he and his public have been able and lucky to enjoy the recognition. In a 2004 interview with John Rousmaniere in *WoodenBoat*, Olin commented,

© MICHAEL BRASSERT, HOUPLA

There can be no question that Olin loved *Dorade*, the only boat he ever owned. In the fall of 1957, in a two-part feature for *The New Yorker*, Morton M. Hunt profiled the Stephens brothers. Olin, not yet 50, had yet to launch his America's Cup Twelve Metres, but he had already amassed a worldwide reputation in a career career over 30 years long. His latest great design was *Finisterre*, drawn to the evolving CCA rule, which had handicapped *Dorade* out of the winner's circle. A beamy, centerboard yawl, *Finisterre* had won the first of three consecutive Bermuda Races in 1956. Describing *Finisterre* for Hunt, Olin revealed his lasting affinity for *Dorade*:

'"The Rule isn't always helpful to the designer," Olin remarked to a friend not long ago, marvelously understating the case. "It's intended to give any reasonably good boat a fair chance in a race, but it has discouraged the building of more boats like *Dorade*. Yet *Dorade* is as good a boat as she ever was – she can slice through a leftover slop of a sea, go to windward very well, and steer nicely in all conditions. But nobody would order a boat like her today. I'm proud of Finisterre, of course, but personally I prefer the way *Dorade* moved. She was a lovely boat to sail." His voice trailed away on a note of sentimental reminiscence.'

"When Dorade was restored, they made her exactly as she was in 1930. Because she was like the original, my experience when I went aboard in 1997 was personal and deeply emotional. They had replaced the steering wheel with a tiller, just as she had when I first sailed her, and when I took hold of this tiller a feeling went over me like a wave. I came up breathing the same air as everyone else and was soon thinking analytically again, comparing one boat against another. But I was deeply moved. When I was her navigator on ocean races in the 1930s, I slept on a special bunk that was made up on the chart table. Most charts were stowed in a shallow space under this combination chart table and berth, with food or utensils under that, and shelves for books at the head. In the main cabin there were lockers with doors that used details from some home furniture. All those details from 1930 were there when I came aboard Dorade *in 1997. These things hit me hard."*

They hit the classic yacht movement hard, too. Nardi had shown what could be done with a great classic and Olin had underscored her importance and reminded the world of what *Dorade* had meant in terms of defining a change in design. The yacht herself went on to make sure that the racing community knew that she was more than a lovely antique but was also an ocean racer able to justify her importance as a singular design. Within weeks of relaunching in June 1997, she stormed through the Mediterranean classic yacht circuit, winning Les Voile d'Antibes in Juan-les-Pins, France. She took class honors in Prada Sailing Week at Porto Santo Stephano. At the Trofeo Almirante Conde de Barcelona in Palma she won, this followed by honors back in Italy at the Vele d'Epoch in Imperia. Olin sailed her in some of these events. She was the toast of the Med, she was very, very fast and Olin's youthful genius and good fortune with his first ocean racing design brought forth an historically interested and enthusiastic public that wanted to see more. There followed a host of important restorations in the 50- to 60-foot range, a rebuilding of ocean racers to populate the growing fleet of beautiful and usable classics. The revitalized classic yacht movement delighted owners, sailors and observers, and *Dorade* had again served as a turning point.

The Gazzoni-Frascara family loved and enjoyed the simple yawl, cruising and racing her, sometimes in company with *Dag*. Cruising started with weekend trips from Argentario to nearby Sardinia and extended to a 3 ½ week cruise to Elba and Corsica with Giuseppi's son, Tomaso, his wife and two friends. In 1998, McLoughlin skippered the boat in early season races before taking *Dorade* around the boot

Top—Peter Frech and Olin aboard *Dorade* in Antibes, with a crew ready to race.

COURTESY
JEROEN FRECH / *L'ILLIAD*

Bottom—Peter Frech, with Olin, Cannes, 2004.

© PATRICIA LASCABANNES

of Italy to the Greek island of Patmos, where the Gazonnis have a summer villa. With wonderful sailing and beautiful scenery, the yawl found and gave new pleasures in the furthest eastern sailing of her career. Gazzoni's daughter Ederica and her friends sailed and delighted in *Dorade*. On the return to Argentario, the top of the mainmast was swept away when a fitting failed. It was the sixth time that the top had been reconfigured, by choice or otherwise. McLoughlin was not daunted by the mishap. He simply reefed her main, set the forestay and running backstays and sailed her home with a slightly shortened rig. She went to weather just fine. Once the masthead was repaired, *Dorade* was set to rejoin the racing circuit in the fall.

Dorade had sparked in Gazzoni-Frascara a passion for restoration, and Federico Nardi found him another project. The old comparisons with *Stormy Weather* had led Nardi to the Great Lakes where he had found and Gazzoni had purchased Olin's masterpiece from 1934. With her purchase, Gazzoni determined that he should concentrate on his newest project. Suddenly, *Dorade* was for sale. He had added heroically to her condition and had used her in a wonderful way as a racer and a family cruiser, but two classics was one too many. It didn't take well-known Mediterranean yacht broker Michael Horsley long to find a buyer.

Peter Frech was the fourth generation of his family to head Heinrich Hanno & Co. B.V. Founded in 1900, the Rotterdam-based shipping and maritime services company provided shipping, freight forwarding, maritime brokerage and storage. Frech had been involved in marine activities throughout his life but had not been active in ocean sailing, instead having sailed a traditional barge on Holland's inland lakes. His son, Jeroen, was destined to become the fifth generation to head the family company but, as is so often the case in long-lived family businesses, concluded that his interests lay in other directions. He wanted a career in yachting. Although disappointed, the senior Frech supported his son in the purchase of *L'Iliad*, a 78-foot ketch designed by Frenchman Francois Camatte and built in 1935. With a plan to launch a sailing and diving charter business in the Mediterranean, Jeroen set out on an independent course. The year was 1999, and the family business had just been sold on the eve of its 100th birthday. Peter Frech—not unlike Roderick

193

Stephens Sr. nearly 70 years earlier—was to find for himself a new interest in pursuit of his son's passion for ocean sailing. Mike Horsley of Edmiston Company in Antibes had found *L'Iliad* for Jeroen and, like any good yacht broker, had a suggestion for his father. The listing for *Dorade* was presented and, in late April, Peter Frech very quickly became the owner of his first ocean-going yacht. He had no experience in ocean racing and knew little of the yawl's history. He only knew that it was love at first sight. *Dorade*'s beauty had captured another admirer. As Frech came to know her fame and significance, he could hardly believe what he had found.

Giles McLoughlin helped Frech bring the boat from Argentario in a very rough passage, not the ideal conditions for Frech's first exposure to the open ocean. However, he was immensely impressed with how the yawl handled in difficult conditions. She was berthed in Port Gallice, Antibes, just 15 miles from Cannes, on the dramatic and famous Cote d'Azur. Her years under Frech were spent in the daysailing, classic-yacht circuit—regattas like

Carrying a dramatic spinnaker with a leaping dorado, *Dorade* reaches under full sail.

© FRANCO PACE

Les Voiles d'Antibes, Vele d'Epoca di Imperia and Argentario Sailing Week. The Regates Royales in Cannes in the fall generally finished the racing season. On several occasions, Olin sailed with Frech, and they both delighted in *Dorade*'s performance on the European circuit.

In 2001, the 150th anniversary of the yacht *America's* triumph in the race around the Isle of Wight was celebrated and the gathering of great classic yachts was unprecedented. Dozens of restorations had been completed in the previous five years, and the designs of S&S, Fife, Charles Nicholson, Rhodes, Nielsen, McGruer, Abeking and Rasmussen, and many others flocked to the Solent by any means possible. Arriving on their own bottoms, by submersible yacht transporters, as deck cargo and on trucks and trains, the immense fleet gathered in Cowes from North America, Europe and Antigua for a celebration of the America's Cup and of yachting in general. It was the greatest yacht gathering ever. Peter Frech was not going to miss the event; *Dorade* was loaded on a truck and delivered to England. She was welcomed with the reverence that was her due. Along with *Stormy Weather*, *Bolero*, and J Class Boats and Twelve Metres from the America's Cup, *Dorade* was featured in programs and reports throughout the week. Olin attended and sailed aboard both *Dorade* and *Bolero* in the regatta.

Her English tour done, she returned for racing in the Med in the fall. Through all of this, Peter Frech was her captain. He was intent on driving her, and she performed well under his hand. Despite his care, *Dorade* suffered a well-observed, post-race grounding on St. Honorat Island at the harbor breakwater in Cannes. She was pounded on the rocks by passing motorboat wakes. Such things happen, especially when a boat is actively campaigned. Frech organized her management without a permanent paid hand and grew increasingly devoted to her and her history. Paintings and photographs of her hung in his homes in France and Holland, and he became protective of her. However, in 2005, Peter Frech's health began to deteriorate and it became impossible for him to handle the boat as he had for the prior six years. He did not wish to engage a captain to sail her for him; reluctantly, he decided to sell her. Mike Horsley was engaged to find a buyer.

It might seem that a yacht like *Dorade* would be easy to sell, but she is not. Despite the abundant romance of her history and the obvious elements of her beauty, she is still the narrow, wet, crew-intensive, old-fashioned "rollermaniac" of her original creation. Cramped berths, a deep interior, shallow cockpit and demanding sailplan all combine to bring many romantics up short as they closely consider her for their own. With her moderate sail area, she can easily be sailed shorthanded in a heavy sea, but this is not obvious. Her stunning beauty draws them in, but she is an antique in many ways, and the interest quickly fades. It takes a special buyer, and several emerged. Peter Frech narrowed the field of purchasers by his demand for the right kind of owner and he could afford to be picky. Several candidates did not seem as happy or uncritical of the boat as Frech required and their interest was turned away. However, by the spring of 2006, Sparkman & Stephens presented a buyer, one whom Frech never met, but of whose approach and background he approved. The deal was done. *Dorade* was destined to return to the United States.

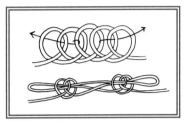

Homeward Bound

Mitch Gibbons-Neff never lost track of *Dorade*. He was determined to find an American buyer for her if he could. That sentiment in no way reflected remorse at having engineered her sale a decade earlier to a European. Her rebuild and return to racing in the Med had been a triumph of which he was proud. He just felt that it was time for the great yawl to come home. He had taken one buyer to Peter Frech only to have the suitor turned away during dinner after a sail. The Dutchman had not appreciated the prospective buyer's mention of a broken spreader. Neff's next candidate was to become her owner and lead her into yet another unique and, in some ways, nostalgic chapter in her long life. Edgar Cato is a "Son of the South," a wiry, trim octogenarian with an easy smile and an infectious enthusiasm for a lot of things, yachts amongst them. Growing up in South Carolina, in a family whose plantation roots reach back five generations, to a time before the Civil War, Cato had entered the University of North Carolina only to have his studies interrupted by the World War II. He had grown up sailing in Charleston with his father and brothers, and his experience in the Navy added to his passion for the ocean. Serving on an ocean rescue tug in the North Atlantic, Mediterranean, South Atlantic and Caribbean, Cato learned to navigate and perform deep-sea dives with the heavy, cast-brass helmets and weighted boots of the day.

He returned after the war to finish his studies in journalism. The Cato family had interests in cotton, pecans, peaches, textile mills and real estate, and his father, feeling that his two sons needed a platform for business, bought a small town clothing and notions store with the thought that his boys could grow it into something. Each was given a third of the small business, and their father kept an equal share. With Edgar's brother the opportunity took, and Cato Stores has become a major ladies clothier throughout the small towns of the South with its slogan "Big City Fashions at Small Town Prices." However, Edgar Cato soon discovered that he was "not cut out for a life as a ribbon clerk," and he lasted less than a year. Armed with a college degree and an abundance of charm, Cato found his way into the State Department, becoming a press attaché in Buenos Aires, Argentina. His life there, bolstered by income from his family holdings, was grand indeed. His diplomatic duties were supplemented by polo, sailing and a very active bachelor's social life.

—opposite—

Edgar Cato and his crack crew.

© BENJAMIN MENDOLWITZ

Two Heart's that Beat as One, the sailors' use of the traditional Sheepshank in series, is a classic knot tied on a bight.

ASHLEY KNOT 1166

197

Edgar Cato and Paul Buttrose
in the cockpit of *Dorade* in
Newport.

By the time that *Dorade* became a part of Cato's life, he had amassed thousands of miles of sailing, much of it singlehanding in the Bahamas and down the chain of islands to South America. He developed a great love of offshore sailing, preferring it, by far, to around-the-buoys competition. As his interest in and collection of yachts grew, Cato came to own a double-ended 36-footer, which he singlehanded through the Caribbean, as far as Venezuela. He raced Melges 24s, won a Florida State Championship in his Etchells, (sail No. 1000), and campaigned his Farr 40. He became a member of yachting institutions like the New York Yacht Club and the International Yacht Restoration School in Newport, Rhode Island. The excitement of the classic yacht scene excited him, too, and in late 2005 he was presented with a pair of interesting opportunities. The first was the beautifully restored S&S sloop *Sonny*, a near sister to *Stormy Weather*. Rebuilt by Nardi, she was fast, beamier than *Dorade*, with a more comfortable and very original interior. Aboard the CM 60 *Hissar* on the return from the Ft. Lauderdale-Palm Beach Race, Cato discussed *Dorade* with his sailing colleague Brad Read. Cato had previously mentioned his interest in *Dorade* to Paul Buttrose, his yachts manager, but they both thought the yawl had been sold. When Read mentioned the boat was available, Cato immediately set to research on *Hissar*'s onboard computer. After finding the listing, Cato called Buttrose by mobile phone. "He asked me in my capacity as broker to look into it," said Buttrose, who knew Cato well enough to know that "look into it" means "this is the boat to chase."

Paul Buttrose is an Australian and a very experienced yachtsman. He has raced aboard legendary yachts like *Windward Passage*. He skippered a Swan 48 and the aluminum, S&S racer *Sirona* for James Michael, who owned *Dorade* from 1941 to 1943. Buttrose, with the capability of an astute businessman, had combined his love of sailing with the business of yachts by representing Nautor's Swan line in Rhode Island and Florida. He met Cato in the 1980s, when Cato chartered a Swan 48 and later purchased a Swan 53, trading up from his Tartan Ten. By 2001, Cato's fleet, many named *Hissar*, included a Farr 60, KZ5—New Zealand's "Plastic Fantastic" Twelve Metre from the 1986-'87 America's Cup—a large rigid inflatable to tow KZ5 around, a Hinckley Picnic Boat and a Beetle Cat. Buttrose managed this assemblage as Cato, past 80 and full of vigor, began to expand his interests beyond yachting, polo and racehorses to include antique airplanes. Buttrose was just the man with the management ability to direct all this traffic. Cato doesn't stay anywhere for very long, and his air force gave gave him the ability to pilot himself to new adventures. When Cato purchased *Dorade* in 2006, Buttrose was managing eight airplanes and all of the yachts.

Armed with the comment to "look into it," Buttrose contacted Mitch Gibbon-Neff, who brought him up to speed on the failed negotiations with Frech earlier in the year. They prepared an offer, which was sent just before Christmas, accompanied by a letter outlining Edgar Cato's qualifications as potential custodian for the historic boat. It mentioned Cato's restoration of two classic Abaco dinghies built by Joseph Albury in the Bahamas, his three-year restoration of a 1965 Trumpy, and the Twelve Metre KZ5, which Cato had taken to the America's Cup Jubilee in 2001, where Frech had sailed *Dorade*. It also included a paragraph on Cato's South Carolina plantation, "where abundant wildlife habitat is maintained along with wooden sluice gates regulating water flow to the original rice paddies." The offering price was $25,000 lower than one Frech had turned down earlier in the year. Mitch Neff was sent to work to complete the negotiations and Buttrose commented of Neff "although we first met in 1972 when I was skipper of Jim Michael's Swan 48 which Mitch was commissioning, the *Dorade* negotiations over the next few months offered a true insight to Mitch's character as I discovered the intensity of his dedication to Olin, his passion for Sparkman & Stephens and, of course, *Dorade*." The offered price of $600,000 was agreed to within three days, but the deal was not done yet and was subject to a survey and sea trials after the first of the year.

However, Edgar Cato's active racing intervened. At Key West Race Week, he was thrown across the cockpit of his Bruce Farr-designed CM 60, fracturing his femur. He requested a postponement of the sea trail as a result. Frech responded, "I am sorry for Mr. Cato that he broke his hip but due to that mischief I am loosing (sic) money and time." Not overly sympathetic to an octogenarian yacht driver! The sea trial was waived, and the deal closed on April 23, 2006.

Paul Buttrose was charged with getting the boat to Newport in time for Graduation Day at the International Yacht Restoration School, of which Cato was a trustee. What could be more fitting than to have the great yawl lying dockside for the students and the school's supporters? Buttrose retained Marcus Capon in France to prepare the boat for shipping out of Toulon, but, as preparations were made, a surprise emerged. It was not to be the first bit of surprising news for the new owner. The boat was found not to have a bill of sale to Frech, the Dutch flag was invalid and, therefore, the boat had never officially been imported to France and could not be exported. This was solved by simply having Capon deliver the yacht out of France to La Spezia, in Italy, flying an Italian flag. Shipping was arranged from there. All preparations for *Dorade* to go as deck cargo with masts stepped were made, but came apart when the designated ship was found to be too lightly loaded and cargo on deck would have resulted in a dangerous and unsafe rolling rate. Another ship would be available soon, but the spars would have to come out. Capon made arrangements for a crane to pick them, and he ensured that the new loading arrangement was safe.

As these plans were being made, the Italian authorities decided that the 76-year-old boat carrying an Italian flag was "archeologically significant" and refused to grant an export license, which would dilute Italy's "national treasure". Buttrose worked through it all, finally convincing the officials that she was really "American goods returned." *Dorade* finally landed in New York on June 6, after nearly a decade out of the United States. French flags, Dutch flags, Italian flags, American flags… *Dorade* was home. She was towed to Newport, only to arrive five days after IYRS Graduation Day.

Dorade looked fine and was dry, only leaking slightly from a section of the bow. So they took her racing, and that first summer back home they raced her hard. Her first contest was the Opera House Cup in Nantucket. It was *Dorade*'s first summer of East Coast racing in seven decades.

Cato's crew included Buttrose and internationally-known sailor, Brad Read, a past champion in boats ranging from Twelve Metres to J/24s. Also along were six-time America's Cup campaigner and professional sailmaker Mike Toppa and crack sailors who crewed on Cato's other big boats. Fall approached and, over Labor Day, *Dorade* entered the Museum of Yachting Classic Yacht Regatta. Olin was invited to join in, and he happily accepted. Mitch Neff and his two sons, TM and Paul, found slots aboard, along with Crayton Walters and Jim Allsopp. The race proved to be an important turning point. In breezy, downwind conditions, the mizzen staysail was set and, with a snap, the mizzen rig collapsed overboard. With Olin in the cockpit in 25 knots of breeze, the whole of the aftermost mast broke in two. As the one who urged the crew to set a staysail, Olin assumed the blame, but it was simply a back-stay failure. They finished the race, but the season was over. *Dorade* was scheduled for a winter of relatively minor repairs—mizzen-mast rebuilding and sprucing up. It was not to be so minor.

Peter Cassidy and his business partner, Ed Van Keuren, run Buzzards Bay Yacht Services. Cassidy is a former software entrepreneur and a devoted fan of Sparkman & Stephens designs, owning and racing the beautiful and successful New York 32 *Siren*. Van Keuren is a former financial services executive. Together, they are quiet, competent and very exacting with regard to the yacht rebuilding they manage. In the fall of 2006, at the urging of Mitch Neff and with the support of Paul Buttrose, Cato handed *Dorade* to their care, in a shed in Portsmouth, Rhode Island. She was to have her mizzen mast repaired and undergo routine maintenance and storage over the winter.

As they jockeyed her into her shed, Cassidy thought that something wasn't right. She seemed to deform under the pressure of the travelift. The interior of the yacht is built with a ceiling—a series of narrow longitudinal battens over the frames on the inside of the hull—up to about the level of the bunks. Although she had been surveyed by Nardi prior to her purchase by Cato, the ceiling had not been removed to expose her frames, particularly at the turn of the bilge. Upon examination, Cassidy and Van Keuren found frames that had deteriorated badly. Ten years had passed since her rebuild in Italy, but Cassidy described the material as "soft brown bread." Contributing to the damage were her bronze cross straps, splines added to her top-sides seams in 1998, and epoxy on her bottom. The grounding incident in Cannes

Edgar Cato at the helm, with Olin Stephens on the left, in the 2006 Museum of Yachting Classic Yacht Regatta. The mizzen has been strapped down aloft after breaking. The Eight Metre *Angelita* and the New York 32 *Siren* follow.

could be to blame. Nevertheless, given the presumed condition of the boat, Cassidy was surprised and quickly shared his finding with Buttrose. A major structural re-do would be required.

When Paul Buttrose broke the news to Cato, the discouraged new owner wondered if it might be best to just donate *Dorade* to a museum and let them deal with the broken frames. Perhaps, they would even make *Dorade* a static museum exhibit. His disappointment with the Italian rebuild could not be hidden. But, at 7:30 the next morning, the irrepressible Cato was back on the phone with the man who managed his yachting and flying treasures. Overnight, he had concluded that he needed to be faithful to his role as caretaker of the great yacht. He told Buttrose to proceed with the expensive, second rebuild. In an interview published in the November 2007 issue of *Sail*, Buttrose commented, "I'm sure they did what they were asked to do, and that they did it well.... She's an old boat, and old boats often do need work." Again, *Dorade* was lucky in her ownership.

201

Over the course of the winter of 2006-'07, Buzzards Bay Yacht Services managed the project. For expert structural help, they enlisted Jim Titus and his crew of experienced wooden shipwrights from Mt. Hope Boatworks in Newport. Together, they removed and reinstalled most of *Dorade*'s interior, and fabricated 35 pairs of new frames and 10 planks on each side of her bottom. Given the amount of work to be done, Cato launched into an effort to return *Dorade* to her 1930 configuration, with a fervent devotion to authenticity. She had sailed all of her early years without an engine, and this had made her lighter and faster. The engine was not original, and it had to go. The propeller aperture, so carefully crafted on the centerline in 1941, was structurally rebuilt and filled in. The watermaker was removed. Interior appointments not originally drawn on the plans were eliminated. Replacing the teak deck was discussed, but ultimately left for another day, despite the fact that white pine had been originally used. Cato pushed the project along with his clear eye to the issue of not just "time" but of 'time remaining." The whirlwind octogenarian wanted to get on the water and race against his NYYC friend Joe Dockery, who had purchased *Sonny* and brought her to Newport. Cato wouldn't waste a season.

The need for a major rebuild caused quite a flap. Cato had presumed that the job had been completed thoroughly by Cantiere Navale dell' Argentario. Nardi had done what he was asked to do by Gazzoni at the time. Frech had sold the boat "as is," and the inspection by Nardi did not include the frame ends. The boat didn't leak, but Buzzards Bay had exacting standards. Articles appeared in *WoodenBoat* and other publications alluding to the matter, and people lined up on different sides. Olin found the dispute unsettling, after so much had been made of the Italian rebuild, and he was devoted to Nardi and his yard. Olin was quoted in an extensive article on the rebuild, written by Joshua Moore in the June, 2008, issue of *Woodenboat*, as saying "I felt strongly, and I still do feel, that Federico and the yard there did what was expected of them. She was, I think, offered to Edgar as what she was, and the fact that he wanted virtual perfection—which is always hard to achieve—I believe that upset Federico greatly." During the course of the discovery of problems, Mitch Gibbons-Neff, so integral to the boat and her resurrection and return to the United States, was diagnosed with lung cancer. By February 2007, the head of Sparkman & Stephens was gone. He had sailed his last yacht race with his sons and Olin aboard *Dorade*, a yacht he treasured, had sold to Europe and had finally brought home.

Over the course of the winter of 2006-'07, the boat came back together. Much of her interior was removed. Behind the bulkhead, forward of the head, Cassidy found fibrous stuffing, which had been there for decades. He presumed it to be seaweed used for sound deadening. The interior furniture had oddly changed slightly in dimensions from the original drawings. Some of it may have been altered; some of it may have been changed during the course of her building in 1930. No one could be sure, but they put her back to what they thought was original. The final touch was to remove the bronze plaque at the top step of the companionway ladder, put there after the Italian rebuild. A new one was installed, replacing Gazzoni-Frascara's name and Cantiere

Being rebuilt again in Newport, *Dorade* comes back together during the spring of 2007.

AUTHOR'S COLLECTION

Closing up the propeller aperture reduced turbulence and returned the boat to the original 1930's configuration.

AUTHOR'S COLLECTION

Navale dell'Argentario with a plaque honoring Minneford's, citing 1929, the date of her keel laying, as opposed to 1930, the date of her launch. It heralded Rod Stephens' contribution to her construction, and it was signed by Olin.

In the early summer of 2007, she was ready to go again. The season's agenda included the races in Maine surrounding the Eggemoggin Reach Regatta, the classic yacht contests in Newport and Narragansett Bay, and the Opera House Cup in Nantucket. The New York Yacht Club Cruise beckoned, as well. *Dorade* sailed between venues, assisted by her ever-present RIB tender, to be certain that the yawl without an engine found her way without incident.

203

Castine, Maine, is an exquisite and welcoming pre-Revolution American town on the eastern shores of Penobscot Bay and is home to the Maine Maritime Academy. The Castine Yacht Club held a celebration of *Dorade*'s return and of the launching of *Anna*, a beautiful, modern—but still classic—cold-molded interpretation of the great *Stormy Weather*. Peter Cassidy and Ed Van Keuren described *Dorade*'s history and restoration to an attentive audience at the Maritime Academy campus. Olin Stephens had been scheduled to attend and race. The disappointing report came that he had fallen and would not make the trip from Hanover, New Hampshire. *Dorade* lay at the town dock, and as you walked down the hill toward her, you could see her distinctive raked masts stretching above the pier before you could see her hull. Cato opened her to any visitor, allowing those who had never boarded the famous yawl to enter her interior, walk her decks and be photographed at her tiller. The town was delighted, and talk in the shops and restaurants seemed to always include some mention of her.

Top—This plaque replaced the one presented by S&S in 1997.

Above—*Dorade* and her rigid inflatable tender head to the starting line for the Castine to Camden Race.

AUTHOR'S COLLECTION

The Castine to Camden race was held the next day as part of the series of three races leading up to the Eggemoggin Reach Regatta. The yawl, with Cato and crew, was towed alongside her RIB to the starting area and cast off. She headed to the west to sort out her sail combinations. It did not take much distance to realize how small she really is as she moved away toward North Islesboro prior to the start. The race to Camden found her trading tacks within her class, jockeying with the likes of Thomas Watson's old S&S yawl *Palawan*, the first of a series of yachts bearing the name. The race was satisfactory, but *Dorade* did not win. The Camden to Brooklin Feeder Race followed, and she showed them her heels, winning in moderate air. The Eggemoggin Reach Regatta was completed with a second place, and she returned to Newport, Rhode Island, to win The Museum of Yachting Classic Yacht Regatta, the event that led to her rebuild just one year earlier. She was back on the American circuit, still collecting silver.

In the spring of 2008, *Dorade* celebrated the 78th anniversary of her launch in May, and Olin celebrated his 100th birthday on April 13th. In a remarkable exhibition of persistence and vigor, Stephens had tried for many recent years to accept every invitation possible to sail in classic regattas on boats such as the NY *32 Falcon*, *Bolero* and *Dorade*. He was the toast of every gathering, large and small, and he

Dorade and *Palawan* cross tacks in the Castine to Camden Feeder Race, August, 2007.

AUTHOR'S COLLECTION

was always gracious and courtly to the throngs of admirers who saw the chance to speak with him as an enormous honor.

But Olin was wearing out. The New York Yacht Club planned a birthday party to honor him in July, and there was some concern that he would not be able to attend. Still game, he made it, and was welcomed by 650 guests at the New York Yacht Club outstation, "Harbour Court", on Newport Harbor, but on the way back to Hanover is reported to have remarked "I'm glad I don't have to do that again for another 100 years." He was grateful, but tired. In August, he watched *Dorade* win the Castine to Camden Race from David Bicks' committee boat, calling it his best birthday present ever. Olin had been famous in yachting circles for nearly 80 years. He had been a celebrity at the age of 22 and had shared his talent and friendship with royalty, heads of state, business leaders and famous familes, as well as with thousands of ordinary yachtsmen and yacht builders the world over. His genius as a designer of the objects they loved—coupled with his grace and charm—had expanded, enhanced and sustained his close relationships. He had done it all. On September 13th Olin slipped away and the world lost its most famous yacht designer and one of its grandest gentlemen.

Olin at the helm of the New York 32 *Falcon*.

"The near sea is a changing, turbulent sea,

but the distant sea looks smooth.

Life and work find their way across both."

Olin J. Stephens II

Looking Back

Eighty years have passed since *Dorade* was drawn by Olin Stephens and christened at the Minneford Yacht Yard on City Island. Her numerous owners have raced her and cruised her in the Atlantic and Pacific Oceans, in the Baltic and the Mediterranean Seas. Well after she was rendered obsolete by the yacht-design advances she helped to precipitate, she remained a threat on the racecourse, and she is still hard to beat today. She has never been forgotten or marginalized by the care given her, and even when her maintenance has been less than fully rigorous, her value and the value of her name in yachting history have always made her precious. She is intimately associated with many of the great ocean races of the world—the Transatlantic, Transpac, Bermuda, Fastnet and Swiftsure—and, in the last decade, she has reemerged as a glamorous and prominent participant on the classic-yacht circuit on both sides of the Atlantic. She is importantly original, having never been allowed to deteriorate on the hard somewhere and, although not as all of a piece as the astonishingly complete *Brilliant*, she stands as a remarkable artifact of the boatbuilders' art as practiced in 1930. She and Olin Stephens are inexorably linked, and they benefit from each other's fame. Rod Stephens' water-trap ventilator is the partial currency of her prominence. All of these aspects make her notable, but is *Dorade* truly a defining yacht, truly a breakthrough? Taken from the perspective of yacht design history, there can be no mistake. *Dorade* really was a turning point, a unique mark on the course of yacht design development.

The first touchstone in that history involves *Dorade*'s place at the intersection of several trends. She is the most prominent inflection point of that intersection. Until the late 1920s, ocean racers were seen as the outgrowth of only those yachts clearly worthy of the challenges of the open sea. Their designers drew confidence from the tested heritage of fishermen schooners or European pilot cutters. They were modified to make them faster than either of these types, but they were not, at their core, equivalent to inshore racing yachts. Ocean racers were more heavily built and were specified to hold internal ballast to provide a better and safer motion at sea. Real racers were lighter and deeper, with external ballast and rigs that were large and, consequently, unstable in severe conditions. Ocean racers cut those rigs down. The

The True Lovers' Knot, tied as a ring in a continuous line.

ASHLEY KNOT 2426

notion of purposefully designing a racer type for ocean work, rather than altering a workboat for racing, was new. Starling Burgess's *Niña* of 1928 was a first step toward a racing yacht designed for the ocean. Her success in the Santander Race of that year made an impact, but she was still a schooner, relatively heavy and beamy in her build.

Olin Stephens combined in *Dorade* all of the elements of a fast yacht with the requirements of an ocean racer. She was lightly built. She carried her ballast externally and low. Compared to the conventional fisherman approach, *Dorade's* lateral plane was smaller, which some thought would make her difficult to heave-to and too quick for comfort. Neither assumption proved true. Her sailplan was large, initially a little too much so, and her mainmast was positioned aft of many prior designs to give her greater balance and handling ease, a less than obvious change that greatly benefited her ocean work. She was narrow and wet and cramped, but still large enough to take a crew safely across the Atlantic. And she did so repeatedly. She was like an inshore racer in her quest for speed but still designed for the open sea, all in a small package. She was really the first to combine all of the design elements that were, within just a few short years, to become absolutely standard in competitive offshore design.

Out of her introduction came controversy. Those who doubted the concept of such a racer had to be convinced by her success in the trials of the North Atlantic—particularly her first Fastnet victory in heavy weather. She so devastated the Fastnet fleets with her wins in 1931 and 1933 that the combination of economic downturn and her obvious ability caused the British to nearly allow the race to wither and die. In some ways, they didn't know what hit them.

After 1931, *Dorade's* racing success and safe passages had proven her case. The design world followed. Not entirely and not all at once, but in increasing numbers, designers emulated Olin's approach. First came the ocean racers *Stormy Weather*, *Sonny*, *Edlu* and *Edlu II*. There followed *Avanti*, *Blitzen*, *Zeearend*, and *Gesture* from the board of S&S. *Bloodhound*, *Ortac*, *Maid of Malham* and many others in Britain derived their basic features from *Dorade*. In his excellent history and analysis, British Ocean Racing (1960), Douglas Phillips-Birt makes the case strongly for *Dorade* as a breakthrough design. "*Dorade* set the course of future offshore design and pointed clearly away from the earlier, working-boat tradition," he writes. "*Dorade* was the most important step yet taken in the yachtsman's search for his own type of fast, seagoing vessel, developed for his special purposes and uninfluenced by earlier and often irrelevant models of pilot cutter or fisherman."

The trend established by her design continued through the centerboard boats of the 1950s and only ended in the 1970s, with the advent of separated keels and rudders and the International Offshore Rule.

Dorade marked another turning point in yachting—she was designed to be sailed by amateurs, without a paid crew, and was certainly configured below as such. While the Stephens and later owners employed professionals as cooks and even

The author, with Olin Stephens, Port Madison, Washington, 2002.

CHARLES FOOTH

deckhands, *Dorade* wasn't set up with a hand forward. This trend did not necessarily catch on as swiftly as did the other features of her design. Many S&S boats that followed were configured with the paid crew forward of the mast, including large yachts like *Baruna* and *Bolero*, but also smaller ones, such as New York 32s. *Dorade*'s accomodations marked a departure that was to become increasingly common with the growing democratization of yachting.

Importantly, *Dorade* defined what many considered to be the best in beautiful yacht proportions. Her delicate stern coupled with a stronger and slightly foreshortened bow gave her a balance that looked just right. Her clean decks and low, short house allowed the eye an unfettered focus on the shape of her hull. Her raked rig made her look swift. She was, and is, unique; on one hand, lovely and dainty, and on the other, purposeful and determined. She is still an icon of a certain beauty in yacht design, arguably amongst the most widely photographed and modeled yachts in the world. Her exploits were boasted of in the 1931 advertising in *Yachting* for her builder Minneford's, and she was still being featured in 2009, in full page ads appearing in *Sail* for North Sails. She was mentioned over 200 times in the *New York Times* between 1930 and 1936. There is no other racing yacht with her enduring fame and public presence.

And so this is the defining and beautiful ocean racer *Dorade*, continuously loved and still sailing. May devotion to her care and the burnishing of her history continue for another 80 years.

Coda

Over Labor Day weekend of 2008, and days before Olin's passing, *Dorade* again participated in The Museum of Yachting Classic Yacht Regatta in Newport and her spars continued to fall. In a collision with *Falcon*, she caught her mizzen on the Q Boat's headstay, snapped the mast at its base and dropped the rig onto her starboard rail and overboard. She finished the race and her season in a tangle of rigging, having broken her mizzen twice in as many years. She retired that fall to Joe Loughborough's shed in Portsmouth alongside *Sonny*, *Skylark* and her competitor *Falcon*, a truly astonishing collection of restored classics from the 1930's huddling in the fabric draped shed. She remained on the hard all through the summer of 2009. Edgar Cato was consumed with other projects including racing his Twelve Metre and, although *Dorade* was offered selectively for charter, no takers were found for the engineless ocean racer. Her mizzen was rebuilt again and her interior was refinished by Green Brett.

In early 2010, with the 80th anniversary of her launch approaching in May, Cato informed Paul Buttrose that he had decided to part with the boat and she was listed with an asking price of $950,000. With S&S designs such as *Baruna*, *Tomahawk*, *Argyll*, *Sirius*, *Circe* and *Manitou* for sale, the market was flush with great classic yachts. But there is only one *Dorade* and her unique place in yachting history made her a market unto herself. Cato had brought her back to the United States and lavished her with care. He launched her and as she floated to her mooring in Newport harbor many hoped that an American buyer would emerge to keep her close to home. Sure enough, in August, Mathew Brooks, a fifth generation Californian, member of the St. Francis Yacht Club, record-setting round-the-world pilot and avid mountaineer, became *Dorade's* fifteenth owner. Raised in the Bay Area, Brooks runs real estate investment and mountaineering equipment companies, and had been looking to acquire a classic yacht with an important history. He had sailed and raced on San Francisco Bay and envisioned a Fife as his ideal yacht. *Dorade* came to his attention through Christine Kaplan who, with her husband Paul, own *Santana*. *Dorade* demands a romantic owner and Brooks fits the bill. His objective is to return her to ocean racing with a reinstalled engine and new mainmast, possibly ready for even a transatlantic crossing or Fastnet Race. Now in her ninth decade, eighty years after her great Transatlantic Race triumph of 1931, the famous yawl has found another devoted caretaker.

Olin aboard Dorade in 2007, armed as always, with a camera.

Dorade Major Ocean Racing Results

The Bermuda Race

1930: Second in Class B, third overall, winner of All-Amateur Trophy

1932: First in Class B, eighth overall

1934: Fourth in Class A, fourth overall

The Transatlantic Race

1931: First to finish, first overall

The Fastnet Race

1931: First overall

1933: First overall

Olso-Hanko

1933: First place

The Honolulu Race

1936: First to finish, first in Class B, first overall

1939: Fourth in Class B, ninth overall

1953: Seventh in Class B, eighteenth overall

The Swiftsure Race

1947: First in Class AA, second overall

1948: First in Class AA, second overall

1949: 10th overall

1950: Third in Class AA, sixth overall

1951: First in Class AA, third overall

1952: First in Class AA, third overall

1954: First in Class AA, sixth overall

1955: Sixth in Class AA, ninth overall

1956: Sixth in Class AA, seventh overall

1957: Eighth in Class AA, 15th overall

1961: Third in Class AA, 47th overall

1963: Third in Class AA, 30th overall

1964: First in Class AA, 18th overall

1979: DNF, DSQ

On the wind.

Bibliography and Sources

Adamthwaite, Paul. "Stormy Weather." *Maritime Life and Traditions.* 3. (1999): 30-45.

Allen, Frederick Lewis. "After Hours, Ahoy!" *Harper's* (July 1951): 94-95.

Ashley, Clifford W. *The Yankee Whaler.* Cambridge, MA: The Riverside Press, 1926.

Blanchard, Norman C., and Stephen Wilen. *Knee Deep in Shavings: Memories of Early Yachting and Boatbuilding on the West Coast.* Victoria, BC: Horsdal & Schubart Publishers, 1999.

A Book of Designs of Deep Sea Racing Craft Issued Under the Auspices of the Royal Corinthian Yacht Club. London: Ernest J. Day & Company, 1932.

Bourne, Russell, and Francis S. Kinney. *The Best of the Best: The Yacht Designs of Sparkman & Stephens.* New York: W.W. Norton & Company, 1996.

Brooks, John. *Once in Golconda: A True Drama of Wall Street 1920-1938.* New York: Allworth Press, 1969.

Compton, Nic. "Boat Yards, Working Class." *Classic Boat* (Sept. 2001).

—. *The Great Classic Yacht Revival.* New York: Rizzoli, 2004.

—. "Sailing Stormy with Olin." *Classic Boat* (Sept. 2001).

Coulson, Robert, and Everett B. Morris, eds. *Racing at Sea.* Princeton, NJ: D. Van Nostrand Company, 1959.

Crane, Clinton. Clinton Crane's Yachting Memories. New York: D. Van Nostrand Company, 1952.

Doane, Charles J. "*Dorade*'s Second Wind." *Sail* Nov. 2007: 58-61.

"The Dowagers." *Latitude 38* (June 1982).

Flood, Allen, and Robert Mullen. *City Island: Her Voyage Through History.* New York: Bronx County Historical Society, 1947.

Fox, John D. *Across the Atlantic in* Dorade. Unpublished, 1931.

Fox, Uffa. *Sailing, Seamanship and Yacht Construction.* London: Peter Davies Limited, 1934.

—. *Uffa Fox's Second Book.* New York: Charles Scribner's Sons, 1935.

Garland, Joseph E. *The Eastern Yacht Club: A History from 1870 to 1985.* Marblehead, MA: Eastern Yacht Club, 1989.

Gerard, Philip. *Brilliant Passage: A Schooning Memoir.* Mystic, CT: Mystic Seaport Museum, 1989.

Golby, Humphrey, and Shirley Hewitt. *Swiftsure: The First Fifty Years.* Victoria, BC: Lightship Press Limited, 1980.

Halabisky, Bruce. "Cantiere Navale dell'Argentario: Restoring America's Classic Yachts." *WoodenBoat* (June 2001).

Hoyt, C. Sherman. Letter to Herb Stone. 12 June, 1933. *Sparkman & Stephens Technical File: Dorade.*

—. *Sherman Hoyt's Memoirs.* New York: D. Van Nostrand Company, 1950.

—. *Yachting* (Nov. 1933): 23.

Hunt, Morton M. "Up From Corker." *The New Yorker* (7 Sept. and 14 Sept. 1957).

Kinney, Francis S. *You Are First: The Story of Olin and Rod Stephens of Sparkman & Stephens.* New York: Dodd, Mead & Company, 1978.

Last Will and Testament of J. Franklin Eddy. Seattle: King County Superior Court, 1978.

Livingston, Kimball. *St. Francis Yacht Club: 1927-2002.* San Francisco: St. Francis Yacht Club, 2002.

Loomis, Alfred F. "Myth of Malham Wins the Fastnet." *Yachting* Oct. 1947.

—. *Ocean Racing: 1866-1935.* New York: Arno Press, 1967.

MacNaughton, Bruce Daniel, and Lucia del Sol Knight, eds. *The Encyclopedia of Yacht Designers.* New York: W.W. Norton and Company, 2006.

Mitchell, Carleton. *Yachtsman's Camera.* New York: D. Van Nostrand Company, 1950.

Moore, Joshua F. "The Mother of Modern Ocean Racing." *WoodenBoat* (April 2008): 64-71.

Museler, Chris. "Racing Classic Yachts, Managing the Growing Pains." *WoodenBoat* (April 2008).

Neuhaus, Eugene. *The Art of Treasure Island.* Berkeley, CA: University of California Press, 1939.

Ogilvy, C. Stanley. *The Larchmont Yacht Club: A History, 1880-1990.* Larchmont, NY: Larchmont Yacht Club, 1993.

Pace, Franco. *Sparkman & Stephens: Modern Classic Yachts.* Brooklin, ME: WoodenBoat Publications, 2002.

Parkinson, John Jr., *Nowhere Is Too Far: The Annals of the Cruising Club of America.* New York: Cruising Club of America, 1960.

Phillips-Birt, Douglas. *British Ocean Racing.* London: Adlard Coles, 1960.

—. *An Eye for a Yacht.* New York: A.S. Barnes and Company, 1955.

—. *The History of Yachting.* Briarcliff Manor, NY: Stein and Day Publishers, 1974.

Pileggi, Sarah. "Two Grand Dames at Sea." *Sports Illustrated* (7 June 1982).

Pratt, Albert. *Journal: Summer 1933.*

—. *Photos: Summer 1933.*

Pritchard, Keith. "*Dorade*: A Breath of Fresh Air." *Classic Boat* (Jan. 1999).

Rabinowitz, Neil. "Great Yachts: *Dorade.*" *Sailing Magazine* (Nov. 1988).

Robinson, Bill. *A Berth to Bermuda.* Princeton, NJ: D. Van Nostrand Company, 1961.

Rosenfeld, Morris (photographs) and William H. Taylor and Stanley Rosenfeld (text). *The Story of American Yachting.* New York: Bramhall House, 1958.

Rousmaniere, John. *Fastnet, Force 10: The Deadliest Storm in the History of Modern Sailing.* New York: W.W. Norton & Company, 2000.

—. *A Berth to Bermuda: 100 Years of the World's Classic Ocean Race.* Mystic, CT: Mystic Seaport Museum, 2006.

—. *In a Class by Herself: The Yawl Bolero and the Passion for Craftsmanship.* Mystic, CT: Mystic Seaport Museum, 2006.

—. "Restoring the Classics." *WoodenBoat* (July/August 2004): 50-53.

Rousmaniere, John, ed. *Desirable and Undesirable Characteristics of Offshore Yachts.* New York: W.W. Norton & Company, 1987.

Scandlin, Horace W. *Photographic Impressions of the White Star Liner Homeric.* New York: White Star Line.

Ship's Log of Dorade: *From Newport to Plymouth, 1931.*

Ship's Log of Dorade: *From Larchmont to Oslo, Cowes and Lyminton, 1933.*

Ship's Log of Dorade: *From Cowes-Fastnet to Cowes-Larchmont, 1933.*

Smock, Jack. Transpac: *A History of the Great Race to Honolulu with a Short History of the Transpacific Yacht Club and Notes on the Eleven Races to Tahiti.* San Diego: The Transpacific Yacht Club and the Maritime Museum Association of San Diego, 1980.

Stephens, Olin J. II. *All This and Sailing, Too.* Mystic, CT: Mystic Seaport Museum, 1999.

—. *Lines: A Half-Century of Yacht Designs by Sparkman & Stevens, 1930 - 1980.* Boston, MA: David R. Godine Publisher, 2002.

—. "Along the Great Circle Track in *Dorade.*" *Yachting* (Sept. 1931): 44+.

Warren, James R. *The Centennial History of the Seattle Yacht Club 1892-1992.* Seattle: Seattle Yacht Club, 1992.

Weinstein, Robert A. *Tall Ships on Puget Sound: The Marine Photoraphy of Wilhelm Hester.* Seattle: University of Washington Press, 1978.

The Yearbook of the Cruising Club of America, selected years.

Photograph Reference

Index

Turtleback Mountain stretches
in the background over West
Sound as *Dorade* lies quietly at
anchor.

OWNERS OF *Dorade*

Roderick Stephens Sr.	1930 - 1932
Olin J. Stephens II and Roderick Stephens Jr.	1932 - 1936
James Flood	1936 - 1941
James Michael	1941 - 1943
Ralph James	1943 - 1947
J. Franklin Eddy	1947 - 1978
Mystic Seaport Museum	1978 - 1979
Antonio D. Gomez	1979 - 1982
Gerard Bosco	1982 - 1984
Charles Chalmers	1984
Mike Douglas	1984 - 1996
Giuseppe Gazonni-Frascara	1996 - 1999
Peter Frech	1999 - 2006
Edgar T. Cato	2006 - 2010
William Mathew Brooks	2010 -

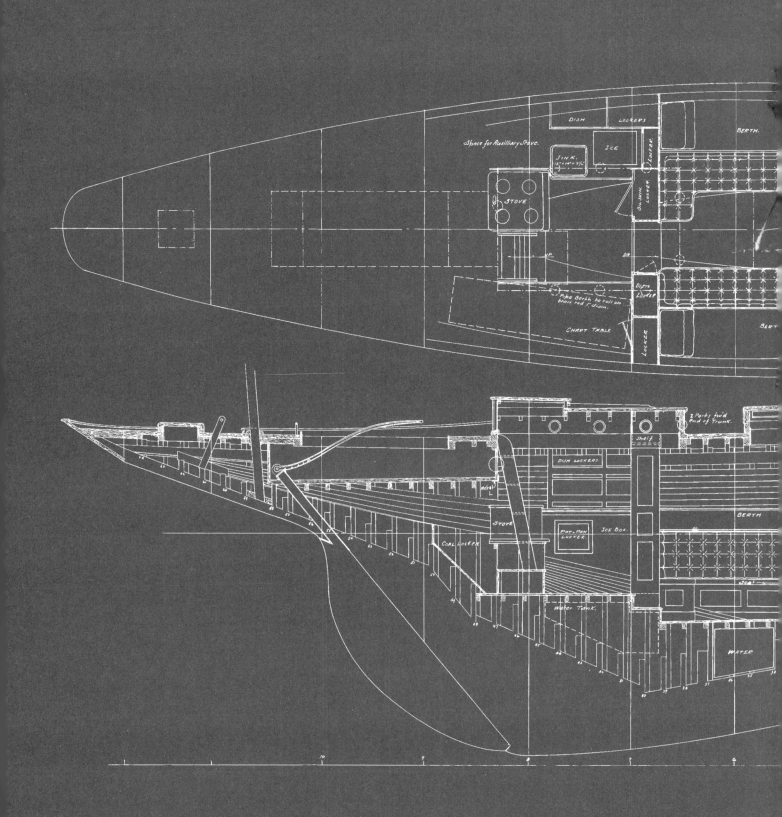